THE EVOLUTION OF A PARTY GIRL

PREYA C. SHAH

Copyright © 2016 Preya C. Shah
Any unauthorized use, sharing, reproduction, or distribution of these materials by any means, electronic, mechanical, or otherwise is strictly prohibited. No portion of these materials may be reproduced in any manner whatsoever without the express written consent of the publisher.

Publishing services provided by **Archangel Ink**

ISBN: 978-1535234771

There is no greater gift in life than the gift of a loving and devoted mother.

I dedicate this book to Sheila Ann Shah in appreciation of the unyielding love and support my mother has given me in my life. From her solid foundation I have been blessed to experience this wondrous world.

***

Contents

Preface 7

Introduction 9

Chapter 1: Facing My Mortality 11

Chapter 2: Back In The Party Scene 19

Chapter 3: Opening My Spiritual Eye 23

Chapter 4: Formulating A Plan 33

Chapter 5: Japan: Kuzuu 39

Chapter 6: Japan: Oyama 51

Chapter 7: Japan: Karasuyama And Nikko 61

Chapter 8: Japan: District Conference, And Tokyo 73

Chapter 9: Japan: Kyoto, And Fujisan 79

Chapter 10: Pitstop In The 'D' 89

Chapter 11: India: A Month In Mysore— The Shala 93

Chapter 12: India, Month In Mysore —Teachings 115

Chapter 13: India, A Month In Mysore —Bylakuppe 133

Chapter 14: India, A Month In Mysore —Goodbye 141

Chapter 15: India: Kovalam Beach 153

Chapter 16: India: My First Return To Mumbai 159

Chapter 17: India: A Month In Kutch 167

Chapter 18: India: Back To Mumbai 189

Chapter 19: India: The Family Vacation 195

Chapter 20: India: Calangute Beach, Goa 201

Chapter 21: India: Escaping Goa.................................... 207

Chapter 22: India, Safe And Sound In Mumbai 227

Chapter 23: India: Sivananda Yoga Teacher Training 231

Chapter 24: Nepal, Chaos In Kathmandu 251

Chapter 25: Nepal: Mount Everest................................. 255

Chapter 26: Nepal: The Farmhouse 271

One Last Thing… 279

Connect With Me 281

About The Author... 283

PREFACE

My personal journey began at exactly the right time. This is the story of searching for the purpose of my life by exploring the world and beginning to traverse my inner world. My path to truth started with cancer and led me through healing, growing, and ultimately unraveling my entire view of reality. I made an extraordinary transformation from the party girl of Detroit to a woman that finally feels the beauty of inner stillness and peace.

I had to journey around the globe to realize that the answers to my life's purpose were found deep within. I first searched in many failed relationships, then at the bottom of many bottles of expensive red wine, then onto the tops of the tallest mountains before I finally found clarity.

The true purpose of life and happiness is free and available to anyone who wants to take their journey inward, as I have done. This is the ultimate transformation from standing on my feet feeling ungrounded to standing on my head and finally feeling grounded.

INTRODUCTION

I went back to my hotel room and packed up my bag. I was shaking as I put my money belt on with my passport, cash, and credit cards tucked safely inside. I dressed in my sweat suit with my running shoes and put a pocketknife in my sports bra. I hadn't dressed like this in the many months I'd been away, but I felt like I was preparing for battle. I had everything on my body that I would need to get back to the USA in case I had to drop my bag and run. I left money on the bed to pay for the hotel room. I didn't tell them I was leaving.

I knew if I could get to the village of Chaudi, twenty minutes away, I would a have safe refuge. But getting a taxi would be a hurdle. My phone was still being jammed, and I hadn't been able to leave town the day before—all the drivers were under strict instructions from their 'boss' not to let me leave, no matter how much money I offered them. Today I was desperate—and determined—but by the third driver I asked, tears were welling up in my eyes. I was being watched and followed now by at least a dozen men—this was my only chance to escape.

The third driver seemed empathetic. While the others had made calls and gotten a strict "no," this one didn't pick up his phone. After a long pause, he agreed to drive me to Chaudi for 1,000 rupees. I quickly agreed, and we were on our way.

I was panicked and confused. Between glances behind us to see if we were being followed, I wondered what had happened during my week in Goa. For the first time in my travels, I truly felt that my life was in danger. And I was leaving behind the first Indian man I had really been attracted to. My father had told me never to go to Goa. I was beginning to understand why…

***

Chapter 1
FACING MY MORTALITY

It was the first time in my life I had really wondered if I was dying...

***

This journey began when I was diagnosed with papillary carcinoma of the right lobe of my thyroid. I was just thirty years old. Thyroid cancer was a disease I had never heard of until I was diagnosed. I thought I knew my own body until I got the results from my MRI.

I had been having neck pain intermittently for about two years at that point. I was a physical therapist at a large hospital in Detroit, and I had attributed my neck pain to my physically demanding job. I helped patients to get out of bed and walk the day after major orthopedic surgeries. One day at work, I was helping an obese patient in her mid-forties walk when she suddenly turned limp and began to code. My adrenaline kicked in, and I lifted the 300-pound woman onto a chair. I started yelling for help. A nurse quickly came in, and we heaved her into bed. I left the room just as the doctors were arriving to resuscitate her. The patient survived, but my neck and arm were more painful and numb then they had ever been in my life.

The next day I talked to my boss about my injury and went to corporate health to be evaluated. They had seen me for similar right-sided neck pain the year before, so they immediately ordered an MRI and put me on steroids. I had been hesitant to get an MRI before, but this time the pain in the right side of my neck, arm, and chest wall was so intense, I was easily convinced.

Chapter 1: FACING MY MORTALITY

I had the MRI about two days after my injury. My boyfriend was a resident at the hospital and was able to get the result to me right away. The test showed that there was one disc herniation in my neck, but it was central and could not be causing my right-sided pain. However, the test also showed a dime-sized mass on the right lobe of my thyroid. Since my neck pain was always associated with lifting, I had never imagined it could be a tumor.

For two years, I had been experiencing strange symptoms. Along with the neck pain that radiated down my arm, I also developed small blister-like skin lesions throughout my body that were most alarming and painful on my vagina. I went to my gynecologist for the blisters. I was devastated and had no idea what was happening. The only logical conclusion was that my boyfriend had cheated on me. After seven days of waiting and repeatedly calling my doctor's office, I finally got my test results. All of the STD tests were negative. I was relieved, but I still had skin lesions all over my body, and things continued to not feel right. I had my gynecologist run the tests again. They came back negative once more, and she said she was stumped.

I started to think it must be all in my head, a psychosomatic response to stress in my relationship with my boyfriend. I also noticed this strange striated pigment pattern on my lower left leg. I became obsessed with my 'sickness'; my family and my boyfriend started thinking that I was a hypochondriac. I was constantly searching the web, trying to correlate all of my symptoms. Every time I searched, I came up with a new disease.

I was thirty years old and ready to start the nesting chapter of my life. I had been living with my boyfriend for about two years and had convinced myself we would be getting engaged soon. I was in good shape; I exercised regularly and taught aerobics two days a week at the community center. My Standard American Diet (SAD) included—dining out, microwaved food, fast food, and drinking too much alcohol.

The next few months after the biopsy confirmed that I had cancer were very emotional and I experienced deep grief. I did a lot of crying. I blamed myself and struggled with feelings of guilt and desperation. I was on the computer constantly, trying to establish some sense of control in my life. I was obsessed, and used the Internet day and night to research my disease and to numb my mind. My lifelong friends Colleen and Kristina and my boyfriend had to endure the brunt of my emotions. I lived a fast-paced life. I was a successful, educated, professional young woman. It didn't seem fair.

I was active in the Detroit party circuit, and my social life was as important to me as my career. My love life was blossoming and I was living with a man for the first time in my life. On the surface, I had a life many would have been envious of. The truth was, though, that things were not going well in my relationship. I had been trying to hold it together for many months, and now as I was coming unglued, my relationship was falling apart. He was moving to Milwaukee for his career, and I was waiting for an engagement ring to move there with him. I remember during that time wanting to be married so badly. It was the first time in my life I had really wondered if I was dying.

As I faced my mortality, I started to question the purpose of my life. What was I on this earth to accomplish before I died? I spent many hours in the darkness of my mind; it was a battle I had to take on alone. Not having any children, I didn't fully understand motherhood, but I think learning that your 'baby' has cancer is a devastating experience for a mother. My mom was trying to emotionally support me, but her own fear was only compounding my sadness. My boyfriend was wrapped up in his career and generally emotionally unavailable. During the darkest time, he escaped by moving away for his residency to Milwaukee. I never got the engagement ring I was hoping for, and we decided we would try a long-distance relationship. I maintained a facade of strength. I told very few people about my thyroid cancer. It was a lonely time of isolation, sadness, and illness.

In preparation for my surgery, I decided to make some dramatic lifestyle changes. I gave up eating meat and drinking alcohol. The glamorous parties I used to crave no longer appealed to me. I ramped up my exercising to seven days a week as I prepared my body and my mind. I had spent many years in hospitals working, but this would be my first experience as a patient. I researched ways to detoxify my body to prepare for the anesthesia and the many chemicals I was going to have to

Chapter 1: FACING MY MORTALITY

take. After reading a few publications, I found a detoxification diet that seemed sensible and not too extreme. Three weeks before my surgery, I started on this detox, the goal of which was to not eat any chemically laden food so I could clear the accumulated toxins from my body.

I ate all organic food. I gave up processed food, alcohol, meat, caffeine, and salt. I ate only whole grains, raw nuts, beans, fresh fruit, and vegetables for the three weeks before my surgery. It was the first time in my life I had ever eaten so healthy, and it felt great. It required a lot of discipline and was difficult at first, but after feeling the results, I was encouraged to stay on it. I had so much more energy and I could handle the stress better.

This detox diet allowed me to understand my body in a completely new light. Once I cleaned up my diet, the blisters healed themselves naturally. I thought I would feel tired after giving up caffeine, but I had more energy than I'd had in months. I thought I would be bored and depressed not drinking or going to parties. I was, however, finding myself happier and dealing with my diagnosis and my boyfriend moving out of state even better. My family did not support my decision to become a vegetarian right before my surgery. This new lifestyle made me feel vibrant, and no one could convince me to going back to feeling sick and tired. After only a few days of being on this detox, I began to understand how significantly and quickly dietary choices influenced my health. It was a grounding time for me, and other than exercising and working I stayed home. I learned to enjoy the art of cooking simple whole foods and making my food with love and healing thoughts. This was my first successful detox diet, but the lessons I learned would stay with me a lifetime.

On September 1, I had my thyroidectomy. It was a successful surgery, and my boyfriend flew back to Detroit from Milwaukee to stay with me in the hospital. I had my mom, my dad, and my boyfriend all taking shifts, and I was lucky to have people that loved me with me around the clock. Even though the surgery had been successful, I felt awful. I couldn't swallow, my entire body hurt, and my parathyroids were not functioning. My electrolyte levels were severely off balance and causing intense muscle cramping throughout my body. It was eight long days and nights in the hospital before my body started regaining proper function. During my hospitalization, I was on blood draws to monitor my calcium levels. Every four hours, day and night, someone came into my room and poked me until they were able to get two vials of blood. My arms were covered with scabs and bruises.

The treatment protocol for thyroid cancer involved spending the following eight weeks depleting any remaining iodine and thyroid hormone in my body, then delivering a radiation treatment via iodine. The thyroid is the only tissue in the body that can absorb iodine, so the radiation would go straight to my thyroid cells. This would completely eradicate any potentially cancerous thyroid cells left anywhere in the body. It is a very successful treatment. This is why thyroid cancer treatment has such a high success rate; I consider myself lucky to have had the only cancer with a 95% cure rate.

I spent much of my eight-week recovery in Milwaukee with my boyfriend. I was on a strict iodine-free diet in preparation for my radiation treatment. I became more committed to my vegetarian diet and became disgusted by the idea of eating organs and flesh from other animals. I grieved after I lost a tiny piece of my body; I couldn't bear the thought of taking the life from another creature and then eating it. I became more exhausted each day as the final remnants of thyroid hormone left my body. I was able to find iodine-free recipes on the thyroid cancer web site, but cooking became a chore. I slept a lot, re-watched every episode of *Sex in the City*, and was extremely emotional as my thyroid hormone level dropped to zero. In hindsight, this difficult time was the final nail in our relationship coffin. I needed someone to support me, and after spending long hours with patients every day at work, he couldn't handle coming home to another patient. I still tried to hold our relationship together, even though my life had been turned upside down. I hoped that I could salvage my dream of getting married, having a baby, and being the perfect doctor's wife.

By late October, my life was getting back on track. The scar on my neck was healing beautifully, and I was starting to get my energy back. I had returned to Detroit, and I had finished my

Chapter 1: FACING MY MORTALITY

radiation treatment. My cancer scan was negative, which meant the cancer cells had not spread anywhere else in my body. I was about to finish my medical leave and return to my full-time job at the hospital. I decided to transfer to the outpatient physical therapy department to reduce the physical demands of lifting bedridden patients.

My boyfriend surprised me with a romantic weekend in Chicago. I flew there, and we stayed in a five-star hotel. We spent most of the weekend in bed together. He also arranged front-row center seats for *Wicked*, the musical. It was a beautiful weekend. I could finally eat out at fancy restaurants again, and I was stabilizing emotionally from this traumatic chapter of my life. I had started on my thyroid replacement hormone, and glimmers of the 'party girl' were starting to re-emerge. We were connecting again; there was so much joy and love between us that weekend as we celebrated surviving this challenging chapter together. Life was good. I had endured the storm and now the sun was shining down.

I came back home feeling more in love with him and sad to say goodbye. We had bought tickets and were going to meet in Florida in a few short days to celebrate my thirty-first birthday.

Then the dreaded phone call came. He wasn't ready for kids, this cancer chapter had been too much for him, and he needed to just focus on his career. He didn't have anything left to give me. WHAM! He ended our three-year relationship with me over the phone. After having just survived my battle with cancer, I thought this would be small, but at the time it seemed bigger. I was a mess again. I spent the next few weeks in a deep depression, spending most of my days struggling to get through work and most of my nights crying, looking through our pictures, and rereading his letters to me. I felt so empty and hopeless about my life and my future.

I could see no joy left in the world and searched every day for reasons to live. I started talking to a therapist; I wanted to find a way to emotionally heal myself. I spent about a year reading psychology books about attachment disorders, codependence, addictive personalities, and borderline personality disorders. I met with my therapist once a week for about a year; she was instrumental in helping me begin my eye-opening journey of self-evaluation. It was important for me to have someone educated to facilitate my self-exploration, but I realized that happiness and finding my life's purpose were not going to be achieved in a therapist's office. I learned a lot about my personality and myself, but deep in my heart I continued to feel empty.

Chapter 2

BACK IN THE PARTY SCENE

For the first time in so long, I felt my internal strength starting to resurface...

***

I got back into the party scene and starting drinking a lot. I couldn't stand to be home alone in my house—the house we once shared. I went out almost every night, even if I had to sit in a bar alone. It was better than crying at home with the constant reminders of my ex-boyfriend and my cancer. I needed to embrace a positive and healthy lifestyle, but instead I was back in the fast-paced party scene, drowning myself in alcohol and unhealthy relationships. I dated a lot, partied a lot, and cried a lot for the next year. I stayed on my vegetarian diet, and the only thing that got me through many lonely weekends was my strong commitment to my yoga practice.

Exercise has always been my salvation. I love to exercise—I've always felt so joyful and happy when I was done working out. However, traditional aerobic classes no longer motivated me. My therapist suggested I try yoga, and I was so desperate to find health and happiness that I was willing to try anything. The yoga studio she suggested was located right downtown and was close to my house.

My first yoga class was awesome and mortifying at the same time. The instructor, Rob, had a mohawk and was covered in tattoos; he blared hard-rock music and used the "F" word throughout class. By all practical descriptions, he was a total freak. By this point in my life, I was in search of the 'silly spiri-

Chapter 2: BACK IN THE PARTY SCENE

tuality.' Instead, I felt like I was at a heavy-metal concert turned yoga studio. But even through the outrageousness of this experience, I felt connected to yoga and his class. When I left his class, I felt my internal strength starting to resurface for the first time in a long time. I went back the next day and the next; I was hooked. I now had a reason to stay home and stay sober on the weekends, so I could make it to yoga in the morning. There was a lot of socializing and flirting that went on at this 'super-cool' studio, but I stayed out of it. I didn't talk to anyone, other than to go up to my instructor after every class and thank him for sharing yoga with me. The only thing I found that gave me a lasting sense of peace and happiness was yoga. Growing up, I watched my Indian grandfather do yoga every morning, and stand on his head until he was over 70 years old. This practice, however, looked nothing like my grandfather's yoga. Finally, between all the therapy, self-help books, and yoga, I was learning how to weather the storm of cancer and a broken heart.

As I learned how to center myself, I wanted to start connecting with nature again and backpack. My ex-boyfriend had been my backpacking partner, so in an attempt to find people to backpack with, I joined an outdoor club. I am not much of a club person, and as expected, the club was mostly filled with socially awkward people. For the most part it was a total bust. The only silver lining was my new friend named Kerry and my HOT backpacking instructor, Craig. I dreamed one day Craig would be my new backpacking partner.

As I tried to enjoy and embrace the single life, I started making friends with other single women over thirty. I made one special friend who changed my life. I had crossed paths with Cassie several times in the past, but this was the time that our relationship really clicked. Cassie was one of the students in the Tuesday night abs, glutes, and thighs class I continued to teach. She was an attractive, well-educated, successful single woman. She was truly charismatic, and her personality was magnetic. I could always find Cassie at a party because there was usually a crowd of people around her. We were similar in many ways, but we came from very different spiritual backgrounds. I was raised atheist and spent many years fighting the concept of organized religion. She was raised in a Catholic family and went to Catholic school but was also resistant to organized religion. Cassie was always learning and reading about different forms of spirituality and new age philosophy. From the first time we met up for wine at the local bar, I had a feeling our new friendship was going to change my life for the better. We spent a few nights a week drinking fine wine and talking about our lives, our heartbreaks, our careers, and our families. She taught me new skills to be a strong and successful woman. Cassie was an influential person and was on the VIP list at many of the events in the Detroit 'scene.' We enjoyed spending our weekends together going to upscale events. Cassie had recently lost her stepfather and I had lost my boyfriend. Together we grieved, emotionally bonded, and drank a lot. But even with my newfound friendship and exploding social life, I felt empty.

I grew up in a very Catholic neighborhood. A few times throughout my childhood, I was excluded from the neighbor's birthday parties and events because we were not Catholic. I blamed these snubs on religion and spent years forcefully rejecting the concept of religion and God. Cassie taught me that spirituality doesn't have to mean organized religion. Once I disconnected my traumatic childhood experiences with organized religion to my personal relationship with God, I was excited to learn and grow spiritually. I read some of the books Cassie suggested to me and applied some basic concepts to my life. Using positive thinking, manifesting, and the laws of attraction, I saw positive changes in my life. Between the yoga, the psychotherapy, my vegetarian lifestyle, and my new spiritual development, I was starting to feel a new level of love and respect for my life. I knew somewhere deep inside of me that I was going to be OK no matter what new challenges life handed me.

Chapter 3
OPENING MY SPIRITUAL EYE

I started to feel connected to the infiniteness of the world and the universe; I realized what a quick moment in time my life really was...

***

It was almost time for my one-year cancer checkup. The cancer scan involves an eight-week process of going off my thyroid medicine and depleting my body of thyroid hormone. I decided the best way to do this was by taking another medical leave from work. My lifestyle had changed significantly over this year, but I was sickened by the looming thought of my cancer coming back. I felt like I was standing at the edge of the Grand Canyon again, about to jump off into the dark abyss of depleting my body of thyroid hormone and iodine. I'd learned from my previous experience that this would cause me to feel exhausted and constantly cold. With this in mind, I asked one of my lifelong best friends, Kristina, if I could stay at her parents' condo in Florida for four weeks and rest in the warm climate. Her parents graciously gave me the key and instructions to reopen their condo, which had been closed for months.

I first flew to North Carolina to spend a week with Kristina. Many days in my college years had been made easier by her sage advice. Kristina has always been the friend I want to be around during difficult times because her witty sense of humor was uplifting. One night over my final bottle of wine, I told her I needed to feel strong to start the second round of testing and possible treatment, but I still felt beaten down by my life. I told her I had always wanted to have superpowers like Wonder

Chapter 3: OPENING MY SPIRITUAL EYE

Woman and I also like the look of her blue streaked hair. The next day, she arranged for her hairdresser to come to the house and make my superhero dream a reality. I was a 31-year-old professional woman with bright blue streaks in my hair, about to continue my battle with cancer. There is something liberating about having cancer because everything else seems small. Why not do or try anything? After my week in North Carolina, now armed with blue Wonder Woman hair, I flew to Bonita Springs, Florida.

The plan was for me to spend the next four weeks reading, relaxing, practicing yoga on my iodine-free diet, and preparing for my cancer scan and possible radiation treatment upon my return to Michigan. Things didn't go quite as planned; I ended up only staying three days at the condo because my body was covered in bites. Cassie came down to stay with me for a week, and we moved to her dad's condo in Barefoot Beach, the next beach town over. It was a beautiful penthouse condo overlooking the Atlantic Ocean. I was very thankful Cassie was there to help me through it. I was exhausted and, emotionally, I couldn't manage the situation on my own. Cassie left after a week, and I moved to a hotel. My mom came to stay with me for my final week.

My relationship with my mom is a work in progress. We have a long-established dysfunctional pattern in our relationship. Our pattern is that my mom gives unsolicited advice trying to 'help' me, I feel enmeshed and angry and react negatively, and she then becomes the 'victim.' This pattern started when I was a teenager and although it has improved, we still went into our unhealthy pattern regularly. I know that compared to the many possible unhealthy mother-daughter relationships, this situation was pretty mild, and deep in my heart I felt lucky to have such a loving mother. When I was sick and actually did need to be 'rescued,' things worked much better between us. When I picked my mom up from the airport in Florida, I needed to be rescued. My energy levels were dropping significantly every day as my thyroid hormone medicine slowly left my body. Having my mom there to cook my iodine-free diet was a true blessing.

One of our final nights in Florida, over a spaghetti dinner, we had the opportunity for a heart-to-heart conversation. There were many things about my childhood that I'd wanted to talk to her about for a long time. I finally got to tell her that I thought my childhood was very traumatic. Our house had been filled with constant conflict and bickering. She told me I was turning into an emotionally abusive adult, and it was time that I grow up and take responsibility for my actions instead of blaming my childhood. I told her that I thought she was manipulative and mothered me to fulfill her own needs and not my needs. We both cried. I am not sure if either one of us truly understood everything we were saying, but I think we both needed to vent, and it felt good to finally say these things after so many years of thinking them. It seems that many people with cancer need to clear past childhood issues with their parents, and this was my attempt to release some of my anger over my childhood. Facing childhood anger that had manifested into adult resentment was an important part of my emotional recovery from cancer.

As my thyroid hormone level continued to drop, I became an emotional mess. I had a lot of challenges to deal with, and I could no longer cope with even the smallest thing; I would just cry. I felt angry, depressed, and out of control. I was at my wit's end; I just wanted to take my scan and get back on my thyroid medicine. It was time to be done with this cancer chapter once and for all! I drank my radioactive tracer and then I went into the scanner. The machine scanned my body to see if any cancer cells had taken up the radioactive iodine.

On November 1st, two days before my 32nd birthday, I got the best present ever. I was cancer-free! It had been a long year of waiting. A negative one-year scan was a positive sign that I was completely cured of my thyroid cancer and needed no further radiation treatments. I felt like I had a new lease on life. I was finally able to feel joy again. The dark cloud that had been looming over my head for the last few years was finally gone. I thought about all of the people who never get to hear that they are cured from cancer, and in that moment I sent love to all those in the world struggling with cancer. I felt overcome with gratitude for all the love and support I had received, and for my body's resilience. I was thankful for my mom's unyielding support even through my outbursts of anger. I had gratitude toward my dear friends Cassie, Colleen, Dyanna, and Kristina

Chapter 3: OPENING MY SPIRITUAL EYE

who experienced my fear and sadness with me. During this time, I realized that crying was my body's way of telling the world that I needed help. I decided never to abandon someone who was crying and made a commitment to help people who cry rather than become frustrated with them. I wanted to pass along the love and gift of life I had just been given.

I was cancer-free and back on my thyroid hormone medicine—it was time to celebrate! My first big party after my treatment was the opening gala for the Detroit Institute of Art (DIA). Cassie asked me if I wanted to join her as a hair model at the gala. It was the party of the year in Detroit; every major politician, business owner, and donor in Michigan would be there. My official title for the party was a 'human arrow,' which meant I was to help direct people around the museum. I drove down to the DIA at 2:00 p.m. for my hair appointment and was quite surprised by what I saw. There was a team of hairdressers from Spain who were creating these beautiful, but very extreme, hair sculptures. They worked fast and used a lot of spray color, props, and wires as they created these amazing creations with hair. It was my turn, and as soon as I sat in the beautician's chair, the frenzy began. There was a lot of spraying and tugging at my hair. She was using copper wires, and I saw a large rubber snake go up into my hair. When I turned around, my head was the apple tree from the Garden of Eden—the Tree of Knowledge. She must have perceived my new path of spiritual growth! I had three hours before I had to get back downtown for the gala, and my head was a biblical garden. I tried to drive home, but my tree kept hitting the roof of my car, so I had to drive home with my tree sticking out of my sunroof. It was quite a sight!

The gala itself was amazing; the DIA was decorated more beautifully than I had ever seen it, and everyone was dressed in the most beautiful gowns. It was an exhausting night of standing on marble floors in high heels. My official job was to give directions, but I mostly stood around and hobnobbed with the elite guests. Once the dancing started and the event was winding down, Cassie and I found a back table and snuck a few glasses of wine and even a few dances. That night I met the mayor, the governor, the CEOs of all three automakers, and the director of the DIA. I was very surprised in the morning to get a call from the event coordinator to tell me my picture was on the front page of the *Detroit Free Press*. There I was with green glitter painted on my eyes and a large apple tree on my head, looking very proud because of everything it had taken for me to be there.

I continued on my conflicted path of spirituality and hardcore partying throughout the winter. I practiced yoga about five days a week, I read about religion and spirituality, and I continued to go out on the weekends and get hammered.

I had always been an environmental advocate, but as I started to heal, I started to feel more and more connected to the earth. In February, just as winter was starting to take its toll on me, I met up with Cassie in St. Martin. We stayed at her mom's beautiful penthouse condo, went out for many gourmet dinners, and danced the night away at a few nightclubs. However, the highlight of my trip was our time spent in nature. Hiking in the tropical jungle was a new and thrilling experience. One day we hiked to the top of Paradise Peak, the highest point on the island.

St. Martin was an island my ex-boyfriend and I had visited several times together, and I was concerned that being back on the island would stir up many emotions associated with my breakup. One of my first nights back on the island, I watched an entire lunar eclipse for the first time. We opened a few bottles of wine and lay on the lounge chairs as we watched the three-hour eclipse from our private rooftop pool deck. It was such an amazing display of nature—no clouds, very little light pollution, and the sound of the ocean crashing on the rocks below us. It was like watching an Oscar-winning movie by Mother Nature. I started to feel connected to the infiniteness of the world and the universe and realized what a quick moment in time my life really is. During that lunar eclipse, on the island we visited many times together, I finally said my final goodbyes to my ex-boyfriend. I had a powerful wave of forgiveness take over my body, and for the first time, I experienced acceptance and peace toward our breakup. I felt how nature's rhythms affected my body, my mood, and my thoughts. That night on our private roof in St. Martin was one of the best 'parties' I have been to with Cassie.

My desire to protect this amazing planet became an undeniable force within me, and I started doing volunteer work. On Earth Day, I convinced Dyanna and my friend Colin to join me handing out compact florescent light bulbs door to door. We weren't selling anything, just giving away free light bulbs, so it should have been easy—WRONG! I was surprised how unwilling people are to change. Even with us coming to their door and giving them free environmentally friendly light bulbs, most people said, "No thank you." I quickly made the connection to my own life and how unwilling I had been to change my old ways as well. Drinking too much, socially smoking, continuing my negative thought patterns—I did all this despite going through cancer. I needed to find a way to clear my mind in order to create space in my life.

I started to become more and more interested in Eastern religions, especially Buddhism. It is a religion based on emptying your mind and using compassion and nonviolence to find answers within yourself. My therapist mentioned in one of our sessions about a Buddhist monastery outside of San Francisco that she had gone to for a retreat. I had been trying to find some kind of yoga vacation or spiritual holiday, so I searched the web and found it. I knew that this was the next step in my healing and spiritual growth. I filled out the online application and awaited my phone interview with one of the monks.

Professionally, I was starting to grow and develop as well. Physical therapy was becoming too narrow for me. As much as I wanted to stay mainstream and out of the dangerous professional grey area of alternative techniques, they kept appearing in my professional path. Pain is such a complicated experience, and to treat someone's pain only through treatment of the bones, ligaments, and muscles was leaving a large group of patients without complete healing. From my personal experience with my neck pain, I was introduced to craniosacral therapy (CST). Craniosacral therapy is a very gentle manual technique in which a practitioner uses their hands and their intention to release restrictions in the craniosacral system and improve the flow of cerebral spinal fluid, allowing the body to heal itself naturally. I started taking courses in craniosacral therapy and continued with my personal practice of yoga with the intention that one day I would also become a yoga teacher.

It was ironic that during my lunch break on the third day of CSTII class that the call from the monastery came. Two major changes happening in my life at one time was confirmation I was on the right path. I had the first conversation I'd ever had with a monk. She was a pleasant and straightforward-sounding woman. She asked me several questions about why I wanted to come to the monastery. I briefly told her about my recent encounter with cancer, how I was looking for a new spiritual path. She seemed open to my answers and invited me for a week in early May.

My aunt lives in San Francisco, so I took this opportunity to spend a few days with her before going to the monastery. My aunt is an amazing street artist and my walls have always been decorated with her beautiful paintings. Growing up, I usually saw my aunt once a year. During my difficult teenage years, she helped me work through my conflicted relationship with my parents. My favorite day with her on that trip was visiting the redwood forest near San Francisco. We spent the day walking in a fairytale forest of amazing trees. We talked openly about our lives; it was a rare moment of deepening the connection we shared.

My aunt did not follow the rules set up by society or our family. She blazed her own trail, lived outside of the box, and lived a very unconventional life. Spending that time with her confirmed my belief that I didn't have to follow the 'rules' to have a happy and successful life. We said our goodbyes at the train station and I headed to the monastery.

I spent the next seven days in almost total silence in the golden hills of California. The monastery was a beautifully peaceful place and off the grid. No cellphones, only solar power and a privileged environment of complete silence. We worked on a very structured schedule, which included twice-daily meditations, vegetarian meals, and three workshops a day. During the workshops, we were divided into two groups of about eight people each. That was our time for talking, but not to each other, only to the monks. It was also the time we listened to other

Chapter 3: OPENING MY SPIRITUAL EYE

campers share the most intimate experiences of their lives. It was hard at first to divulge such personal experiences with complete strangers, and it was also hard to listen to other people tell their stories without giving advice or words of encouragement. I learned a lot about negative self-talk, the world of duality, and the many conflicting aspects of my personality. I also learned a lot about projection as I wrote this poem about the moon.

I am the mistress of the night sky.

I sit quiet and powerful every night.

My life is constant; my path is predetermined and perfectly reliable.

As I rise I dominate the sky with my silver glow. I have powerful energy.

When I am full, it is a time of letting go; when I am new it is time to create.

I reflect only the sun as I move beautifully, powerfully and consistently across the sky.

Through this life-changing week, I lived in a hermitage, a small freestanding hut in the woods. My hermitage had a bed and a window but no electricity. No mental distractions such as books or music were allowed. During the day, the temperature inside the hermitage was over 100 degrees, and at night it was cold, down into the 50s. I went to the bathroom in a nearby outhouse.

I was happy living this simple Buddhist life of silence. By the end of this week, I had started to understand self-love and had this beautiful love growing within me for myself. Living in silence allowed me to hear my negative self-talk and replace it with self-love. I learned a lot about the basis of my inner conflicts, and I started to integrate many of my conflicting personality traits. The long process of disassociating my personality traits from the real 'me' started this week.

This was the first spiritual vacation of my life, and I loved it. I came home feeling like I had progressed further along my path of healing. I was better and stronger for taking this time away, not broken and exhausted as I typically felt upon returning from my party vacations. I now sensed that many of the hardest days of my life were behind me, and I had new tools to help me through my life.

Even enjoying a more natural, spiritual path, I still held on to my previous vices. I rejoined my bowling league in the spring. I thought bowling would be a great way to meet some new people, but this time I did not enjoy it at all. Being in that dark bowling alley with all the drinking, smoking, and small talk no longer appealed to me. I no longer wanted to be in low-energy places. I had a similar experience when I joined about fifteen people on a houseboat trip to Lake Cumberland in Kentucky. The trip consisted of too much drinking and many low-energy activities. When I was around people partying, I could feel something flip inside of me, and I would quickly fall right back into the party scene—lots of drinking and one infamous game of strip blackjack. After my retreat at the monastery, I had developed improved awareness of my disassociated personality types and started to question why I was still engaging in the 'party girl' behavior.

During this period after the monastery, I had many of these experiences where I tried to participate in some event that I would have really enjoyed before my spiritual growth and it no longer amused me. In fact, I had a real internal struggle as I let go of some of the friends who no longer shared common interests with me. I still spent many weekends drinking too much, but I was starting to change the way I felt about these nights, and I was feeling more unsettled with my life and the fact that it was not aligned with a bigger purpose.

In August I went with Cassie to a Kryon seminar at a beautiful resort area in Michigan. Kryon is a spiritual leader from another dimension that is channeled through a man who gives spiritual lessons from the universe. It was the most 'fringe' thing I had ever been to, but I had learned a lot about being open to new things in the last few years. I was beginning to understand that it is only fear that makes people closed-minded, so I decided to be open to whatever came my way; I felt fearless after my battle with cancer. On that trip I also bought my first healing crystal.

Chapter 3: OPENING MY SPIRITUAL EYE

The channeling was a mind-blowing experience. There was a convincing energy in that room that was far different than anything I had ever sensed before. He explained that DNA carries information of past lives in at least thirteen dimensions. Cassie had an intense experience during the channeling as well; it was my first experience with how strong the universe's energy can be. I left that weekend with many more questions than answers. My current way of viewing the world seemed so narrow and simplified, and that weekend I opened up my mind to many larger concepts.

Through my many years of schooling, I had always seen science and spirituality at odds with each other. I began studying quantum physics, and I realized that science and spirituality are actually merging together. Understanding this connection make spirituality more available to me. My concept of reality had always been analytical and science-based. When I started to see some of the scientific evidence about the power of thought and how thoughts actually carry energy, I made the connection that this could all be happening in the many undiscovered dimensions. The idea that my thoughts can affect the outcome of my life was becoming undeniable to me. What I considered spirituality, the universal energy, Mother Nature, or God could actually be called undiscovered science.

One Wednesday morning in the beginning of October, I had the very sobering experience of a friend committing suicide. I used my grief as a tool to try to connect with my purpose. This trauma strengthened the conflict growing between my professional path, my social life, and my spiritual path. I spent many nights that winter wondering what my life was really about; I had always thought I would be married and starting a family by the time I was thirty-three, but that wasn't the case, so I decided I needed a new plan.

Chapter 4
FORMULATING A PLAN

I wanted to have a clear path for my life's journey, and I felt this unbelievable spark of excitement and freedom from planning my trip. I was no longer waiting for my life to happen; I was creating my own future…

***

The Saturday before Easter, I went in for an interview for an International Exchange Program through the Rotary Club. It was the most difficult interview of my life. There were fifteen Rotarians sitting on a panel, all facing one chair in the middle of the room where I sat. The questions came at me for 45 minutes; I was in the zone. When I walked out of the room, I felt it deep within me that soon I would be heading off on my first international exchange!

That night I sat on my red leather couch drinking a glass of wine when my phone rang. It was Sandy, the group leader for the Group Study Exchange Program; she was calling to congratulate me for being awarded one of the four spots for the Group Study Exchange Program to Japan. I got it! I was going to Japan for a month on an all-expenses-paid trip to study physical therapy. She invited me to the Rotary Club District conference on May 2nd where I would meet the other members of the team I would be traveling with. Sandy briefly described the team members to me on the phone: Michelle, a Canadian police officer; Lesli, a mother of two kids and a music therapist; Andrew, a professional sports team manager who was working as a manager of a hardware store; and Sandy herself, who was a

Chapter 4: FORMULATING A PLAN

mother of two teenagers and had a previous career as a product engineer.

On Saturday May 2nd, I drove up to Frankenmuth, Michigan, eager to meet the rest of the team. I was very excited for my upcoming adventure. Our team had a brief meeting at lunch where we introduced ourselves and set up a schedule for our next three meetings. During these meetings we would prepare for our vocational exchange and prepare our presentation in Japanese. Our exchange program was in Tochigi Prefecture, which is a state about 40 minutes north of Tokyo. We had a lot to prepare for before our trip. During our meetings, we would create a presentation and handouts, order uniforms, study the Japanese language and culture, and get to know each other.

I left the district conference with mixed feelings about the other team members. When I got to work Monday after an exhausting weekend, I was surprised to see about twenty emails in my inbox from two members of the team. I'd had an initial impression that one of the members was obsessive and would be a thorn in my side, and my jammed inbox confirmed my initial impression. In the planning stages, there was a lot of paperwork, and the drastic differences in our approach to these tasks became quite apparent. The four of us were from a wide variety of professions, two different countries, and were at different stages in our lives; it's not surprising that we approached this exchange differently. That summer we had our three meetings—and exchanged *thousands* of emails.

One night during that summer, I was driving home from work, tired, hot, and exhausted, when my mind started to wander. I had been feeling less and less satisfied at my job. I had been working as a physical therapist at the same hospital for the last six years. I had changed my practice drastically after my cancer experience, becoming more holistic with my physical therapy treatments and integrating craniosacral therapy, nutrition, and yoga. I was having more success with my patients, but my boss and I were not agreeing on my new holistic approach. We both tried to avoid confrontation by limiting our interactions, and he only talked to me when he had major concerns. For the first time since becoming a physical therapist more than ten years ago, I would wake up in the morning and dread going to work.

My hospital was in an urban area, and most of my patients were obese and unhealthy. We saw many of the same patients year after year for the same problems, and I felt disgusted by this cycle. I attempted to encourage long-term lifestyle changes, but the medical system was not ready for this formula.

As my mind wandered, I remembered my last trip to India about six years prior. I had toured a charity hospital in my dad's village and the patients were in desperate need of physical therapists. This memory made me feel unappreciated and frustrated with my current position. When I got home, I started searching the Internet to find the name of that charity hospital. After hours of searching and a few phone calls, I found their website. I learned they ran an annual camp during the month of January. I started thinking about everything that had happened in the last few years of my life, feeling like I was constantly fighting an uphill battle. I was frustrated, I was lonely, and was finding myself being drawn back toward an unhealthy lifestyle. I knew once and for all I was ready to heal myself physically, emotionally, and mentally. It only took me one moment to make the final decision—it was time to quit my life and build a new one. In addition to my trip to Japan, I would go to India and work at the charity hospital.

I spent that summer doing a lot of research online, and I worked three jobs to prepare for my travels. I was trying to save up at least $10,000 spending money for my seven-month journey. I stayed in and cooked dinner by myself most nights to save money and to empty out my cupboards.

I wanted a clear path for my life's journey, and I felt this unbelievable spark of excitement and freedom from planning my trip. I was no longer waiting for my life to happen; I was creating my own future. I heard a motivational speaker talk about being the CEO of your life, and I finally felt like I was. I had this unique feeling of being the one driving my life. I had thought these drastic changes—quitting my job, moving out of my house, and traveling throughout Asia—would be difficult to digest, and yet it felt much easier than continuing my current life. I was in search of deep answers to many of life's questions, and I knew they wouldn't be answered in my current life. I wanted to create a life of health, wealth, love, and adventure. I

Chapter 4: FORMULATING A PLAN

needed to feel like my life was aligned with my larger goals in life. Something inside of me was awakened during that time, and I felt more alive than I had in years. This was one of my first experiences finding true happiness within myself. I was ready and I was committed to this journey. Now I had to share my news with my parents, who were typically not so enthusiastic about my choices.

As soon as I started on this new path, I felt doors opening for me as all the doors of my old life kept getting heavier. I was elated in July when my sister called to tell me that she supported my trip, so she and her husband were going to use their air miles to pay for my plane ticket to India. A few weeks later, my brother, Vik, called and told me he and his wife Alisa also supported my trip, and they were planning a family trip to India to visit me. Vik and Alisa were also the first family to come visit me after I moved to New York City in my twenties. I felt very thankful that my siblings were both supporting me on my journey.

My parents had known of my trip for a few months, but we both avoided the topic in our day-to-day interactions. When my trip did come up, the conversations never went well. They would first recite all the terrible things that would or could happen to me in Asia. When that didn't sway my opinion, they would explain why it was crazy to quit my well-paying job when so many people were out of work and would love a stable job. I had dealt with my parents' disapproval for most of my adult life. When I was 24 years old and bought my 'death trap' soft-top Jeep Wrangler, I heard all the horror stories of the people that died while driving Jeep Wranglers. When I was 26 years old, I moved to New York City, "the most dangerous city in the country," and heard about the crime, and the danger of a single woman living alone in NYC with no family. Every time it got easier to accept their disapproval of my life choices. Even though my parents were putting forth a strong effort to persuade me not to go, I knew once I was traveling they would not only give me any help or support I needed, they would probably come to India to visit me. When I was younger, I would doubt myself if they disapproved, but this time I knew I was doing the right thing. My deep intuition was that I was on the right path. I was secure in my decision.

The first lesson of my trip had already started—I was learning better communication and acceptance of my parents without triggering my anger. After many years of trying, I was slowly mastering this challenging skill set. During those months, I learned a very simple statement that I used often to head off the unproductive negative conversation. It was, "I know you are concerned about me taking this trip and I understand your fears. With that being said, I am still going, and I will do what I can to make you feel better about it." I also had to let go of my guilt over being the child whose behavior was frowned upon. Parenting a child is a huge task, and having a child that was a self-described 'party girl' and did not prescribe to the societal norms is more than most parents sign up for. I realized their anxiety was not a product of just this situation, but something that had been around for years. Now I was learning to establish boundaries to prevent their anxiety from creating anger within me. I couldn't prevent them from having it, but I could prevent myself from reacting to it.

Moving is never easy. I spent weeks going through my house and packing. I spent many nights looking through old pictures and rereading old letters one last time before I recycled the old reminders of my lost love. I wanted to grow, and I wanted a different path, so I had to first clean up the 'dirt' of my life to make room for changes. I read through all my cancer reports one last time and looked at the MRI of my tumor for the last time before I alley-ooped them into the recycling bin.

I had boxes of stuff to get rid of, stuff I had spent hundreds of hours working to earn money to buy that I was now giving away. For the first time, I clearly saw the irony of my material existence. I thought acquiring all of this stuff would make me feel happy and less lonely, and now working so hard to get rid of the same stuff to find happiness seemed ludicrous. This move brought a heightened awareness that most of my stuff was actually a bandage on my loneliness.

When I moved out of my house, I felt like I was finally ending the party girl chapter of my life at the age of 33; I was at the far end of the bell curve. I felt lost when I pulled out of my

Chapter 4: FORMULATING A PLAN

driveway, and I remember having no sense of where I should drive; I was officially homeless. I went to my friend Sheldon's house, and we reminisced about the many nights of wine, sushi, and parties we had shared at my old house.

I spent most of my final two weeks at work covering other therapist's patients and planning my trip. They arranged a farewell party at a local bar. Many of my coworkers and friends came out to celebrate my new chapter. We smoked cigars and drank lots of wine. It was a bittersweet feeling; I was excited for my adventure and sad to say goodbye to the coworkers I had spent the last six years with. Appropriately enough, I went into my final Friday of work with a serious hangover.

Sept 30, New Moon Manifestations:

I bring these things into my life now for the greatest good of all concerned:

*A time to travel and experience all that the world has to offer on my quest for personal growth and achievement. A true love of all people.

WANTS: *A big party on my homecoming, a new piece of jewelry, $20,000 for my life journey, a translator, a new bed and car when I get home, and new carpets for my old car.*

NEEDS: *HEALTH, WEALTH, LOVE, AND ADVENTURE!*

*understanding of Japanese culture and language

*compassion, tolerance, and ability to learn from all people and from all walks of life—patience, Preya!

*clean water, clean food, and clean beds

Desires: *sex with a man in Japan*

*health, wealth, and love!

*a magnetic personality

*love waiting for me when I come home

DREAMS: *Better understanding of Eastern medicine and how to successfully incorporate it into my practice*

*an Intensive Chronic Pain Clinic that incorporates my paths of yoga, craniosacral therapy, physical therapy, spiritual growth, vegetarian diet, positive thoughts, and self-love for patients who really want to heal, with abundance of referrals and leading to financial success

*healing of one » healing of all » world peace

*a new level of clarity between myself and the universal energy field.

*respect for women of the world to be successful leaders

***

Chapter 5: JAPAN: KUZUU

About ten Rotarians with welcome signs, applause, and huge smiles met us at Narita International airport. Japanese people have the most welcoming smiles in the world. We were swept away on a luxury coach for our long drive to Tochigi Prefecture, where I would be spending a month. We stopped at a noodle-shop for dinner. I was unshowered and exhausted, sitting across from men in crisp suits, most of whom didn't speak English. We were delirious and silly from our lack of sleep. Sandy, Andrew, and I all giggled about our first picture in Japan being the three of us face down in our tempura udon soup bowls. They drove us back to our hotel, and after a few minutes of struggling with the Japanese keyboard, I managed to get off a quick email to my family that I had arrived safely. My brother quickly responded with an email saying, "Have fun, learn, and be careful." Cassie responded, "'Have fun, learn, and be careful,' says your brother…' 'Party, drink lots of sake, and have sex Japanese-style,' says your best friend!"

Our first three days we stayed at a hotel to recover from our long journey and acclimate to the time change and culture. There is a thirteen-hour time difference between Detroit and Japan, so we needed to completely reset our internal clocks. During these few days, I experienced many first introductions to the Japanese culture, the most memorable being sake, Japanese rice wine. I am no lightweight when it comes to drinking wine—I could drink six to seven glasses of wine on a big night out and still be relatively put together. Sake is a different story. When we were getting over our jet lag, Andrew asked me if I wanted to go out and experience some of the local nightlife. Years ago, I'd had a bad night drinking sake back in Detroit, but I believe that, "While in Rome, you should do as the Romans do," so I gave up my 'I am never drinking sake again' policy for this trip. Andrew and I headed out to experience Sano nightlife. Sano is a suburban town about 50 miles from Tokyo. It took us 20 minutes of walking to belly up to a bar; it was the only place we found that had live music. I was amped up about my first night out in Japan after days of traveling, and we started pounding sake. The bar was empty, the band was playing whatever we asked, and my glass of sake was filled before it was ever emptied. After the first few glasses of sake, the bartender pulled out a bottle of absinthe.

Absinthe is a legendary drink in America because of its history of being illegal. It is a combination of distilled herbs, most notably an ingredient called wormwood, which makes you hallucinate. This was my first time trying absinthe. By the end of my drink, I was on stage with the band and dancing. By the next song, they had gone to their van to get the tambourine that I requested. I was singing Bob Dylan songs, and we lost track of time. I got back to the hotel just in time to meet the owner of the hotel who invited me to join them in their VIP room for karaoke. I staggered to bed very late and very drunk.

The next morning we were meeting our first host family, and I was sick. I was throwing up every time I moved, and it seemed as though my old demons of drinking and partying had already found me abroad. I had to use all the strength I could muster to pack up my suitcases between many trips to the toilet. I had one of the worst hangovers since my 'I am never drinking sake again' policy had been enacted back in Detroit. I finally made it down to be greeted by the Sano welcome committee. They were all distinguished-looking men in suits, while I looked haggard and smelled like sake and vomit. I made quite an impression that morning—I was physically sick and had to sit down during the pictures because I was about to faint. It was a very embarrassing situation, but I was so sick I couldn't do anything to make it better. I barely survived the lavish luncheon. I didn't eat anything but managed to hold down some water and by the end I'd started to feel human again. Having a large plate of sushi in front of me for that entire luncheon was probably the biggest punishment of all. I met my host and gratefully got into his Mercedes to drive to his house. He was a doctor and very concerned about my illness; I had to tell him it was just a wicked sake hangover. He was very eager to show me Japan, and I was very eager to sleep.

The presentation that night at our Rotary orientation dinner was my first presentation in Japanese, and I barely got through it. The pronunciation of the Japanese language is very difficult for me; the sounds are different than sounds I am used to making in English. I think I was still a little brain dead from the

Chapter 5: JAPAN: KUZUU

massive hangover earlier that day, despite the nap I managed to get in that afternoon. I turned down many offers of sake that night.

The next morning, I completed my first yoga practice in Japan. It was great, and I was feeling much more comfortable in my host family's house. The two young children of the family kept opening my door to watch me do my yoga and then would start giggling and slam the door. It wasn't the most peaceful yoga, but it was fun to play and teach them some easy poses. The father of the family, Dr. Tommay, went to work, and Hickory, his seventeen-year-old eldest daughter, and her grandmother and I left to go walking around town.

Hickory was a beautiful young woman with a shy presence. Japanese women I had encountered thus far took the role of the submissive, well-behaved woman. They rarely make eye contact, cover their mouths and look down when they talk, and giggle in this sweet, childlike way when listening. Hickory went to a private school where English classes are taught from the age of seven, and she spoke beginner's English. I can speak very basic Japanese and we developed a nice way of communicating with each other. The grandmother had a firm and graceful presence, but she spoke no English.

The first place we walked to was a Japanese cemetery. We followed an uphill trail through towering cedar trees, passing by a koi pond. Then the forest opened up into the cemetery. The cemetery was very elaborate with large black granite headstones, which looked like thrones. Most Japanese people are Buddhist and therefore cremated, the ashes placed in a special chamber in the burial vault of a family plot.

I could feel that this was a spiritual place, and an inner peace filled me as I walked thought the cemetery. The dense cedar forest surrounding the cemetery blocked out the noise and disturbances of the city, thus keeping the cemetery sacred. The grandmother showed me their family plot where her husband's ashes were. My grandfather had died earlier that year, and I spent much of my time in that cemetery thinking about him and experiencing my suppressed emotions regarding his death. The grandmother and I could not speak, but I tried to understand how devastated she must be to lose the man she'd devoted her life to. I felt very connected to her and this family.

We walked to a small town park where there were several temples and shrines. I put my 100 yen in and took a fortune card. Hickory was very excited to see I got the best fortune card of all. She said my trip to Japan would be filled with good luck and that I had a great plan ahead. I agreed and saved the fortune card in a special place in my wallet.

After meeting my host Tommay for lunch, we all drove to a very old Buddhist temple in Tochigi city that is set high up on a mountain, with rivers and waterfalls throughout. I was surprised to see statues of Hindu deities mixed among the statues of Buddha. I quickly learned of the purification ritual that must be done prior to entering any temple in Japan. Outside of Buddhist temples there is always a large fountain with a gold ladle. Before entering the temple, you must use the ladle to wash your hands and wash out your mouth, then pour clean water down the handle of the ladle before placing it back in the fountain. After the water, we walked by incense and used our hands to direct the smoke over our heads and bodies to cleanse our impurities. They all took the 100-yen fortune cards, but I did not want to test my luck with another fortune since my morning fortune was so lucky. After saying some short prayers in the temple, we headed back down to the car.

There was a definite mystical feeling in this air. Learning about spirituality in a book is far different than feeling it inside your body. All of these feelings were new to me and difficult to understand or explain. I was overcome with inner stillness as we approached the temple; it was a familiar feeling that I had also attained after yoga classes back home. It's a peaceful and loving feeling. It was a beautiful day in Japan full of new experiences, love, and generosity. My fortune was very lucky indeed.

For my first vocational day, my host mother drove me to Sano Kosei General Hospital. I was meeting the rest of my team there at 9:00 a.m. Unfortunately, this seemed to be more a political visit than a clinical visit. I was only able to have a short five-minute conversation with a PT who worked in the Impatient Rehabilitation Unit (IPR).

IPR units are located in the hospital and are for patients to receive intensive therapy after a major life-changing event such as a stroke or spinal cord injury. Through my conversations with the medical staff, I understood that there is a fundamentally different mentality about the role of the health care system in Japanese society. One example of this is the average length of stay in their IPR unit. In Japan it is three months, while in the US it is less than two weeks and dropping quickly. Insurance companies are the driving force behind the shockingly short stays in the United States. Another contributing factor is that, in the US system, our patients receive three hours a day of therapy. In the Japanese system, they only receive one hour of therapy a day. In the ten years since I'd become a PT, there has been a dramatic move to get patients out of the hospital very quickly. In the US, we send patients home when they are medically stable. In Japan, they send the patients home once they are *healthy*. I have always thought a good way to understand a culture is to see how they treat their sickest and most helpless members. Spending time in the hospital, I saw respect toward the sick and elderly members of their society.

The Japanese hospital overall was set up much the same as a US hospital. I thought that they would have an Eastern medicine influence, but this was not the case. The physical therapy department had most of the same equipment as at US clinics; it even had the same American branded exercise equipment. The hospital staff included fifty-nine doctors over seventeen different specialties. The hospital was divided into many of the same departments as most American hospitals. We spent some time in nuclear imaging and, as this was my first time being back in a room with a nuclear scanner since my illness, it brought back many feelings and emotions that I had not felt in a long time. I was overwhelmed by the memories associated with my cancer. I saw the people lined up to get their cancer scans and knew this would be a day they would never forget.

At first, I wanted to run out of that hospital. However, I was playing the role of diplomatic ambassador of my country and the Rotary Club, so I repressed those emotions. I wanted to sit down and laugh and cry with all of those patients on one of the scariest days of their lives; I again buried those feelings. I managed to survive those long ten minutes without anyone knowing how dramatic of an experience it was for me. Somehow I held it together. In the few short days that I had been here, I had already become good at these two skills—a plastic smile and maintaining a poised demeanor in the midst of conflict in order to fit into my role as a Rotarian in Japan.

After our trip to the hospital, we viewed a judo demonstration at the local police station. I sat next to Andrew during the event and we talked for the first time since our crazy night out in Sano. Through our giggling, it seem he may even have been flirting with me. After dinner at home, my host family took me to the local shopping mall, and Hickory and I walked around the mall together. After I promised not to tell her parents, she opened up and shared some of her 'boy trouble' with me. For the first time in my life, I had the pleasure of playing the role of the older sister giving advice. The boy trouble she shared with me sounded so familiar to my high school romances and all the drama surrounding them. Aging is something you don't really notice until something slaps you in the face. Thank God I had learned so much about life since those high school days. However, only a short time ago I had been trying to piece my life back together after my most recent heartbreak, which had left me feeling like a high school girl all over again. I explained to her that I had developed many of my best qualities through struggling through difficult situations. Learning how to let go of someone is one of the most difficult experiences of growing up, and many adults, including myself, still struggle with it. I tried to boost her self-esteem and shared all the things I thought were wonderful about her. I wish I had known when I was in high school how unimportant those romances would turn out to be in my life.

After I had been in Japan almost a week, we went on a tour of a limestone excavation site. As we drove up to the site, I saw *him*—my first hot Japanese man. He was tall and muscular and had a chiseled face. He was a young Rotarian who had come up from Tokyo to spend the day with us. Perfect! This good-looking, young Japanese man took away my dread of the tour. The potential for a Japanese romance was still on my mind.

Chapter 5: JAPAN: KUZUU

It is difficult to turn on the charm and flirt during a Rotary meeting, but we managed to flirt a little. I learned that Teppai was a salesman for the explosives that they used during mining. His career flew in the face of my environmental beliefs, but I stayed poised and decided to overlook it. After lunch he would be accompanying Lesli to a pediatric center for the disabled, but I was supposed to go with the rest of the group and tour a home manufacturing company. I decided it would be much more aligned with my professional goals to accompany Teppai to the pediatric center, despite the fact it meant spending the afternoon with Lesli. So I convinced the Rotarians to change my schedule, and I followed my hormones...I mean, my 'professional goals.'

That afternoon at the pediatric facility was one my best days with Lesli. She was wonderful with the children. I had never worked with a music therapist professionally, so I really wasn't clear what they did. When Lesli started singing and playing with the kids with Down syndrome and cerebral palsy, they came alive. I really understood how beneficial music was in motivating these kids. They were singing along and dancing, even though it was in English. The kids loved her, and I could see she loved them back. Lesli inspired me to get down on the floor and follow her lead; we laughed and smiled all afternoon. There is something about children that brightens up the rainiest days, especially kids who are so full of energy and life.

The story of my massive sake hangover must have been the talk of the week. As Teppai was driving me back to the sayonara party to end our time in Kuzuu, he stopped at a 7-Eleven. I wasn't sure what he was buying. I joked to Lesli when we were sitting alone in the car that he was probably stopping to buy some condoms, which got Lesli upset at me again. After a few minutes, he came back out with a few small cans that looked like soda cans. There was writing in Japanese, and he told me it was called Ukon No Chikara. He said I should drink one before the party that night and one after the party so I didn't get a hangover. I took his advice and drank the first one down; it tasted similar to Red Bull. As he dropped me off at the party, we said our goodbyes, and he said he would try to see me later in the month in Tokyo. That was the last time I ever saw Teppai, my first hot Japanese man. Based on our conflicting value system, it was probably for the best.

By time I got to the sayonara party, I had hives all over my arm. I had a massive allergic reaction to the Ukon No Chikara. Hickory saw them and wanted to tell her dad, but I insisted that she didn't. The last thing I wanted to do was create a scene at the sayonara party after working all week to recover from the terrible first impression I'd made at the welcome party. The party was held in a private room at a deluxe restaurant, and I mostly talked to Hickory.

My host Tommay gave a really nice speech about how much they had enjoyed having me in their home and I also stood up and expressed my gratitude to all the Rotarians. Luckily, I had a translator, so I could speak comfortably in English. I had brought some American Spirit cigarettes from home because I had been told how much Japanese men smoke, and the rumor was true. I brought a pack to the party, handed out the cigarettes, and we all smoked one together. I left in the morning. Hickory wrote me a really nice note and she cried when I left.

Chapter 6

JAPAN: OYAMA

I looked beautiful, I felt beautiful, I was an American Geisha…

***

As our Rotary group moved on to our next host city of Oyama, the group dynamics were starting to weigh heavily on me. I had never traveled with people that were so different from me. Our schedule was stressful, and there was rarely a free minute. The Japanese society is very orderly and formal and from the time I woke up in the morning until I retired to my room, I was constantly on stage. Our team was basically four strangers with different lives and views on the world and being together 24-7 was difficult. Sandy and Lesli, the two mothers, were constantly trying to 'mother' us. They dealt with the lack of control with constant small talk and directions, which was very annoying to me. On the bus ride to Oyama, I was sitting with Andrew and we were laughing about something when Sandy shushed me. I hadn't been shushed in years and had forgotten how demeaning it feels. Andrew and I sat in silence the rest of the bus ride; he was as frustrated with them as I was.

Sumia, my host in Oyama, was going to be spending the day with us. The Japanese culture is very punctual, but Sumia was a little scatterbrained at times and she mistakenly told us that the meeting was at 10:00 a.m. when it was at 9:30 a.m. By 9:33 a.m., she had received three calls wanting to know where we were. In American culture, there is usually a ten-minute grace period. In Japan, everyone gets to meetings ten minutes early, and by one minute after, you are considered late. We got there

Chapter 6: JAPAN: OYAMA

at 9:45a.m., a whopping 15 minutes late. I could tell it was a big deal to them; they were all speaking to her about it in Japanese. I didn't understand exactly, but it seemed stern.

It was going to be another packed day with many Japanese cultural events. The first stop was a Buddhist shrine. The winds were howling and blowing the bus as we traveled through a level-three typhoon. An old Japanese priest who was wearing a light purple traditional Japanese outfit greeted us at the temple. In broken English he instructed us through a ceremony where we offered a branch of a tree to the food God. The ceremony was very precise—I had to start walking up to the altar with my left foot, move the branch from my left hand to my right hand, bow twice, clap twice, and then place the branch on the altar. My walk back to the pew also started with my left foot. It seemed that even the religious rituals of Japan were not immune to the order and precision that pervaded every aspect of Japanese life.

I stayed quiet on the bus, still trying to work through my general feeling of irritability. The five days of constant rain were likely adding to my moodiness. We arrived at Mashiko Pottery village just as the storm was passing and the sky was clearing. Mashiko pottery is the premier brand of pottery in Japan. The factory is a collection of old Japanese buildings on sprawling grounds with many gardens. It is set up in the mountainous part of Tochigi, and the view of mountains all around added to the quaintness of this village.

I sat next to Andrew as we enjoyed our formal lunch on the grounds at Mashiko and shared how many of the days on this trip reminded us of elementary school. We remembered how funny tornado drills used to be as we both comically assumed the bracing position when the typhoon was passing through. I tried not to make too many references to our almost ten-year age difference. When he was in elementary school, I was finishing high school.

Once our stomachs were filled, we went into the studio to learn how to make pottery. The studio was a large room with two long rows of pottery throwing wheels. The master potter sat down and explained to us how to make Mashiko bowls, and then we all donned our blue aprons. We crowded around and listened intently. He made it look so easy, but I knew how difficult it really was. During the winter after my breakup with my ex, my friend Colleen and I had taken an eight-week wheel-throwing pottery class. It was quite therapeutic because we were all healing through art and friendship. I never became a master potter, but I developed a great respect for the skill of a potter.

It was really fun getting messy and playing with the clay, and I again found it therapeutic to work on the throwing wheel. I caught Andrew staring over at me a few times when my hands were dripping with wet clay and I was giggling like a schoolgirl. I don't know if it was the lasting impression of the classic Demi Moore and Patrick Swayze scene in the movie *Ghost* or there is just something really sensual about making pottery, but my mind couldn't help but fill with dirty thoughts. I once again realized the healing power of art. I left that studio feeling much lighter and far less irritable.

That night I was awoken from my sleep in the midst of a nightmare. I had many emotional nightmares the first few weeks in Japan. I don't know if it was the enormous amounts of sushi I had been consuming, the anxiety of being on display all day, or both. This vivid nightmare started out romantically. I was at my old house in Ferndale and had a surprise visit from my ex-boyfriend. He showed up at my house with flowers and wanted to get back together, saying all of the things I spent years after our breakup hoping he would say to me. It felt so real, and I was elated. We continued on to the bedroom, and I had one of the most vivid sexual dreams of my life. The next morning in my dream, I was dressed up to attend a wedding. It was *his* wedding, as I watched him marry someone else. I woke myself up that morning sobbing. I took a bath and smoked a cigarette as I tried to clear the dreadful nightmare from my head.

The next day was a vocational day at Jichi Medical Center, one of the largest university-based teaching hospitals in Japan. Lesli and I were given a tour by Dr. Mariko Momoi, a pediatrician and an inspirational woman. She had a graceful presence, but when she talked, she commanded respect. She spoke perfect English and was one of the best pediatricians in all of Japan. The hospital system had a separate pediatric hospital, which was where we all met and started our tour. The pediatric hospital had 135 beds and only two PTs; the main hospital had 1,130 beds and thirteen full-time PTs between the inpatient rehab and outpatient departments. There is a major PT shortage in Japan. There is also a PT shortage in the US, but the number of PTs in this huge hospital system was unbelievably low. Dr. Momoi told us that the national healthcare system had created a large shortage of healthcare providers in Japan. The benefits of the system are that Japan has a very low infant mortality rate and the total cost of health care in Japan is very low compared to the US. But the healthcare workers are overworked and underpaid.

That afternoon, Lesli and I, along with my hosts Sumia and her father G, went to a small Eastern medicine hospital. This hospital had an entirely different feel to it than the huge modern facility we'd toured that morning. It was small, and the beds looked old, but the energy in the building was very peaceful and soothing, not chaotic like Western hospitals. Learning Eastern medicine techniques was my focus for this entire exchange program, and I was finally getting this experience. I spent the afternoon learning about Kampo, an ancient form of Japanese medicine using herbs as medicine. Kampo is covered under the national healthcare system, and about 75% of physicians in Japan prescribe it. I studied a large chart similar to a periodic table of elements of the 148 different Kampo herbs.

In this system, the doctor's visit is similar to that in America—first a subjective report and then a physical exam. The doctor then mixes the appropriate Kampo numbers (representing different herbs) and gives it directly to the patient. Lesli and I were both a little congested, so the doctor made us the Kampo formula for a cold. I was leery after the hive incident with the Japanese hangover drink, but I tried it anyway. The Kampo was a greyish powder, and we had a large teaspoon of it with some water; it tasted bitter. I think it helped my congestion a little, but it was difficult to make a definitive statement after only one dose.

We moved to a different part of the hospital and learned about acupuncture. We were given a very brief introduction to the concept of the Ki (chi). Ki is the main unified energy

THE EVOLUTION OF A PARTY GIRL

source of all beings, and when it is blocked or out of balance, disease develops. Acupuncture uses very thin needles that are hooked up to an electrical charge to reestablish proper flow of Ki through the energy channels of the body. I volunteered to try it and had one needle placed in my hand. It was so thin that it didn't even draw blood. It was not painful, like typical needles; it was actually soothing.

After the acupuncture, we went to a different part of the hospital to learn shiatsu massage. A master sensei of shiatsu was coming to teach us. Lesli and I each spent an hour on the bed being a patient. I mostly watched while he worked on her, but every now and then he would teach me a technique and let me participate. The massage felt amazing. Surprisingly, I had had only one professional massage in my life up to that point. The shiatsu massage was quite different than the American style spa massage. The sensei spoke almost no English, so it was difficult to fully understand the philosophy, but with my physical therapy background, I learned just by watching him. He primarily used pressure from his thumbs to open up blockages of the energy lines or meridian lines in the body. He started on the skull and moved through the entire front side of the body. Then he moved to the back side, starting at the head again. Sumia tried to translate, but it was difficult with her limited English. He clearly stated that my right side liver meridian line was very tight. He said that I am cold too often, and I drink too much.

We couldn't speak the same language, but just by using his hands on my body he was able to zero in on problems with my health. I was always cold because I no longer had a thyroid, and I had struggled with drinking too much for years, which I am sure affected my liver. He looked at my hands and said that it would not be good for me to be a shiatsu therapist because my thumbs were too narrow and did not hyperextend.

When we finished up, Sumia had to pick up her daughter Caho from school. Lesli was really missing her children and said she would enjoy going to Caho's school with us. The school day was just about to end when we arrived. We went to the front office where Sumia introduced us to the principal. He came out and said he wanted to tour us around the school. We peeked in a few classrooms and all the kids' faces lit up

Chapter 6: JAPAN: OYAMA

when they saw us. When we arrived to Caho's class, they were just being dismissed. The energy in those kids was unbelievable; the kids swarmed us, and we were all hugging each other and laughing. Lesli became very emotional and started to cry, saying she missed her kids so much. I felt total joy with those kids as my maternal clock, which I had already hit the snooze button on several times, started to scream.

The next day, Sumia and I headed out early to start my glamour day. It was the first time in my life I was going to wear a kimono. We arrived at the kimono shop a few minutes late, again, and the other team members were already in the dressing room getting dressed. Andrew had arrived early since it was his host's family shop, and he was already dressed in a traditional samurai outfit. He looked great, and we pretended to sword fight with his prop sword. I wore my long hair up in a French twist; Younan told me all women put their hair up when they wear a kimono. The owners guided me to a rack of about twenty different kimonos and told me to pick out the one I wanted to wear. They were all attractive, and I would have been more indecisive if I wasn't already running late. I picked out a mostly black kimono with large pink flowers. The material was heavy, almost like thick polyester, but it was made to feel like silk. As I walked into the dressing room with my kimono in a box, I saw the other girls being dressed in their kimonos. Each person had two Japanese women working quickly through the many layers of fabric. They were laughing and having fun, playing dress-up. There was this beautiful little Japanese girl dressed in a kimono for her special five-year-old picture. She was so cute, my maternal instincts kicked in again, and I had to take a picture. She wore a bright pink kimono and ruby red lipstick, and had beautiful black hair.

I stood motionless and took in all the excitement in that dressing room. I must have looked confused; two Japanese women quickly scurried over to me and shuffled me into a dressing room. I first went into a private dressing room where I stripped down to my underwear and put on the first layer, which is a thin white cotton petticoat. Then I came out to the main dressing area and put on very funny socks. They were called *tabi* and were thick, white, and webbed between the first and second toe, and were worn with wooden clogs called *geta*. Next, I put on the second layer called a *nagajuban*. This layer was very similar to another kimono, but it was lighter material than the actual kimono; mine was light pink. The nagajuban was bound up very tightly at my waist. These Japanese women were small, but they moved quickly and were strong; they knew how to bind these layers tightly. The third layer was the actual kimono. It was many yards of beautiful flowing material. The sleeves were very confusing because the large sleeves from the nagajuban needed to be layered inside the even larger kimono sleeves. It was a hot late-fall day. I began to sweat with all the layers of polyester, and my makeup started to run. I was starting to feel uncomfortable. The kimono was getting heavy, and then they started to tightly tie the sash around my waist. The last step is tying the decorative obi, which is the large ornate bow in the back.

By the end of the 20-minute process, I had about ten pounds of fabric on, and I was hot and could barely breathe. Then I turned around and stared into the mirror. I looked beautiful, I felt beautiful, I was an American geisha! The layers of pink flowers and black fabric flowed so elegantly when I walked. In America, whenever I want to feel sexy, I always put fewer clothes on. That day I learned a lesson in modesty. I felt more beautiful and sexy than I had felt in years and yet I had more yards of fabric on than I had ever worn in my life. We had professional pictures taken of us, and then we made an outing in the kimonos. Getting in and out of the car was difficult. I am used to walking with my large New York City stride length, which is impossible in a kimono. Between the layers of tightly bound fabric and those wooden shoes, there is no way to walk other than a shuffle. Japanese women always have this very dainty walk, and now I too had mastered it. We went to a Buddhist temple and took many outdoor pictures in our kimonos. The weather was glorious, and we all felt beautiful. I had read the book *Memoirs of a Geisha* several years before and had always been intrigued by the lifestyle of the geisha girls. The Rotarian men couldn't help but stare at me in my kimono, and it reconfirmed my impression that I would have been a great American geisha girl.

Chapter 6: JAPAN: OYAMA

After our morning of playing dress-up, I was a little sad to put back on my boring khakis and Rotary uniform shirt. We had a few hours before our next event, and Sumia and I went to the mall. I was excited to see they had one of my favorite outdoor clothing shops—Montbell. Andrew and I had a plan to climb Mount Fuji after the official four-week exchange ended. Every host family that I told about my plan to climb Mount Fuji became very fearful and tried to convince me not to climb it. There is only a four-week official season where it is 'safe' to climb Fujisan. I was planning on climbing it for my 34th birthday, November 3rd, about five weeks after the 'safe' season, when it would be ice-capped and treacherous. Sumia was also very nervous about my climb. She told me a story of her father's friend who had died trying to climb it in the off-season when he was blown off the mountain by high winds.

I hadn't had space to pack my extreme weather hiking gear, so while at the mall, I tried on a raincoat, and Sumia really wanted to buy it for me. It is a tradition that the host families buy a gift for the people they host, but this was far more expensive than a token gift. She insisted and I finally agreed. When we left the store, we were both giggling, as we often did. When we looked up, there was a full rainbow covering the sky. We agreed it was a sign I was going to have a great climb up Mount Fuji.

This day was one of my favorite days of the exchange, a day of dress-up and shopping with Sumia, my favorite Japanese woman. The day continued to get better as we headed to our first formal tea ceremony. Hickory, my first host's daughter, had done a small tea ceremony for me, but this was going to be performed by a world-renowned master tea sensei. This master had spent his life training in the art of tea ceremonies. He was in his late 40s and was dressed in an all-black traditional Japanese outfit. He was married, and his wife was his assistant. Behind his house there was an ornate Japanese-style garden, a small Buddhist shrine, and a traditional tea ceremony house, where the ceremony was performed.

I sat next to Andrew at our farewell dinner in Oyama, and it wasn't long before we were drinking beer and laughing about some of his crazy experiences with his host family. His host owned a private male-only karaoke club with an attached hotel. I guessed these karaoke clubs were pretty close to what we consider a 'gentleman's club' in the US. The waitresses were all young women from nearby Asian countries, and I speculated that they were full-service 'waitresses.' Andrew had looked very tired and hungover for the last few days, but after getting a few beers in him, he finally shared with me some stories of his late-night karaoke club experiences. I'd had an idea that he'd had some wild nights that week, but they were crazier than I had originally thought. I learned that most of these very formal and rich Japanese Rotarian men led a dual life that involved many women at these 'karaoke clubs.'

After our banquet and a touching speech by Sumia about me, we headed home. G, Sumia's dad, opened a bottle of sake, and we spent our last night together with many laughs. I felt very connected to this family, and I gave them each another gift. I'd bought G a pair of Montbell gloves, and I gave Sumia one of my favorite books, *The Secret*, translated into Japanese. She had shared with me that things in her marriage were very difficult, and she wasn't sure if she should stay married. I had shared with her the devastating breakup that I was still healing from. *The Secret* was given to me by my coworker Lauren and it helped me develop a positive outlook on the world in the face of adversity. I hoped it would help Sumia, as well. We shared some laughs and tears that night. I went up to my apartment a little drunk and packed up for my move to my next host family. Even though we live on opposite sides of the globe, have different cultures, and speak different languages, I once again understood how similar our struggles are as women.

The morning I was leaving, I shared some final laughs with Sumia and G. Sumia surprised me with a bottle of Tabasco for the rest of my trip. I missed Tabasco and quickly opened it up and put it on my cheese and onion sandwich. They were shocked at how much I put on. G, not knowing what Tabasco was, put some in his miso soup. He tasted his soup and nodded in approval and said "oishi," which means delicious. Then he put some more Tabasco in his soup. Next he loaded his piece of toast with peanut butter with Tabasco. He really liked the Tabasco. I put Tabasco on my apple, and Sumia put Tabasco in her green tea. At this point G, Sumia, and I were all in tears, laughing at our Tabasco-off. I said my final goodbyes with Sumia, and I cried.

Chapter 7
JAPAN: KARASUYAMA and NIKKO

Even after a few weeks of living under this tightly regimented society, I understood how strong the pressure is for people to conform and the negativity it created...

***

Karasuyama was a very small town with a small Rotary Club; therefore, Sandy and I were both staying at the same host family's house. I thought this would be very good for us because our conversations were quite limited these days. After the first few weeks of struggling to relate to the suburban housewives of our group, I had basically thrown in the towel and found it easier to remain quiet than entertain the superficial conversations. I thought this opportunity to live with Sandy would help reconnect me to the group that I felt obligated to stay connected to.

As Andrew and I became closer and closer, we became more distant from the rest of the group. We looked forward to seeing each other every day. We usually sat together and had authentic conversations. Our relationship was developing into a potential romantic connection.

Our first day in Karasuyama was a welcome slowdown from the insanely busy schedule I had been struggling to maintain. I enjoyed my first midafternoon nap in weeks. The assistant governor came over to our host's house to meet us. He was the town psychiatrist and we talked about suicide rates in Japan, which are one of the highest in the world. Suicide is the number one cause of death in people under 30 years old in Japan. I was not entirely shocked to learn this; I had sensed some level of emotional emptiness and sadness in many of the Japanese people I had met. It's hard for me to fully articulate, but underneath all of the organization, efficiency, and outward appearances that had to be maintained, I felt that there was a strong undercurrent of emotional disharmony. Even after just a few weeks of living under this tightly regimented society, I understood how strong the pressure is for people to conform and the negativity that created. I was stressed and having nightmares almost every night. I felt overwhelmed and conflicted by some people's strong judgments of me. Needless to say, the hospitality they continued to extend was unparalleled. Nobuko, my host 'mom,' cooked a huge dinner for us. She made Asian green beans and grilled fish, and, of course, we washed it down with some local sake.

Our time in Karasuyama was mostly spent eating a special local fish, having quiet dinners with our host family, and of course drinking sake. We also toured the local beer factory, Kirin Beer. After the brewery tour we went to our first Japanese *onsen* (natural spring water baths). All onsens are split into male and female baths since you are required to be naked. This bathhouse was elaborate and I felt I'd been transported to an ancient European spa. It was a perfect fall day and I chose to be in the outdoor baths. The three other women in my group continued to small-talk with each other and stayed at the indoor onsen. Large white marble pillars and trees with autumn leaves surrounded the bath, the sun was shining bright, and the air was crisp. I was the only person in the outdoor bath, with bubbling, hot natural spring water embracing my nude body. I felt like a Greek goddess in my private bathhouse. I started doing my yoga and taking in all the natural beauty of Japan. I didn't feel that words could add to this experience, so I chose solitude even if the others felt like I was being antisocial.

In the morning, Nobuko and Toshio our host couple, drove us to our next stop, the tourist city of Nikko. Yoshia, a lovely Japanese woman about my age, who would be our translator and escort for the next four days, met us. She was a nice looking, confident, single woman and spoke excellent English. She explained our itinerary for the next four days as we drove to Kanaya Hotel, the oldest hotel in Japan, for lunch.

The hotel was beautiful and ornate, and it reminded me of a special hotel room I had shared with my ex-boyfriend. I was feeling homesick. My mind started to wander as I lamented my many failed relationships. I was going to be turning thirty-four in two weeks, and I never thought I would still be single at this age. I was tired of feeling like I had to constantly uphold this inauthentic restrained image of myself. I was always around people in Japan, but inside I felt very lonely. In a moment of weakness, I misused my Internet phone and called Troy. Troy and I had casually dated on and off over the past year, and it was the closest thing I'd had to a relationship since the breakup with my ex. I had not talked to him since he had cheated on me while on a trip to Rio de Janeiro five months ago. The conversation from Japan was very short. Troy had been a family friend since my childhood. I thought he would be a loyal and stable partner, but we were on totally different paths. I wanted to grow spiritually and achieve my personal goals in an equal partnership. He wanted to be a billionaire playboy in an open marriage, with plenty of low-class women on the side. I thought talking to him would take the edge off my loneliness, but I should have known better. Every time we got back together, I would hope he would see the light and outgrow his frat boy ways, but I once again hung up the phone feeling utterly disappointed. That was the last time I ever called Troy. As one relationship ends, it usually creates an opening in the universe for a new relationship to manifest, and I was still hoping for some romance in Japan.

After lunch, Yoshia took us to a shrine and explained the history of the buildings. As we were taking off our shoes to go into the main temple, she told us there was a private attached room only for the shogun of Japan and his direct descendants to pray in. The main temple was beautifully carved wood and that familiar inner stillness came over me.

Tension was continuing to mount in our group. Lesli was becoming unglued, as the stress of this month pushed her to her breaking point. She barely talked to me at all, and if she did, it was usually a rude and abrupt jab. Michelle tried to play both sides by complaining to me about Lesli and complaining to Lesli about me. Andrew continued to be my salvation, as the bond between us grew stronger. Sandy tried to keep our group together, but our massive personality differences kept the tension high.

Even so, in the midst of the thousands of people outside at the annual parade in Nikko, I could find peace within when I was in this powerful temple. Before this trip I had visited hundreds of temples in my worldly travel, but I had never felt connected to temples like I did on this trip. I would visit temples because they were historic places that tourists visit, but now I wanted to go to temple to experience that beautiful feeling of inner quietness that I had recently discovered. I sat on the floor and began to pray, and then Yoshia told us the director of the temple was here to escort us into the private room of the shogun. She explained it was a huge honor; she had taken tours to this temple hundreds of times and had never been invited into this sacred room. It was amazing. The entire ceiling was covered with ornately carved wood tiles of phoenixes and other scenes from historic Japan. In the center of the room was the large family crest of the shogun family. Underneath that exact crest, in that exact room, eighteen shoguns had prayed for over a thousand years. I was humbled by the thought.

We were staying at a hostel that night in Nikko. I had never stayed at a hostel, but it was nice, and the atmosphere was somewhere between a college dorm and a standard Holiday Inn. It was Friday night, and we were just about to break out the bottles of vodka that I had bought on the airplane when I made an astonishing discovery. My black Coach purse was not with me, and my passport was in that purse. I emptied all of my bags with no luck and went into red alert. I told Sandy, who was eager to help. We went to the front desk, and they let me use their phone. I called Nobuko and Toshio's house where I had left that morning. No one answered, and I left a voicemail. We called back and Sandy tried to leave a voicemail in Japanese. I was panicked; I couldn't think of who to call. I didn't have Yoshia's phone number, so I called Sumia, my previous host, who spoke better English, and asked her if she could call Nobuko and Toshio and ask them to search their house for my purse. She understood and said she would do whatever she could to help. I was in a state of panic.

The rest of my group was also upset about my passport situation. I went back to my room and sat, feeling stressed. I decided to use the crystal I'd been carrying with me ever since I'd attended the channeling with Cassie. It is a Tibetan quartz crystal, which is known to be very powerful. At that moment of chaos and fear, l held my crystal tight and said, "With all my power and all the power in this crystal, please help get my purse and my passport back to me." At that very moment, there was a knock on the door. It was the lady from the front desk. She said that Nobuko had just called and my purse was on their front porch. The universe delivered my purse back. I had never prayed so powerfully for anything to come back to me before, but the results were instantaneous. I couldn't believe what had just happened, but this type of experience would become more common in the coming months.

Andrew was the only person in my group I could share something so personal with. After the red alert passed, our group sat around and had some drinks in Andrew's room. We had two rooms: the four of us women were to share a small dormitory style room with four beds, and Andrew had a huge traditional Japanese tatami-style room to himself. We made some impromptu apple martinis, and we all were feeling in a mood to celebrate. We played cards, cracked jokes, and shared some of our most embarrassing stories. This was the first time in weeks our group had been together alone, without any Rotarians, and we could finally feel relaxed.

Eventually, the other girls were ready for bed, but I wasn't. I wanted to stay and chat with Andrew, so I went next door, got my stuff, and set up an extra futon in Andrew's room to spend the night in his spacious living quarters. We talked for a bit, finished up the cocktails, and went to bed. He made a suggestive comment to me for the first time on this trip. He said he wanted to sleep in my futon, not across the room from me. We were both a little buzzed and lonely, so I said goodnight and acted like I hadn't heard him. We woke up early and I got ready in Andrew's room because the other three girls were all sharing one bathroom. We packed up our bags and moved to an upscale hotel that night, not speaking of what he'd said the night before.

It was finally time to head to our hotel after another long and eventful day. We checked into the Park Hotel and we were pleased to see we had four separate rooms. I managed to squeeze in a quick bath and was dressed and dolled up for dinner in 45 minutes. It was one of the first events in a long time that we didn't have to wear uniforms, and I wore my black open-back shirt with black leggings and my knee-high boots. I felt sexy. We headed to an exclusive private dining room at the hotel. Andrew's jaw dropped when I came into the room, and he told me I looked beautiful. I sat with Yoshia at dinner, and Lesli sat across the table, shooting jealous glares at me through most of the dinner. Then she started talking about how loudly Sandy had snored in the dorm room they'd shared the previous night. I tried to be as polite as possible when I said, "I don't think that is a very nice dinner conversation, Lesli, do you?" After all the mothering they had been doing to me, I felt justified in mothering back. She was enraged—I could see the flames coming out of her ears, and if looks could kill, I would have been dead.

Aside from Lesli's insecurities, it was a nice dinner. I had Yoshia on one side and Andrew on the other. We drank many glasses of fine red wine, ate lots of sushi, and laughed the night away. After dinner I needed some time away from the group, especially Lesli. It was Saturday night, and I wanted to go out by myself. I found a karaoke bar and after much coaxing from the owner and a Bombay Sapphire on the rocks, I sang "I Will Survive" by Gloria Gaynor. It was exactly what I needed to go back and face my group

When I got back to the hotel, Sandy and Andrew were in the lobby drinking beer; I think they were waiting up for me. We talked briefly, but they were pretty drunk and so was I. I said I was heading to my room and Andrew said he would walk me back since our rooms were next door to each other. The hotel was a huge maze and very easy to get lost in, but I don't think that was his only reason. He asked me if I wanted to stop by his room and have a glass of tea before bed; I said okay and before I knew it, it was happening. We were on his bed and making out.

He said he had been waiting for this opportunity for weeks, and things got hot and heavy quickly. It didn't take long before most of our clothes were on the floor. It took all the willpower I had not to have sex with Andrew that night. I had not had sex in more than three years since my breakup with my ex, and I wasn't going to break my streak like this. After that breakup, I had promised myself that I wasn't going to have sex with anyone unless I was in a healthy, committed relationship. I'd continued to be true to my goal through many superficial relationships, and to the frustration of many men over the last few years. I wasn't going to give up on my goal in a moment of drunken loneliness. Andrew was shocked when I jumped out of bed and said I had to get out there. He pleaded for me to stay as I quickly got dressed and went to my room, hoping none of the other team members would see me leaving. In my hurried exit, I left my sexy black underwear in his bed.

The next morning was my first major hangover since that dreaded first day in Sano. I woke up and buried my head in the pillow and laughed about the events of a few short hours ago. I had to face Andrew first thing in the morning. Usually after drunken hookups, you don't have to see the other person ever again or at least for a few weeks. In this case, I still had to spend every day with Andrew for the next two weeks. We saw each other in the morning and neither one of us was eager to make eye contact. He looked as hungover as I did, and we were heading to the Kinu River to go on a boat ride. Not good for the nausea, but maybe the fresh air and natural beauty would do us both some good.

I sat next to Yoshia on the boat, and she told me how much fun she'd had with me last night at dinner. Michelle also sat next to me on the boat and opened up to me for the first time. She told me that Lesli was also driving her nuts and she wanted to hang out with Andrew and me more. I could see Lesli glaring at me again with jealousy as Michelle, her 'BFF,' and I sat and talked and laughed together. The boat was large and reminded me of a gondola; it had a man in the back using a large pole to steer and he was wearing a traditional Japanese straw hat. The boat ride was beautiful, but between the hangover and the awkwardness, I had a very hard time enjoying the ride.

Chapter 7: JAPAN: KARASUYAMA and NIKKO

We headed to a place called Edo Wonderland after the boat ride. It was a park that was reconstructed to represent the Edo time period of Japan. It reminded me of a renaissance festival in the USA. All the people were dressed in traditional clothes of the period, and Yoshia told me they were speaking old-style Japanese. The Rotarians wanted us to see a traditional-style Japanese animated show. We sat on the floor in a dark room while an animated character jumped all over the screen and spoke loudly; it was awful. I decided to take the opportunity to meditate for the first time in weeks. I reached into my bra and took out my crystal to give me strength and guidance on how to deal with Andrew and even how to handle Lesli. I meditated on finding answers during the 25-minute play.

During mindful meditation, I looked at a problem and tried to peel the layers away, like an onion, until I came up with answers within myself. I realized that the purpose of all of these experiences was to teach me something about myself. Traveling with this group brought my lack of patience and tolerance, and my overdrinking to the forefront. Having to sacrifice my independent spirit and always conform to the group definitely led me to drink more to cope. All the fancy parties and the drinking, which the Rotarians encouraged of their guests of honor, was something that I was trying to get away from in my life back home. I had also totally lost focus on my yoga practice, was struggling with the lack of vegetarian options, and had no time for reading or meditating. All of my internal mechanisms were failing, and I felt a total lack of control over my life. I continued to 'show well' as I struggled every day to put on a smile, be elegant, and represent myself and my country well while not ever complaining about wearing these awful uniforms that Michelle and Lesli had picked out. I kept going deeper and deeper through my layers of anger and frustration until I came to love and compassion; love and compassion for Lesli and Andrew, and gratitude for this amazing opportunity I'd been given. I had only one week left of the Rotary exchange and would certainly miss the high life on the next leg of my trip, living in India.

When the lights came back on after the show, I was rejuvenated and at peace and ready to talk to Andrew again. I broke the ice with some light comments about how terrible the show was, and Andrew and I spent the rest of the time together at the park; we both acted as if nothing had happened the night before.

Our lunch was another gourmet meal, but we were all very tired of Japanese food. Many times Michelle was served a different meal because she was allergic to shellfish and doesn't eat any seafood. This time she was served a sizzling steak, and we were served more sushi. Lesli got up from the table and ran to the bathroom. Soon after, I also went into the bathroom and found Lesli sobbing. She said she hated this food and it was so unfair that Michelle was served steak. She said she missed her family and she wanted to go home. Just yesterday, Lesli had complained to Sandy about me, and part of me wanted to just walk away. But I'd made a promise to myself after my cancer to not walk away when someone is crying out for help. That day I was her angel, helping her through her almost-public meltdown. I told her it was hard for all of us, and that she was doing a great job representing Canada. I told her she was setting a great example for her children, and it would broaden their horizons. It worked and Lesli started to perk up. I reminded her that after being home for a week and back in the role of mom, she was going to wish we were back being served top quality sushi in Japan. She agreed and we both starting laughing.

We arrived back at the hotel pretty late, but Sandy was determined that we had to practice our presentation. We hadn't presented in Japanese in almost a week and she wanted us to run through it before bed. We all sat in Sandy's room and I watched Andrew and Michelle flirting like crazy. I couldn't believe what I was seeing. After last night's failed hookup, he was now trying to pursue Michelle...unbelievable. I went to bed as soon as we were finished, so I didn't have to watch the display. I was disgusted with men!

I woke up early and went down by myself to the onsen. I came back to my room in my hotel-supplied yukata (a light kimono) and saw Andrew in the hall locked out of his room. Was he just leaving Michelle's room and I'd caught him? Or was I being jealous and letting my mind run away with me? He looked like a deer in the headlights when he saw me. I smiled and said good morning, went into my room, and tried not cry. I went to breakfast in my yukata. I sat at a table in the corner, but I could barely eat, contemplating the thought of Michelle and Andrew hooking up last night. Sandy and Lesli came down and said they'd tried to wake up Michelle, but she said she was skipping breakfast. Was that another sign? Was my mind wandering to the worst-case scenario, or was Andrew just another typical bed-hopping, slimy guy? I went back to my room and got dressed.

We spent the morning touring two local art museums. My body was at the museum, but my mind was in a fog. I felt bad—I did not really want a relationship with Andrew, but I certainly did not want him hooking up with someone else the night after we did, and having it in front of my face. A camerawoman stayed with me most of the time. I was smiling and talking, and I tried to save face. Then she asked me to do an interview. During the interview, my mouth was talking but my mind was so annoyed, I can't imagine the interview was good. I was glad very few people in Japan could understand my English gibberish.

After lunch I started to perk up and decided I didn't want to put any more energy into these negative thoughts. I had a choice to either be annoyed for the rest of the trip or be glad he wasn't my boyfriend and just make the best of my time in this amazing country. Andrew and I were staying in Japan for an extra week after the exchange and traveling together, so I was going to need to figure out how to carry on with him. I decided that the next time we are all together, I was going to flirt with other men and see how he liked it! Our next stop was a police station for Michelle's vocational visit. We had another judo demonstration; I kept my eyes closed for most of the main demonstration but still could hear the slamming and punching. After the group sparring, a tall Japanese man came into the gym dressed in a samurai uniform. I could feel the energy in the room change. He moved very slowly, almost like he was floating across the floor. When he reached the center of the gym, he quickly pulled out his long sword and placed it on the floor. Then he bowed in front of the sword and prayed. After a few minutes of silence, he began his demonstration; it was slow, skillful, and very precise. It reminded me of a ballet, not martial arts. I was so mesmerized by his beautiful work that I totally overlooked the sword. In that moment I developed a new understanding and respect for martial arts. I have been a long-time advocate of nonviolence and I have always believed that violence was an excuse for people to not seek better forms of communication. I always connected violence with the lack of proper education on tolerance, compassion, and love. When I saw that samurai get down and pray before picking up his sword, I understood that this was his form of serving God. Just as my role is as a physical therapist, his role was as a samurai, and I felt compelled to respect that. His amazing poise and discipline was very respectable. This was the first martial arts demonstration that I'd actually watched and enjoyed.

That night we had a dinner we had been looking forward to for days. The Kanuma Rotary Club was taking us out to an Italian restaurant for dinner. Andrew asked if he could sit next to me for dinner and must have noticed my coolness toward him despite my best efforts to move forward. We had an Italian feast in Japan. It was delicious. We had risotto and antipasto salad, and they made me a special dish of fettuccine Alfredo with mushrooms. The dinner was topped off with several glasses of Chianti, Pinot Noir, and Cabernet. After a few glasses of wine, I couldn't help but ask Andrew if something had happened with Michelle the night before. He denied it and made me feel like I was overly jealous for having such thoughts. Who knows the truth, but part of me felt like it was a calculated move to intentionally make me jealous after I'd denied him that night in Nikko. His plan was working—my jealousy was persuading me to hook up with him again before we left Japan.

Chapter 8
JAPAN: DISTRICT CONFERENCE, AND TOKYO

My birthday celebration had begun in the form of a 24-year-old boy toy wrapped up in my bed sheets...

***

The district conference was another dog and pony show. We paraded around in our uniforms, constantly being photographed. We sat in the front row at a large table with our nameplates and listened to hours upon days of speeches in Japanese. If I hadn't been so burned out by this point, it may have been more enjoyable, but after 27 straight days, it was hard to keep my fake smile glowing. Our presentations went well, and on the final day of the district conference, Andrew and I skipped the speeches to go to a Tochigi Soccer Club game.

This was one of the two vocational visits Andrew had during the entire month, since he'd just graduated from college in sports management. Andrew asked if I could come along to the game, and the Rotarian who 'escorted' us bought me a ticket. We got to the game a little late since our Rotarian took us to a sake bar in the morning before the game. The game was really fun. The soccer team was on a horrible losing streak so the stands were mostly empty. We went to the press box and met some of the reporters who had just done a story on us the day before. Then we met the owner of the soccer club, who was a jovial guy, and finally we met the cheerleaders and I got a few pictures of Andrew surrounded by them. Andrew and I were

Chapter 8: JAPAN: DISTRICT CONFERENCE, AND TOKYO

a little buzzed from our breakfast sake, but we continued to drink a few beers at the game.

We left our escort and walked around the field to the fan section. When we got behind the bleachers, he pulled me toward him and started kissing me. This was our first kiss since our hookup in Nikko, and unfortunately, we were drunk again. It was really fun—I felt like I was in high school again, making out behind the bleachers. We were both giddy after the explosive kiss. We made it to the outrageous fan section where many people were covered in body paint and chanting, cheering, and playing the drums. It was total chaos, and in the middle of it, he started kissing me again.

We arrived back to the district conference late, quickly changed out of our soccer-cheering apparel into our formal uniforms, freshened up, and headed down to the banquet hall. The formal dinner at district conference was truly fun. I had a chance to see almost all my host families again. I felt like I recognized most of the 700 people at the conference. In Japan, when dinner is served, everyone gets up and starts to mingle. There is always a sharp end time of the party, so once dinner is over the party is over. I tried to eat a little food after all my drinking at the soccer game, but I was too busy walking around and seeing everyone for my final goodbye. I saw Toshio and Nobuko, who gave me back my purse and my passport, thank God! I saw G, who had another small gift for me. Sumia was not there, and neither was Tommay, my first host, who was working, of course. I saw the presidents from all the Rotary Clubs I had visited over the last month. I met the governor of the Rotary Club of Tochigi Prefecture. He was a powerful man that had a magnetic presence. He came over several times to talk to me, but his English was very limited. I think he was trying to flirt with me, but I had already learned that the lost-in-translation Japanese flirting was unsuccessful with me.

I packed up from my final host family and our group headed to Tokyo to spend the last few days of our exchange at a hotel. The rooms were small, but the hotel was very chic and modern. Just after we checked in, we got ready to go out for dinner. We went to a corporate chain Japanese restaurant. The food was acceptable and the variety could satisfy all our different palates.

THE EVOLUTION OF A PARTY GIRL

After dinner the rest of the group went back to the hotel, and Andrew and I went out. In Tokyo they have vending machines on almost every corner that sell everything from water and tea to cigarettes and beer. We bought some vending machine beers and decided to just walk around and explore Tokyo at night. It was raining, but it was a gentle rain that created a romantic atmosphere. Kids in Japan love video games; they have video arcades on every block and they are filled with people. We decided to give it a try. We played two musical video games; I played one with drums and Andrew played one with a guitar. It was fun, but I was terrible and could barely keep up at the easiest level of the game. As soon as I finished playing, a seven-year-old boy came over to my game. He took his personal drum sets out of his bag and started 'rocking out.' It was amazing. The speed he could move was mind-boggling. I was getting dizzy watching so I decided to dance instead of watch. Andrew joined in. In a surreal moment, we danced together, soaking wet, to an amazing drum set being played by a seven-year-old in a video arcade in Tokyo.

After the arcade, we found this beautiful Buddhist temple that was set high on a hill. We climbed the steps to the main gate and sat and talked. Andrew and I really talked openly that night. We talked about our hopes and dreams, we shared our fears, and I realized that even though he was only 24, he had a mature view of the world. I felt connected to Andrew that night. After these last few days with the group, Andrew and I were going to be traveling together for a week. Not just any week, but my birthday week. I had been thinking a lot about the idea of having sex with Andrew. I thought that being intimate with someone else might bring closure to my relationship with my ex, and this seemed like the perfect time. I was in Japan, I was going to be traveling abroad for the next six months, and it was my birthday. There were several times during the last three years I had thought about how women hit their sexual peak in their early thirties. I had been celibate for most of my early thirties and the thought of missing my sexual peak depressed me. Ironically, I decided on the steps of that temple that I was going to have sex with Andrew.

Chapter 8: JAPAN: DISTRICT CONFERENCE, AND TOKYO

We stopped by a 7-Eleven on the way home to pick up a bottle of wine, and I secretly bought a pack of Japanese condoms. We got back to the hotel around midnight and decided to have our nightcap in Andrew's room. Tomorrow was our first free morning in weeks, and we weren't meeting up with the group until two o'clock; it was a great day to sleep in. We opened up the bottle of wine and it wasn't long before we were making out again. He kissed me very passionately, enough to get me very turned on, but not so aggressively that I felt like I needed to pull back. His lips were soft and his body was firm against mine. We stood in front of the huge window that overlooked downtown Tokyo and kissed and kissed. A few times I pulled back and looked at him, and we would start to giggle. There was something about a forbidden relationship and sneaking around that made it even more exciting. I felt free, not having to pull back, not having to keep telling myself no, finally feeling free to enjoy the sensual experience. I hadn't felt this free in an intimate experience in years. I cared for Andrew; we had spent every day together for the last month. I knew it wasn't love, but I didn't want love—I wanted sex.

He slowly walked me over to the bed and started to undress me. With every piece of clothing that fell off, I felt freer. I wanted to go slow, not because I was afraid, but because I felt so good that I wanted this moment to last. I drank a few sips of my wine and started to undress him in a teasing playful way, sipping wine between buttons, zippers, and giggles. He wasn't enjoying the slow and playful pace as much as I was. He was twenty-four and full of sexual energy. I felt like the older woman having to slow him down and teach him a few lessons along the way. He finally pushed me onto the bed and climbed on top of me. I was ready and so was he. I had waited many years to have sex and couldn't wait any longer to feel that orgasmic bliss. I reached to my purse and grabbed the condoms I had bought. They were Japanese condoms, which should be the same as in America, right? Wrong! Well, ladies, all the rumors are true—the Japanese condoms were tiny. We struggled to get the condom on and broke one. Andrew protested having to wear it, but finally we were ready. After a few more minutes of kissing, we were both over the awkward condom situation

THE EVOLUTION OF A PARTY GIRL

and back in the heat of passion. I was a little concerned it might hurt after so many years.

After we had sex, I walked over to the window and got my emergency American Spirit cigarette out of my purse. I cracked the window and sat naked on the windowsill, my silhouette in the moonlight. City lights cast my shadow through the entire room. Andrew stood behind me kissing and caressing my neck. My birthday celebration had begun in the form of a 24-year-old boy toy wrapped up in my bed sheets.

We stayed in bed naked until noon. We had sex again in the morning, and he said, "I have been waiting for this morning since the first day I met you." He kissed me goodbye, and I snuck back to my room to get showered and meet the group. I had done it, and it felt incredible. I immediately wondered why I had waited so many years.

We spent a thrilling afternoon driving cars at an ice-covered tire-testing track and got home in time for dinner. The girls went out together, and Andrew and I went out for Chinese food. We came back to the room early for another night of orgasms in Tokyo.

The next morning I snuck back into my room early to pack up and get ready. It was the last official day of our group study exchange. I had survived the language barrier, the cultural barriers, and trying to fit into a stereotype that was very far from who I really was. And... I'd had sex for the first time in almost four years. I still had a week left in Japan and six months of traveling in Asia. Michelle and Lesli were also staying in Japan another week and traveling together. Sandy, who was flying back to the US, came into my room as I was packing up to say her final goodbye to me. She looked down at my perfectly made bed, looked at me, and then looked at the bed again; she didn't say anything, but she had to have known.

We checked out, and Andrew and I took a cab to Chris's house. I had never met Chris, but a mutual friend had introduced us on Facebook, preparing for my visit. She had left her apartment keys with the doorman and we went up to her amazing penthouse on the 28th floor. Everything in Tokyo was small and expensive, like my apartment in NYC, but this apartment was a penthouse. It had a full wall of windows that overlooked the Tokyo tower and on a clear day you could see Mount Fuji. It was such an amazing apartment, with a friendly cat, and we had no schedule and no reason to leave. We spent all day just lounging in 'our' penthouse. We watched a movie, we listened to music, and I read.

We met Chris for dinner at a small Mexican restaurant called Junkadelic. It was one of the first places I had been in Japan that had a hippie vibe, and it was a welcome change from the stuffy events I was getting used to. It was strange waiting to meet Chris after we had already spent all day in her apartment with her cat. Chris was a beautiful middle-aged woman from Florida. She had short red hair and was a well-polished American businesswoman. I'd always heard people say that I was very American and I wasn't sure what it meant, but now I started to understand. American women are free and there is a strength and confidence that they possess that I have seen in few other countries. Chris was a vice president of a large US company, and I could tell by her demeanor and her immaculate penthouse that she was a strong career woman. It was so refreshing to talk to another strong American woman. We shared a pitcher of margaritas over nachos and good conversation.

Chris was an amazing hostess; she opened her home and her heart to us. I stayed in the guest bedroom, and Andrew stayed on an air mattress in the family room. Chris left early in the morning for work, and Andrew came into my room. We stayed in bed until almost noon again, packed up, and began the long trip to Kyoto. This month had been so physically and emotionally exhausting, we both felt so happy not to be on a schedule. It was the first day in a month that we'd woken up with only our own schedule to fill. We each left a bag at Chris's house, and she invited us to stay back at her house the night before we flew home. I was excited and nervous to spend a week alone with Andrew; I had not spent a week alone with a man in several years. I had developed walls around myself, and I wanted to relearn what intimacy felt like during our short time together.

Chapter 9
JAPAN: KYOTO, AND FUJISAN

I had spent years learning and unlearning love. I didn't want to turn into a cold, calloused, and lonely woman. I swallowed my discomfort and opened myself back up to his expression of affection...

***

For the first time in a month, we were on our own. We had to navigate to the subway station and then to the train station and get on the correct bullet train, all while carrying our own luggage. We had no translator and no map. We made it to the train station just in time to catch the train to Kyoto. It was difficult, and we had no time to get lunch; I was hungry, cranky, and exhausted. The bullet train was unbelievable; it was like riding a roller coaster at 300 MPH. The views from the train of the Japanese countryside were beautiful and we got our first glance of Mount Fuji out the window. After a long day of traveling and our first mini fight, we arrived at the Rhino Hotel. The hotel was basic, not like the luxury hotels we had stayed in with the Rotarians. Once we were settled, we took the subway to the oldest park in Kyoto, which was along the river. Kyoto had a liberal and artistic vibe that was different than anywhere else I had been in Japan.

Andrew and I walked along the old narrow brick sidewalks, on our first official 'date night.' Kyoto was one of the only cities in Japan that was not destroyed during WWII—the buildings were all perfectly maintained traditional Japanese architecture. It was a full moon, and the streets were alive with a vibrant nightlife. We watched two fire dancers as they performed on the river's edge; it was mesmerizing. Their highly fit bodies were glistening with oil as they performed an almost erotic fire show. We were getting hungry and decided to look for a restaurant. The moment the Rotary exchange portion of the trip had ended, Andrew and I had made a few rules. The first one was a strict policy of 'no more Japanese food.' The second was 'no overscheduling.' There were some of the oldest and finest restaurants along the river's edge, but they all broke our Japanese food moratorium. We walked to another touristy shopping area and found an Indian restaurant. I was sure after a few months in India I was going to be just as fed up with Indian food, but on our first dinner date it tasted like heaven. Andrew had never had Indian food before, and he fell in love with it at that meal. We openly flirted and giggled while sharing my favorite vegetarian foods. We got lost trying to navigate back to our hotel, but all the struggling was worth the freedom.

We awoke to a rainy morning in Kyoto. We had no schedule and enjoyed spending a long morning in bed together. He had a 24-year-old's sexual appetite, and I was experiencing a voracious sexual rebound after my period of celibacy; he was always ready to go, and I was an enthusiastic partner. I was feasting on lots of playful morning sex, which amounted to us never getting out of bed until at least noon.

It was a holiday in Japan, the birthday of the past emperor. The palace grounds in Kyoto only open to the public a few days a year, and luckily this holiday was one of these special days. The emperors had lived in Kyoto for most of the history of Japan; it was only in recent history (1868) that the emperor had shifted the family residence to the Tokyo palace. There was so much to see in Kyoto, but our intimate time together seemed more important than any tourist attractions. Based on our rule of no overscheduling, we decided to only see two of the main attractions of Kyoto.

We went to the palace first. It was now pouring rain, and Andrew and I shared an umbrella. That day we were forced to walk together closely under our shared umbrella, and he spent most of the day holding my hand. I felt really uncomfortable with the handholding. Sex was one thing, but actual intimacy was awkward and scary. We were at a beautiful Japanese palace.

I was trying to act casual and enjoy the sights, but I kept focusing on the fact that he was holding my hand in public. Over the last few years, I had built thick walls around myself to avoid any real emotional connection with a man. I was surprised how uncomfortable his displays of affection made me feel. I was hesitant to step back into the twilight zone of intimacy. I had read a lot of self-help books and spent many hours talking to a therapist, but understanding healthy relationship techniques in a book or an office is totally different than actually applying the tools I had learned. I was afraid, not to travel the world alone, but to experience emotional vulnerability with a man. I was clear that this was going to be a short-lived relationship with Andrew, and I used that as an excuse to keep the walls around my emotions impenetrable. I was, however, curious if some of my codependent relationship patterns would start to surface again. I had spent years learning and unlearning love. I didn't want to turn into a cold, calloused, and lonely woman. I swallowed my discomfort and opened myself back up to his expression of affection. I started to understand our relationship as a safe place to practice new relationship skills. It was a great opportunity to see if I had learned some of the hard lessons I needed to learn from my failed relationships. That day Andrew and I acted like a couple in love.

In the afternoon we went to the iconic golden temple. It was a Zen Buddhist temple built by the third shogun. It was still pouring rain, which added to the mysticism of the experience and helped thin the crowd of all the tourists. The temple was built on an island in the middle of many Japanese gardens and ponds. We were not allowed to go on the island, or tour the inside of the temple, but it was the backdrop of our romantic walk. We spent an hour strolling hand in hand through the gardens. Just as the sun was coming out, we found a small rushing waterfall with the mist creating a rainbow. A beautiful Japanese crane was perched on a tree beside the water and for that moment everything looked and felt magical. I was overcome with emotion by the beauty of the natural world. We sat together in silence, holding hands and breathing deeply. During that moment I was reminded of the beauty of opening myself up to a new relationship.

Chapter 9: JAPAN: KYOTO, AND FUJISAN

At night we walked to a French restaurant by our hotel. We had two bottles of wine, mussels, and a cheese plate. Just what we needed—more aphrodisiacs. I let the wine expose the fears that come out when I start to care for someone. I was starting to become attached to my 24-year-old sex toy, and I was afraid. I had been training my mind to keep this relationship just sexual, but that has never been something I have been able to do. Many of my friends are able to "just have sex" with a guy, but that has never been me. I become emotionally attached to men when we share intimacy. The only people in my life I had sex with were people that I loved and now I was struggling to separate the sex from love. I knew in a few days our passionate love affair would be over. After the second bottle of wine, I started to pick a fight about something irrelevant to keep myself from feeling the connection that was developing between us. I was again becoming a victim to my self-sabotaging behaviors around love and relationship. I was using alcohol to numb the pain. That night I went to bed with my clothes on, drunk and angry. I pretended to be mad at Andrew, but I was really mad at myself.

The best part of fighting is making up, and that morning we definitely made up—in bed, on the windowsill, and again in the shower. We checked out of the hotel and took on the task of again traveling in Japan with no maps and just two Post-it notes with some train numbers on them. Neither Andrew nor I were planners, but we both knew somehow we would always get there. My birthday was the next day and we were on our way to Mount Fuji! There was no direct way to get there; it took five trains to get from Kyoto to the Kwagichicko Station Inn. It took us all day to travel, and we got in after dark. It was an amazing full moon, and yet the dark sky enveloped Mount Fuji.

The morning of my birthday I was so excited to look out the window of our room and see the magnificent Fujisan in all its glory, right in front of our hotel. What a perfectly shaped mountain and it was waiting for me to meet her. It had snowed gently the previous night, and when I went to the front desk, I found out the road up to the fifth station, the starting point for our trek to the peak of Mount Fuji, was now closed. RATS! Our plan had been to take the first morning bus to the fifth station and begin our hike up. There are no overnight accommodations beyond station five so we had to complete our climb in one day. Andrew had wanted to sleep in, and we'd missed the first bus. I was frustrated; my dream of my birthday party atop Mount Fuji was fading fast. We walked across the street to the bus station and sat and waited for the 10:00 a.m. bus. The driver told us the road to the fifth station was still closed, but he would drop us off at the first station. We were on the bus with two loud, obnoxious, stereotypical Americans. They were overweight and had thick Southern accents. They boasted they were from Texas and continued to talk loudly about all their money. They were negative about everything they talked about, from the US economy to the country of Japan. I felt so annoyed, and then they got worse. They started talking to Andrew and making fun of Detroit. I finally broke my silence and said, "Today is my birthday, and I would appreciate as a birthday gift to me if you could keep your negative opinions about my hometown to yourself." I went on to say, "These loud conversations that you guys are having are exactly why so many American tourists get the awful reputation that we have. Please be quiet." They were shocked, and I think Andrew was too, but it was my birthday and so far nothing was going right.

The bus dropped us off right at the barricade in the road by station one. We stated walking up the road. We could see Mount Fuji's summit in the distance; it seemed really far from where we were, and it was already 11:00 a.m. I thought we were going to be on a trail when we hiked Mount Fuji so I had been lugging around my huge and heavy hiking boots for the past five weeks, only to be walking up a road, not a trail. The scenery was beautiful, and the weather was perfect, but this was not the way I wanted to hike Mount Fuji. I was trying to stay positive and make jokes about the situation, but I was disappointed. This day was supposed to be the highlight of my entire trip to Japan. While I had been enduring all the stuffy parties and judgmental women, my mind would always wander to being on Mount Fuji, and I would find the strength to smile and withstand the toxicity. The two loud American men were also hiking the road with us, and I could hear them yelling loudly no matter how fast we tried to hike. We did finally manage to get out of ear range and were able to experience some of the true si-

Chapter 9: JAPAN: KYOTO, AND FUJISAN

lent beauty that only the mountains can provide. The weather had cleared and the sky was this amazing color of blue. The snow-covered summit against the blue sky with the green pine trees was my celebration in nature. Despite all the naysayers and all the times we thought about turning around, we were officially urban-hiking Mount Fuji on my 34th birthday.

We hiked past station two and sat down for lunch at a nice spot before station three. We started to calculate the time we had before we had to get back down to catch the bus back to the hotel. If you miss the last bus, you are stuck on Fuji for the night without a tent. As we were having lunch we saw the 2:00 bus pass us and drive up the road to drop people off at station five—the road had reopened! Now I was even more annoyed that the busses were going up to station five and we were no longer sure where to get the bus back to town. The morning driver spoke very little English, but when he dropped us off, he had clearly said he would be back at 4:45p.m. to pick us up at station one. With the road reopened now, we had no idea if we should try to catch the last bus at station five, or hike back to station one. We finished lunch and decided to hike up to station three, still via the road, and make our decision based on time. We thought maybe another bus would come, and we could flag it down and have them take us up to station five. During our lunch break, the two guys from America caught up to us and were in the same predicament we were. We found out that the louder of the two actually lived in Japan. He must have had an executive job, because he got on his cellphone and had his assistant call a taxi to pick them up and take them up to station five. It was going to cost him $200 USD. He asked if we wanted to join them and split the cost of the cab. Andrew and I were both on a tight budget, and being in a cab with these two yahoos for my birthday hardly seemed like a celebration. We both wanted to go up to station five badly, but we declined just as the cab pulled up and picked them up; we began our descent back to station one. We became afraid that we had missed the last bus of the day, but finally at 5:15p.m. we saw the bus returning from station five. I stood in the middle of the road to flag the bus down to make sure it stopped—there was no way I was going to let that bus pass us and be stranded on the mountain. When we got on the bus, we saw those two Americans again. They ended up only having about 20 minutes to see station five before they had to catch the last bus. They actually tried to console us, telling us it wasn't anything great and that they hoped I still had a great birthday dinner. When we finally got back to our hotel, I was ready to open my bottle of wine and have birthday sex.

We had already asked around and found there was a gourmet Italian restaurant within walking distance from our hotel. It was getting cold at night, and we bundled up and filled a glass of wine for our walk to dinner. We walked arm and arm under the full moon that illuminated Mount Fuji. Our mood was much lighter now, and we had a beautiful evening stroll to dinner, while trying to make rings as we breathed out into the cold night air. After all the drama of trying to hike Mount Fuji, we understood why only 1% of the people of Japan had ever hiked it.

The restaurant was romantic and cozy. We drank Chianti, laughed, and fed each other pasta. By the second bottle of wine, we both had decided to change our plans and try Fujisan again tomorrow. It was a perfect birthday dinner, and afterwards, we walked home and stayed up late. I told Andrew about my full moon ceremonies, and he was eager to try. We performed a mystical ceremony with Fujisan towering above us. I released my fears around vulnerability and intimacy. I was determined to learn how to live my life with an open heart, and find out how to feel safe and secure through human connection.

We woke up early and I made a morning hot spring visit. Luckily, it was so early that no other women were in the tiny bathhouse. It was a view I will never forget, watching the sunrise on Mount Fuji while sitting naked in a volcanic hot spring. The day had already started out right, and I had a good feeling about the bus today. We packed up and checked out and left our luggage at the hotel. We made it to the bus station on time to catch the 9:00 a.m. bus to station five. It was at 7,500ft (2,300 m) and turned out to be a tourist trap, not at all as we expected. It was filled with souvenir shops and restaurants. We grabbed a quick bowl of noodle soup and made our final preparations. We were repeatedly discouraged from attempting to hike it two months after the climbing season. November 4th was my birthday 're-do,' and I was pleased to find the trail was virtually empty.

The hike started out innocently as a wide, flat dirt path. The trees had now lost their leaves, and it wasn't long before we were above most of the clouds. Mount Fuji stands alone. Unlike other mountains that are nestled in ranges, on Mount Fuji the tree and the snow lines are much lower, and the wind gusts are very forceful. The ground was black volcanic rock mixed with black dirt. The sky was clear and vibrantly blue, and the air had a crispness. I felt alive. We were excited —laughing, giggling, and smooching for the first hour. Climbing Mount Fuji is a spiritual pilgrimage for many, and there were several small statues of Buddha covered in ribbons and bells. It wasn't long before we made it to station six. Past this station I saw the first glimpses of snow on the ground. My toes were sore and cold. Hiking for five hours on the concrete yesterday had been hard on my feet. I had forgotten to cut my toenails before we hiked, and they'd cut through my skin, which was now bloody.

The path was rough between stations six and seven. We had to climb about fifty steep rocky switchbacks, and the air was getting thin and cold. All those cigarettes were catching up to me and I was becoming short of breath very quickly. Andrew was doing better than I was, and I told him to hike ahead. The mountain was empty. I had heard reports during peak season of thousands of people being herded like cattle; this was nothing like that. All the stations were closed, and we only saw two people on the mountain all day. Andrew waited patiently and never complained or hiked more than a few hundred feet ahead. We took a long break at station seven and ate lunch just under the summit of Mount Fuji. Knowing I was planning to climb Everest after my time I India, he told me his story of trekking in the Himalayas a few years previously and warned me about how difficult the path to Namche Bazaar on the way to Everest Base Camp was.

We both had put on all of our layers, but when we stopped it became cold quickly. The wind was picking up and the sun was starting to get behind the mountain, and was no longer keeping us warm. We could see the summit, but there was a lot of snow and ice between it and us.

THE EVOLUTION OF A PARTY GIRL

We arrived at station eight, and I was exhausted, cold, and windblown. The gusts on Mount Fuji were like nothing I had felt before—they come quickly and are powerful. I had to get down and lie flat on the trail a few times to not get blown off the mountain. Just past station eight is where the snow line began, and I was legitimately done. Andrew wanted to go farther, but I didn't. It was also 3:00p.m. and we had to still descend in time to get the last bus to town. I told Andrew he could hike farther up on his own, but I didn't think it was a good idea for us to separate.

I had bought a bottle of oxygen with my friend Sumia back in Oyama to take on Mount Fuji. We had no champagne to celebrate our climb, but I did have the O2. We popped the top and set up our own oxygen bar at 10,350ft (3,150m). I had never intended to summit to 12,388ft (3760m); my dream was only of climbing Mount Fuji for my 34th birthday and I had done it! I love to be in nature and in mountains, but never enough to risk my safety. To me it's not about the summit. It is one small point at the top that gets all the glory, but I am inspired by the journey.

We caught the bus to Tokyo after we picked up the rest of our luggage at the hotel. This long bus ride was going to be one of our last times alone before we met back up with the rest of the team to fly home. We got in to Tokyo pretty late and navigated back to Chris's penthouse apartment. Chris was getting ready for bed and we said our final thank-you and goodbyes. I gave her a nice calendar with images of Mount Fuji that I had bought her; Chris had just climbed Mount Fuji during the last climbing season. I had experienced such gracious hospitality on this trip, from her and all the Rotarians. Chris didn't have kids and had an amazing career. She was married, but her husband was a yachtsman, and they spent months apart at a time. I could see a little of my life and my dreams in the lifestyle she had attained.

Andrew and I woke up on time and enjoyed our final morning in bed together. The room had a full wall of windows that overlooked the amazing Tokyo tower and the skyline of Japan. Andrew started to kiss me and touch my body. I think Chris must have heard because she knocked on the door and said that she was leaving. We were both naked and neither one of us were about to get up to say goodbye to her. We probably broke every social etiquette rule as houseguests as we said goodbye to her through the door. It was our last beautiful and enjoyable sexual experience. We ended up staying in bed way too long and were late to arrive at Narita Airport. We checked our bags and ran through the airport as they were announcing our final boarding call. Andrew grabbed me and kissed me passionately, just before anyone could see us. We turned the corner to the gate, and Lesli and Michelle were waiting.

We had a seventeen-hour plane ride sitting next to each other, platonically. Michelle and Lesli were sitting a few rows behind us. They had just returned from a tropical island in the south of Japan called Okinawa. They did not have an amazing week like Andrew and I had. There was another typhoon in the south of Japan, so it had rained most of the week, and Michelle told us she and Lesli spent most of the week fighting. Michelle said she'd missed us so much the last week and wished she had gone to Mount Fuji with us instead. Andrew and I laughed, but we were so glad to have had our secret passionate love affair. The plane ride was good for us; it was a nice transition between romance and becoming friends again. I said a very public goodbye to Andrew, with a distracted hug in front of my parents at the baggage claim of Detroit Metro Airport. I was only going to be home for four days before I left for India. I felt overwhelmed about the million things I had to do to prepare for the difficult next six months of my life. A lot had happened already since I had left Detroit five weeks ago; I had learned a lot about being a diplomat, an international politician, and a cougar.

Chapter 10
PITSTOP IN THE 'D'

It was so nice to be surrounded by my friends and family again. I felt love, and like I could finally be myself...

***

My parents picked me up from the airport, and as we drove home, I felt a wave of depression come over me being back in Detroit. All the trees had lost their leaves, and it was freezing cold. There has always been energy in the fall that makes me giddy and excited when the leaves are changing colors and the air becomes crisp. After the leaves fall, however, and the winter starts to come, I feel lonely and depressed. I don't know if it is seasonal depression, but I feel sad and lonely at the end of every fall.

Detroit looked bleak compared to all the beauty I had been experiencing in Japan, but I loved the freedom of being in America and felt so happy to be free again and not living a life of pretending and performing. Feeling comfortable, appreciated, and understood even for a few days was just what I was craving. I spent the next few days on Asian time rather than trying to take on the jetlag. I had a lot of planning and loose ends to tie up before the next leg of my adventure, and I could get a lot of computer work done at night when everybody else was sleeping.

The next six months were going to be some of the most challenging experiences of my life. This journey would entail charity medical work, traveling with my family, lots of yoga, and becoming a certified yoga teacher, all with the backdrop of

Chapter 10: PITSTOP IN THE 'D'

living in a third world county. The cherry on top of my adventure was going to Nepal and climbing Mount Everest. I had to find a way to make everything I needed, including gifts for my family in India, fit into a backpack and a suitcase, each weighing less than 50 pounds.

On Saturday night, Cassie threw me a fantastic party. I have thrown many parties for my friends, but no one had thrown me a party since I was a child. To have people honor me in such a special way was almost enough to make me eat sushi again.... almost. I had lost weight in Japan, and living back at my parent's house I had access to all my old formal dresses from high school and college. They all still fit, even my dresses from high school. I chose this black open-back dress and decided to tie my Japanese obi around the waist to incorporate my new sense of Japanese style.

It was so nice to be surrounded by my friends and family again. I felt loved, and like I could finally mentally and emotionally relax. Drinking red wine and socializing with my 'tribe,' made me fall back in love with Detroit. There was one surprise guest—Craig, my hot backpacking instructor, showed up at my party. We flirted that night and I thought maybe there would be romance waiting for me when I came home from Asia, but for now I was still mourning the end of my love affair with Andrew. Once the party wound down around midnight and everyone left, I went back to my old neighborhood in Ferndale with three of my guy friends. We danced and partied until the wee hours of the morning. There is always the list of people who say they are coming to a party and never show up, and on this list was Andrew. Our love affair was unceremoniously over.

The next day all my family came to my parents' house, and they also had a birthday/going-away party for me. I said my final goodbyes to all my nieces and nephews, knowing that they would be much more grown up when I saw them again in six months. I spent my final day packing before my long plane trip back around the world. I'd come home the Pacific route from Japan and traveled the Atlantic route to India, which means I flew around the world in five days! It was a long journey. I visited four countries in one day and finally made it to Bangalore,

India. I was three hours late and one bag down, but I was 'home.'

Chapter 11: PITSTOP IN THE 'D'

Chapter 11
INDIA: A MONTH IN MYSORE— THE SHALA

My mind was still, my body was still. This is why I had come to India—to feel the yoga...

***

It was my first day in India. My cousin Bharat, flew in from Mumbai to meet me and help me get settled. The news had come that my suitcase, containing everything I'd need for the last five months of my trip, had never left Detroit. It was an ominous beginning to my trip, but after much hassle, we made arrangements for my bag to be transported directly to my family in Mumbai, India.

My plan was to spend the next month in Mysore at the yoga *shala* (school) of K. Pattabhi Jois, the originator of Ashtanga Vinyasa–style yoga. He had passed away that May at the age of 94, but his daughter and grandson had taken over the school. As we walked up to the world famous shala, I felt a sense of realness to this experience I had been waiting my whole life to take on: backpacking alone through India and reconnecting with my roots. When I walked in the door, I could again feel that stillness come over me. This was one of the most renowned yoga schools in India, and I was about to become a student.

A yoga class was just ending; we waited in the front room for the class to finish up. I had two goals that day: register for my month-long study of yoga and find an apartment. The grand-

Chapter 11: INDIA: A MONTH IN MYSORE— THE SHALA

daughter wasn't as I expected—she was plump and looked like one of my Indian 'aunties.'

I was expecting her to be fit like my yoga teachers back home. I introduced myself with a namaste and told her how excited I was to meet her and to finally be here after months of anticipation. I had sent over lots of paperwork and pictures of myself months ago as part of their formal registration process. She told me she was sorry but she had changed her travel plans and instead of closing the shala for five days in mid-November, she was closing it for two weeks. As my jaw dropped, she tried to reassure me by offering that I could still sign up and pay the large registration fee and do a self-study at her shala. I was lost. I was sleep deprived and now the reason for my month of study in Mysore was no longer open.

I sat with Bharat and his brother-in-law in the hot and stuffy car, contemplating what to do. After we wandered around the area trying to figure out an apartment situation, I met two angels from New Zealand. They had just flown in yesterday as well, had also planned to practice yoga at the shala, and were in the same predicament. They told me the yoga scene in Mysore had changed since the guru had died, and now there was a new teacher that many students were going to instead. They pointed me toward the new Ashtanga teacher in Mysore, Sheshadri. They gave us directions and wished me good luck.

We drove through the crazy windy streets of Mysore, and I felt desperate. After a long journey, I was jet-lagged, overtired, and irritated with the unprofessionalism of this world-renowned yoga shala. I had already had one of my bags lost and a huge debacle trying to solve that situation. After just one day in India, I was feeling fed up, nothing was working out, and I wanted to burst into tears. Bharat suggested I come back to Mumbai with him and stay with our family. He said Mumbai is a huge city, and I could find somewhere there to study yoga. I really did not want to go to Mumbai just yet, but I had just one day to figure out everything for the next month and then Bharat was leaving and I was on my own to fend for myself.

We finally found the other shala; it looked like a brand-new building. It was freshly painted bright white and had orange and blue trim. Bharat and I walked up to the gate and met

Sheshadri's wife. She said that he had just started to teach a class and she couldn't disturb him. She must have seen the complete frustration in my face, and she said, "Well, let me see what I can do to help you out." Five minutes later, bouncing down the steps and toward the front gate was Sheshadri. He was a very small man, less than five feet tall, but he was muscular and did not have an ounce of fat on his body. He spoke English clearly. He introduced himself and his shala with a genuine sense of compassion and love. For the first time since I'd arrived in India, I felt like something was working out. He even followed up with an amazing offer. He had just rented one of the apartments located in the shala to a German woman about my age who was looking for a roommate to share her two-room apartment with for the month. He told me to come back after his class at 7:00 p.m. and he would be able to meet with me and arrange everything.

Just when I was starting to lose faith and hoping that this first day was not an ominous foreshadowing of my next six months in India, I met the amazing Sheshadri. When one doors closes, I have learned to have faith, because it is usually just to create an open space for a new one to appear. We were hungry and had an hour before we could meet with Sheshadri. Bharat, his brother-in-law, and I all went to a nearby restaurant called Mahesh Prasad for dinner. I saw a lot of international yoga students there and felt like it was a good sign. We walked back to the shala at 7:00 p.m., and I signed up for one month of yoga and pranayama with Sheshadri. I would be taking a pranayama class in the morning at 8:00 a.m. and my asana class would be in the evening at 5:00 p.m. The name of his shala was Patanjali Ashtanga Vinyasa Yoga. As I was registering for my classes, a thin woman with very dark long hair and a strong presence came up the stairs. It was Katharina, the girl from Cologne, Germany. We talked shortly; her English had a heavy German accent. She asked me if I wanted to share her apartment and I said yes!

It was after 8:00 p.m. and a chaotic first day in India. Bharat was heading back to Bangalore that night and flying to Mumbai in the morning. I still had no groceries or essentials for my apartment. We went to the Big Bazaar, the 'Kmart' of India.

Chapter 11: INDIA: A MONTH IN MYSORE— THE SHALA

In a whirlwind tour, we bought my cooking utensils, bedding, towels, and enough food for a few days. As Bharat and I sat and waited for his brother-in-law to pick us up, we looked at each other and started to laugh. In one day we had done so much and now he was about to drop me off at 'my apartment' in India. I wouldn't see him or the rest of my family until I went to Mumbai for Christmas in six weeks.

As I got back to my new home, I said my final goodbye and thanked Bharat. There was a note on my bed from Katharina that said "Welcome Home!" I was so tired that I fell on the bed with all my clothes on. The exhausting day was almost enough to let me sleep through the night and overcome my jet lag. Not quite, though—I woke up at 4:30 a.m. when Katharina was getting ready for the morning asana class.

Yoga, as I quickly learned, is far more involved than the physical classes I had been taking in Detroit. Yoga has a total of eight limbs, and the physical poses that we in America call yoga are called 'asanas' by yogis, because it is only one of the eight limbs of yoga. Pranayama, the class I registered for in the mornings, is another limb of the eight arms of yoga.

The shala was located on the third floor of the building. The yoga room was long and narrow with white walls and tiles and all the trim was bright orange. The front of the studio had a large statue of Hanuman, the warrior monkey God of the Hindu religion. He is the God of strength and devotion. Next to the statue at the front of the room there was a large showcase that had pictures of many of the Indian deities. They all looked familiar to me from growing up with an Indian father. However, I had never studied Indian religion, and I couldn't tell one from the other. Along the sides of the long yoga room there were several large windows. The windows were all open; they had no screens, only bars to keep the monkeys out. The doors in the front and back of the yoga room led to the wraparound balcony. The small waiting area in the front opened to a small rooftop deck. The yoga room was clean and simple, and in this room I would be spending many hours transforming myself. Off the roof deck, there were two very basic bathrooms with only cold water. The apartment bathroom was inside Katharina's bedroom, so I would be using the upstairs public bathrooms for the month.

At 8:00 a.m., just as the morning asana class was getting out, I was waiting on the roof deck for my first pranayama class. I would be attending class every other day, leaving my off days to practice pranayama on my own. Sheshadri was full of energy and seemed to be invigorated after teaching the morning asana class. He told me to come in and sit on my mat; the room was hot and you could feel and smell the hard work that just occurred in there. They were about five other people taking pranayama class. Every student was learning different exercises, so after he finished teaching each student individually, he came over and sat in front of me.

He spoke fast with a heavy accent, and many of the words were in Sanskrit. I learned that prana is the vital energy or life force that drives the body and that the chakras are the main energy centers of the body. By using the pranayama breathing techniques, you can purify the body and activate the chakras. There are ten types of prana, and each one is responsible for a different life energy. Each prana is associated with a physiological function in the body, such as excretion, reproduction, and even the energy of your heart and lung function. If any of the ten pranas are unbalanced, a disease will develop in that part of the body. By using different breathing techniques, I would learn how to clear the different energy channels and dramatically increase my prana or life energy. I learned the basic philosophy of yoga in that first class, including one pranayama technique that I was to practice until my next class in two days.

This was my sixth trip to India, so most of the things that would have shocked most Westerners I was already aware of. It had been about six years since my last trip to India, and this was my first trip without my family to drive, translate, and cook for me. I was on my own. When I walked downstairs after my pranayama class, I felt this feeling of fear from the complete freedom of finally being on my own. I no longer had the other Rotary group members to pacify, and I didn't have my family to answer to, either. I was ecstatic to be able to do whatever I wanted without explaining it to anyone, but being in India alone also was scary.

Chapter 11: INDIA: A MONTH IN MYSORE— THE SHALA

There was no stove in the apartment. Katharina had bought a small hot water boiler for us to make chai, oatmeal, and noodles. I made a cup of tea and went and sat on my balcony; for the first time in months, I had a free day to rest and recuperate. I had bought a book at the Chicago airport on the way to Tokyo and had barely had time to start reading it. I decided I would spend the day reading on my balcony and napping. The book was by one of my favorite inspirational and spiritual authors, Wayne Dyer, who was also from Detroit. I spent the day reading about co-creating my universe. I cooked some Indian ramen noodles for lunch. My mind would wander often, and I felt overwhelmed about the journey ahead, realizing that this was only the second day of my six months in India and Nepal.

My roommate was gone most of the day; she came home just as I was getting ready for my evening asana class. I got dressed in my yoga clothes and went upstairs to sit on the roof deck while I waited for class to start. Yogis from all over the world started to arrive around 4:30p.m. Then I saw my two angels from New Zealand. They smiled and walked right over to me. Their names were Jackie and Barbara, and they were both flight attendants. They had gone to their first asana class the night before and said I was going to love it. They asked me if I had ever practiced 'Mysore style.' I said no, so they explained how the class was going to run. Ashtanga yoga has a specific order of the poses: first, start with the sun salutations to warm up, then the standing series, seated series, and lastly, the finishing asanas. This was all part of the primary series of Ashtanga yoga designed by K. Pattabhi Jois They told me the poses were all printed out on cards in the corner of the room for the new students. The more advanced students have it all memorized. Sheshadri would start the class with a few prayers and chants and lead us through our first few sun salutations. After a few minutes he would no longer give verbal instructions, but he would walk around to give adjustments. All the students progress through the asanas in the same order, but at their own pace.

We placed our yoga mats down and made two rows facing each other. Sheshadri sat in the front of the room next to the statues of the deities. I found the two large legal-size laminated sheets with pictures of the primary series and placed them

THE EVOLUTION OF A PARTY GIRL

in front of my yoga mat, along with two small cards with the prayers written on them. I recognized all the poses, but I was feeling a little nervous at the prospect of making a fool of myself and drawing attention to the fact that I was the new girl. I was skeptical and unsure if I was in over my head.

At my yoga studio in Detroit, I'd had an uncomfortable experience with a yoga teacher adjusting me. He was a popular, good-looking yoga teacher and he strutted around the studio like a male peacock, always displaying his plumage. He was one of the owners so I made it a point to go to his class when I first started practicing yoga. He adjusted me three times during that class and they all involved him putting his hands around my lower hips and pressing his body up against mine...yuck! I never went to another one of his classes again and avoided ever going to any teacher that I heard does 'adjustments.'

After the chanting (I was happy to see most of the other students were also reading the cards), we stood up to start our sun salutations. As my body started to move, my mind became lighter and lighter with each movement. I had many stresses on my mind and body going into that class: the emotional roller coaster of my month in Japan, the chaos of arriving and getting settled in India, and my continuing concern about the whereabouts of my other suitcase. Within minutes on the mat, I could feel the stress melting away. It was as if the negativity controlling my mind was replaced by a beautiful energy that calmed me. I loved yoga! Regardless of the emotional garbage I brought to the mat, the practice centered me every single time. As we were performing the sun salutations, I looked out the window and from where I was standing, I could watch the sun setting. It was magnificent, the first of many joyful sunsets in India.

As I looked around the room, it was hard to not feel slightly intimidated by some of the amazing yogis I saw. The energy in the room was powerful. I tried to keep my eyes and my thoughts inward, but I had to look around periodically to figure out the poses. It was South India and the room was hot and sticky. Sheshadri came around a few times to adjust me and, wow, these adjustments were like nothing I had ever felt before. He was a small guy, but he opened up parts of my body that had been tight for years. His adjustments were aggressive and force-

Chapter 11: INDIA: A MONTH IN MYSORE— THE SHALA

ful, but afterwards I was euphoric. After my warm-ups, I started into the primary series. I was already drenched, dripping with more sweat than my body had produced in over a month. I could smell the alcohol pouring out of my body.

The primary series consists of thirty poses that you do on both the right and the left sides. I had completed the first ten poses, and I could barely hold onto any body part because my hand would just slip on the sweat. My body was working so hard I could feel myself panting in exhaustion and smiling in a delirious bliss as I reached my 'yoga high.' I have never had a runner's high before, but I have reached a super elated state in yoga and assume it must be close to what runners get when they go beyond exhaustion into bliss. Sheshadri tapped me on my shoulder just I was starting to wonder how I could possibly get through the complete primary series and told me I had done enough for my first day and to lie on my stomach. He came back a few minutes later and started walking on my back. All the joints in my body were snapping and cracking. The physical therapist in me was concerned since I always told my patients not to let anyone walk on your back, but it felt like exactly what my tight body needed. After, I lay on the floor in a sweaty puddle on my yoga mat for about 30 minutes while the rest of the students finished their class. My mind was still, my body was still. This is why I had come to India—to feel the yoga.

Sheshadri turned out to be the most amazing, skillful, and knowledgeable yoga teacher I had ever been in the presence of. He was so down to earth, cute, and silly, yet he was a strong and disciplined teacher. He was in his mid-50s, married, and had an adult son who also would assist during the class. After class, my body felt like putty. I was so glad all I had to do was climb down one flight of stairs and fall into bed. As I lay in bed, the only way I could describe that class was magical. I had already started to feel the detoxification happening from all that sake, sushi, and excessiveness I was part of in Japan.

I woke up early again on my third day in India. It was around 4:30 a.m. and Katharina was getting ready for her yoga class. When she got up in the morning and unlocked her door, I tried to take advantage of the opportunity and go to the bathroom located inside her bedroom. I lay back down for a minute, but

I was too awake to sleep. I started the pranayama technique I had learned. This was my off day from my pranayama lecture, and I was supposed to work on my own. I propped myself up in bed and tried to sit in lotus position. My body was sore; I could feel every muscle I had used during my asana class the night before. There was no way I could tolerate sitting in full lotus, so I decided to sit 'Indian style.' I practiced the first technique I had learned. It was called *sheethali* and it was a cooling pranayama. According to Ayurvedic Indian medicine, if a part of the body gets too hot, too cold, too tight, or too dry, the energy channels become blocked and disease develops. I am sure I am in general too hot, as most type-A people are. This technique was really weird. I had to roll my tongue into a cylinder and then inhale through the tip of the tongue. After I inhale, I am supposed to close my mouth and use my hand to close the right nostril and exhale out the left nostril. The left nostril is called *ida* and is the negative energy channel. After I complete my exhalation, I roll my tongue again and inhale through the tip of my tongue. After my first few rounds, I started to laugh out loud. I don't know if it was an energy release or just that the thought of me being here in India breathing through my rolled tongue at 5 o'clock in the morning, trying to find the answer to inner peace, seemed so laughable. I completed the sheethali technique for fifteen minutes and it was grueling. I was exhausted from a simple seated breathing exercise, and it took all the discipline I had to keep going for the entire time; I must have opened my eyes about twenty times to check the clock. I was sweating, my tongue was sore, and I was out of breath. I've always considered myself a relatively in-shape person compared to many of my friends and family, so it was hard to believe I could possibly be this mentally and physically out of shape.

I made of cup of chai and sat out on the balcony. That day I would rest my body from the dramatic wake-up call it had just received at asana class last night and now again at pranayama. I sat on my wraparound balcony, and I could hear the students practicing their asanas upstairs. As the class ended they all came down one by one. No shoes are allowed in the yoga studio, so the students left their shoes in front of my apartment door. There must have been about fifty pairs of sandals from all

Chapter 11: INDIA: A MONTH IN MYSORE— THE SHALA

over the world in front of my door. The yogis came downstairs after their class drenched in sweat, but looking better than I had looked last night after my class. It was the first time I got to check out all the advanced yoga students from the morning class, and of course look for any romantic prospects. There were quite a few good-looking guys, especially with their amazing yoga bodies dripping in sweat. It was going to be a good month; I could smell it.

When Katharina came down, she invited me to breakfast with some of the other yogis, to which I readily agreed. Katharina had already been in India for six weeks, and she studied at the main shala with K. Pattabhi Jois's daughter and grandson. It was her first time in India, and she wasn't Indian, but she knew her way around Mysore and was much more comfortable in India than I was. On our walk to the rickshaw stand, she stopped at the flower lady and bought a garland of jasmine flowers; she cut it in half and gave half to me to put in my hair. They smelled so fragrant and I got a whiff of them each time I turned my head. In India there is often a strong stench of pollution mixed with body odor and excrement. The flowers were a great way to disguise the smell. We walked up to the rickshaw driver, and Katharina bargained like a pro, not a tourist. It was about a 20-minute rickshaw ride to Gokulum, on the other side of Mysore, where most of the other yogis lived. We talked very freely the entire ride. I could already tell we had similar views of the world. It was refreshing to talk to her—she was strong and independent, but she also was pleasant and witty. She was taking me under her wing and helping me and for that I was very thankful.

We went to brunch at a place called Anoki's. I recognized many of the faces from this morning sitting at a long table in the dining garden. Katharina introduced me to about ten people at the table: three from America, two from Germany, one from Sweden, one from Ireland, two from England, and a few people at the end of the table I didn't get to talk to, but it sounded like they were speaking French. I was very glad to learn that English was the international language.

After breakfast, Katharina took me on a tour of Gokulum, and she showed me all the yogi shops. Lastly, we went to the tailor and bought a white cotton upper cloth to cover my shoulders and chest in public. On the rickshaw ride back home, she told me that she had rented a car and driver for the approaching new moon day. According to Vedic philosophy, during the full and new moon the yoga shalas are closed because the energies are very strong and people are more likely to get injured. She invited me to join her and some of the other yogis I had met at breakfast to visit the local temples. It was going to cost 400 rupees, which is about nine dollars each for the car and driver for 12 hours. I was trying to figure out how that little money could even cover the cost of the gas.

When we arrived home I was tired. I lay down and took a quick nap before my asana class. At 4:30 p.m. I went upstairs to sit on the roof and wait for the other students for our 5:00 p.m. class. I loved sitting on the roof deck—there were palm trees in every direction, and I could see the large mountain in the background called Chamundi Hill. The roof was the only slightly quiet place I had found above the sound of all the traffic horns and street peddlers.

I again took the same spot in the middle of the yoga room. I had my cheat sheets in front of me and felt much more peaceful starting this class, knowing what to expect. My second asana class was even more magical than my first. I didn't have anxiety, so I could let my mind get to a deeper level of inner peace. I was situated to watch the sunset again as I performed my sun salutations. I finished my sun salutations and was again dripping with sweat as I started into my primary series. I had much more energy and was able to get deeper into the poses than my first class. I finished about half of my poses in the primary series, then Sheshadri came over and told me to try some back bending before I finished. He crouched down behind me while facing me and told me to bend all the way backward. I did as he instructed, and landed with my back on his back. Then he told me to reach down and grab his knees as he stood up and he held onto my lower legs, which were wrapped around his shoulders. Next thing I knew I was suspended in the air upside down with my legs around his shoulders and my hands holding on to his knees, my back against his back. My entire body was getting stretched. He told me to let go of his legs, and he started swinging me from side to side while I was upside down, and my back again started cracking and popping. I came out of it by placing my hands on the ground and kicking over. Lying on the mat, I was a sweaty mess again, and my body felt like Jell-O. I went to bed again right after class, and I had pure joy filling my body.

I woke up early the next morning and could hear the morning asana class pounding on the floor right above my bed. I was still jet-lagged, and I decided to catch up on journaling, but as soon as I opened my journal to write, I felt disgusted. I hadn't felt like journaling since the last week in Japan. To relive everything by writing about it in my journal wasn't how I wanted to start my day, so I just lay in bed and listened to the class do yoga.

Sheshadri always started pranayama class by asking everyone individually how their previous pranayama techniques were going. At my last class, I told him I had been doing sheethali twice a day for fifteen minutes and it was getting much better. I shared with him that I had chronic right-sided chest and neck pain and it flared up while I was doing the pranayama. The pain was familiar to me—it was the same pain pattern I'd experienced before my thyroid cancer diagnosis. He said it was because I had an energy blockage, and my liver was releasing heat and negativity. After all the drinking and drama in Japan, I was sure he was right. I couldn't help but wonder if I could have prevented my thyroid cancer by starting this pranayama when I first experienced the neck pain years ago. But there is no going back to undo the past—everything that had happened had led me to this place, sitting on a mat in front of Sheshadri, learning to channel prana throughout my body.

He taught me another cooling pranayama that day called sheetkari; it was another silly-looking technique. Sheetkari involves inhaling with the tip of your tongue pressed up against the back of your front teeth; most of the inhalation is through the sides of the mouth. To exhale I had to close my lips and use my hand to close the right nostril and exhale out the left nostril. Sheshadri reminded me the left nostril was the negative energy channel of the body. Negative energy causes the body to overheat, so all of the cooling pranayamas involve exhaling through the left nostril. He first demonstrated the technique to me, and then he watched me do it. I continued on for what felt like forever, until my mind forced me to open my eyes. I opened one of my eyes to look around the room to see where he and the other students were doing. To my surprise he was still sitting right in front of me. Sheshadri scolded me for opening my eyes and told me to focus my attention within and not be so easily distracted. I felt like a toddler with my unsettled mind; it was difficult for me to sit still and complete the pranayama. Knowing he was watching did force me to keep my eyes closed, but it also made me aware of my childish tendency to need a babysitter. After a long 30 minutes of sheetkari, he finally told me to rest in savasana; I gladly did.

I went downstairs after class to find my apartment locked up. I hadn't taken my key with me when I'd gone upstairs because I'd assumed Katharina would be there when I got done. I went back upstairs to ask Sheshadri if he had a spare key, and he said he did not. I went back downstairs and sat on my yoga mat in front of the door. I had no money, no cellphone, and not even shoes, so I had no choice but to sit and wait for her to return.

I was feeling some guilt for how far behind I had gotten on my journaling—I assumed the universe agreed as it had arranged a scenario where I'd have no choice but to journal. I think I had become so fed up with everything in Japan that I didn't want to journal about it. All the food, the fakeness, my group, and even my codependence toward Andrew had me at my wits' end. I still hadn't received a single correspondence from Andrew since we casually waved goodbye to each other at the baggage claim.

I sat down on my yoga mat and started to write. It was like I had opened a dam, and my mind worked faster than my pen could move. After about three hours of writing, I was almost caught up. It was now past noon, and I was getting hungry and annoyed. Sheshadri had sent his wife to see if I had gotten back in to my apartment. She was a lovely woman that looked to be about my age, but she didn't speak any English. She brought me oranges and bananas, which I graciously accepted and ate immediately. I finished journaling about the last week with Andrew and was able to explore my feelings of fear. This

Chapter 11: INDIA: A MONTH IN MYSORE— THE SHALA

reoccurring struggle with emotional vulnerability continued as I experienced a similar fear sitting on my balcony alone in India, locked out of my apartment. Around 2:00 p.m., Katharina came up the stairs loaded down with bags. I had been locked out for a total of five hours; I was emotional and hungry after another taxing experience that I was becoming accustomed to in India.

My family from India called to check in on me, but I didn't tell them about my troubles. They told me my bag was in Paris, and they were trying to arrange to get it sent directly to Mumbai. It had been almost a week since they'd lost my bag, and I was starting to get concerned that I would never get it back. It contained all my very expensive mountaineering gear that I was going to use to climb Mount Everest, along with equipment I needed for my physical therapy volunteer work.

I was so looking forward to asana class, as I stood on my mat and began to move my body and unwind from the emotional trauma of the day. When I got deep into certain poses, I felt bursts of sadness erupting and flowing through my body. As I went into marichyasana, Sheshadri came over and adjusted me deep into the spinal twist. As soon as he adjusted me, I felt overwhelmed with sadness about the death of my grandfather earlier that year. My eyes filled with tears, and they streamed down my face as I continued through my poses. As I went into the deep hip stretches, I felt the negative emotions I spent the day journaling about release. That class was filled with releases of many negative emotions, and I spent much of the class with tears streaming from my eyes. I had released some heaviness in my heart and mind. As I came to my finishing poses and went into my headstand, I felt lighter than I had felt in months.

I woke up early the next day and was bright and joyful. When Katharina and I walked into the kitchen to make chai and porridge, there was a huge dragonfly trapped in the kitchen. It was flying about the kitchen in a wild attempt to escape. I said we should catch it and take it outside. She said, "No, we must just open the window and let the dragonfly find its own way out." Then she said that I was like the dragonfly feeling trapped in our apartment; she said she would give me instructions, but it was time for me to find my own way around India. My relationships with men were like that dragonfly, too—I was trying to catch them instead of just opening my heart and letting them find their own way to me.

India is chaotic. The traffic is mayhem, and people drive on whichever side of the road allows them to go the fastest. There is no speed limit. Families of five people travel together on one scooter, and fourteen people can squeeze in one tiny rickshaw. Red lights in India are only for people who can't think for themselves. There is one rule—don't hit anything, especially the cow sleeping in the middle of the road.

There is a constant sound of beeping horns anywhere you go. That day I had a crash course in how to use your horn in India: Use it to say hello if you see someone you know or to ask a pedestrian if they want to ride in your rickshaw. Use it every time you pass a truck or bus to let them know you are there. Use a horn to try to convince a street dog, pig, monkey, cow, or human to get out of your way. If there is a moment of peace and quiet, make sure to use your horn!

The market was just as chaotic. Hundreds of vendors yelled about their products and gimmicks, and thousands of shoppers pushed and shoved through the crowed street, everyone haggling to get the best price. When I was little, my mom used to say that if an Indian man has three mangos, he would eat one to survive through the day. While sitting and praying, he would sell the other two and use that money to buy three more mangos for the next day. In that moment, I saw more truth in that statement than I'd ever understood before in my life.

It was a dramatic contrast to the inner peace I had been experiencing at my yoga shala. I started to wonder how a country that has written the book on peace and nonviolence could be in a state of poverty, disarray, and chaos. I had some baseline understanding of Indian culture from my many family trips to India, but I had never been exposed to the spiritual and yogic practices. Holiness and divine virtues guide all of Indian society.

The extreme organization and efficiency of Japanese culture had left me with a feeling of emptiness. There was an undertone of emotional bankruptcy there. Numerous Japanese people privately shared with me that many people in Japan are lost and depressed. Many Western cultures are ruled by greed, material-

Chapter 11: INDIA: A MONTH IN MYSORE— THE SHALA

ism, and vice, which also cause people to feel lost and depressed. I have found this is by and large not the case in India. Through all the chaotic driving and haggling, and despite the outward appearance of complete mayhem, it seems that the people of India are grounded in their spirituality and don't need or crave the organization or material goods we Westerners need to feel whole and complete. The rhythm and organization of Indian life is based on a spiritual value system. Having a large loving family and a strong spiritual practice is more important than the size of your house, the brand of your clothes, and the profit and loss statement from your company.

Somehow, I made it to Sandya's Kitchen to meet up with Katharina for lunch at 2:00 p.m. I felt totally wiped out—a simple trip to buy fruit in India is a full-day adventure and involves haggling with about ten different people. But, like the dragonfly, I had freed myself from my room and had navigated the streets of Mysore on my own for the first time.

After asana class that evening, I ventured out again on my own for dinner. I ended up enjoying a pleasant meal with a Swiss man who offered to walk me home afterwards. I turned him down, but as I crossed the street to walk back to my apartment, I began to wish I'd accepted his offer. I realized I didn't know which street to turn on. All the streets looked the same and none of the streets had signs, streetlights, or even names. I started feeling panicky; I walked up and down several streets but I couldn't recognize anything. Just as I started to get really afraid, I saw a tall, very good-looking yogi walking toward me. I said, "Excuse me, I just got to Mysore a few days ago, and I am lost. I am living in Sheshadri's yoga shala. Do you know where that is?" He said he didn't know, but he would help me find it. He walked with me, and I tried to figure out where I was. I was calm and comfortable with him, and once I was not feeling afraid, I could actually think. He told me his name was Steve. He had a strong English accent. As we walked, he invited me to his apartment on Sundays and Wednesdays for the kirtans he has. (Kirtan is a yogi and Hindu way of singing in devotion to the Gods. I had gone to a kirtan back in Detroit at my yoga studio and really enjoyed it.) By this time, I had figured out where I lived, and Steve, my knight in a white cotton

THE EVOLUTION OF A PARTY GIRL

dress shirt, left me at the shala. I didn't know anything about Steve, but as soon as he'd come near me to help me find my way home, I'd felt safe and secure. I decided I would attend his kirtans, if only to see him again.

Katharina and I woke up early on the morning of the new moon to enjoy our day off, driving around the countryside in our hired car.

The first temple we visited was a Jain temple on the top of a large hill. My family is Jain, but I knew very little about it. I learned more in that morning about Jainism than I had ever known of my family religion. Most of my aunties in India don't speak English, and my cousins that I can speak with don't follow the strict rules of Jainism. Between the language barrier and my lack of interest in organized religion, I'd learned little about my family religion. Walking barefoot up the 650 steps carved into the side of the mountain made me feel like I was on a spiritual pilgrimage. As I was climbing up the steps, my cellphone rang; it was my mom with my grandma calling from the US to check up on me. I guess this is what a modern-day pilgrimage looks like.

There were twenty-four large statues of Jain Gods throughout the temple. They are not Gods in the sense of a Supreme Being, but people who have attained true enlightenment. One of the monks at the temple performed a small ceremony on me and placed a line of red turmeric between my eyebrows.

It had started to rain and the day was getting long. In the afternoon we went to a temple dedicated to the God Vishnu. In Hinduism, everything in the universe is always in one of three states: creation, preservation, or destruction. The three Hindu Gods personify these forces of nature—Brahma is the force of creation, Vishnu is the force or preservation, and Shiva is the force of destruction or transformation. This temple was built of soapstone during the 12th century, and it rightfully represented the power of preservation. The detailed carvings on the side of this temple were incredibly intricate, and they told the stories of the Indian scriptures. The rain started coming down harder so I covered my head with my white cotton upper cloth. Katharina took a picture of me, and I could hardly recognize the girl in the picture. My hair was pulled back in a tight low ponytail, my only makeup was a large red turmeric religious dot on my brow line, and my head was covered with a white scarf. I was so far away from the parties of my past. As we went to our final temple of the day, a Shiva temple, I could feel the Shiva force taking hold of my bearings as my inner transformation began.

The next day I woke up eager for the return of my yoga routine. As much as I enjoyed driving around the Indian countryside and experiencing these beautiful temples, I looked forward to my daily asana class. I went to my morning pranayama class and was happy to see Sheshadri. He asked me how my moon day had gone, and I told him about the temples we went to visit; he seemed pleased that I went to visit temples on my free day. He said I was ready to learn my first heating technique, which would help purify my blood, lungs, and throat. He taught me Sheda Bhastrika. This was my first easy pranayama technique. I had to quickly and forcefully inhale and exhale through both nostrils for ten cycles, and then I had to rest for one minute before completing the next cycle. He told me to do a total of fifteen cycles, lasting about 15 minutes. This one seemed much easier than the two cooling pranayamas. Hopefully I was achieving a new level of mental discipline.

My body was getting into my yoga groove; I was able to now sweat through the entire two pages of poses. Then Shiva's power of destruction took me by surprise. I was nearing the end of my primary series that evening and going into the lotus pose when I heard the loudest three pops I have ever heard my bones make. My left knee had dislocated. People two mats over asked me if I was okay because they'd heard it dislocate. I went right into savasana and tried to meditate the pain away. I could feel my knee throb. By the time I sat up, my knee was the size of a grapefruit. I tried to walk, but I couldn't put any weight on my leg without feeling like it might dislocate again. I told Sheshadri what had happened, and he carried me down the stairs to my room and got ice from the family that lived downstairs from me. I had some Advil, and I took four of them. I quickly realized this was the most serious knee injury I had ever had in my life. I started to panic, as I felt overcome with fear about being in India alone and with no health insurance. Katharina was very sympathetic to my fears; she went to the pharmacy and bought me about thirty pills of ibuprofen. She spent the night helping me ice and elevate my leg, and thankfully left her bedroom door open for me to hop to the bathroom in her room. I cried myself to sleep with an icepack and my healing Tibetan quartz crystal on my knee. It was clear this yogic path was not going to be a straight linear one.

I woke up the next morning hoping it had all been a bad dream, but I still couldn't put weight on my leg. I hopped around my apartment on my right leg. When Katharina came down after her asana class, she went downstairs and got more ice for me. It felt so good when it first went on my hot and swollen knee. I stayed on 800 mg of ibuprofen three times a day, which is what doctors prescribe in the US. Sheshadri came down after teaching the morning class to check on me. He brought some eucalyptus oil and spent about ten minutes rubbing the cooling oil into my knee. He gave Katharina the name of an Ayurvedic oil to buy for me and said he would come back after evening class and massage it on my knee. Katharina spent the day nursing me, and I spent it lying in my bed whimpering. I was helpless, and she took good care of me over the next few days. I told my family I had hurt my knee, but they didn't know that I couldn't walk on it. Luckily I was able to use my physical therapy knowledge for a speedy recovery. With the help of icing, my medicine, and the Ayurvedic oil that Sheshadri recommended, which Katharina rubbed on my knee every day, I was able to walk gingerly on it after about three days. One of the yogis from the morning class, Sven from Germany, recommended a local hotel where I could pay to use their pool. Swimming was exactly what my knee needed.

The hotel lobby was luxurious. It was my first time in air conditioning since I'd gotten to India. It probably wasn't even that luxurious, but after being in my very basic living arrangement for over a week, my perception had already changed. The floors were all marble, and there was a coffee and pastry shop on the way to the front reception. The pie case had tiramisu, chocolate mousse, and even an apple pie. I decided I would indulge in a coffee and a dessert after swimming. I walked up to the reception desk where the man behind the counter politely said, "Welcome to the Regency. How can I help you, Madame?"

Chapter 11: INDIA: A MONTH IN MYSORE— THE SHALA

With all the fighting and bargaining I'd had to do every day, I hadn't heard anything so polite since my flight had left Paris. I told him I wanted to use the pool for the day, and he registered me and said he would escort me to the pool area. I told him I had hurt my knee, and he said that he would walk as slowly as I needed. When I saw the pool, I felt like it was a mirage. It was a beautiful tropical oasis; there were palm trees all around the pool, and the water looked so blue and refreshing. There were lounge chairs around the pool and a few Western guests. The pool area was built below the street level and there were brick retaining walls around it that were covered with ivy. For the first time in a week, I was able to experience life in India without the sound of constant horns blowing. The pool attendant gave me a blue-and-white striped beach towel, and I went into the shower room to rinse off. I had brought my bikini to India but wasn't sure if I would ever wear it. Bathing suits are not socially accepted in India. It is a very modest country and women swim with their clothes on. I asked Sven if it was okay to wear a bikini, and he confirmed all the female guests would be in bikinis. I turned on the water and couldn't believe what I was feeling— hot water. I stayed in the shower for almost twenty minutes as I tried to wash away my growing pains of life in India.

When I came out of the shower room, Sven had arrived; we set up chairs next to each other, and we talked and read. He was reading a book by Thich Nhat Hanh, a Buddhist monk that is living in exile in France. After about 30 minutes we were hot and sweaty and decided to go swimming. I went into the shallow end because I couldn't climb the ladder into the deep end. As soon as I was in the pool, I could walk again without pain. I spent the day swimming and exercising my left knee in the pool. I even was able to do many yoga asanas in the pool without pain. I swam a few laps at a time, and we ordered lunch at the pool. By 4:00 p.m., we were both ready to leave. I again took a long hot shower before getting dressed. As I left the Regency Hotel that evening drinking a latte, I felt like I'd had my first day of vacation since my trip had begun. My knee was improving, my mind was clear, and I was ready to head out of the gates of the hotel and battle again with the rickshaw drivers.

That night Sheshadri came down after class and instead of rubbing my knee like he normally did, he pressed really hard in the front of my hip. It was firm enough to make me cringe. He said he was opening the blocked energy line above my knee. Between that technique and my swimming, my knee felt about 50% better; I could bend it, I could walk on it, and it began to feel more stable. Katharina told me knee pain has a lot to do with addictions and drinking. She said this was part of the heavy drinking of my past clearing out of my body. I went back to the pool for the next few days, and I used the water and swimming to rehab my knee. After five days, I went back to asana class.

It was good to be at yoga again. My classmates had been concerned about me and were happy to see me. Even though I was in a foreign land, traveling alone, I had developed a support system. My first class I just did my ten sun salutations then went into savasana. The next night I did my sun salutations and my standing asanas. On my third day back I tried to do my primary series again. I still couldn't bend my knee properly, sit in any bent knee position, or twist my knee. I was able to modify and still do most of the poses, though. I had spent the last week wondering how the hell I was going to survive in India alone with a dislocated knee, not to mention how it was going to affect my plan to climb Mount Everest in the spring. I lamented a lot that week, and if it weren't for Katharina, I might have flown to my family in Mumbai. She was my angel during that time. She allowed me to sulk, kept trying to lift my spirits, and brought me ice and food. I was grateful for her.

I stayed on my medicine and icing regimen for about two weeks; the yoga helped a lot. After a week of only going up to yoga, pranayama, and back to my bed, I was feeling really cooped up. Katharina said she was going to kirtan at Steve's apartment and asked me if I wanted to join her. I of course did and was excited to see Steve.

Chapter 12

INDIA, MONTH IN MYSORE — TEACHINGS

I decided this was the perfect opportunity to practice lack of attachment and the yogic concept of "let go and let God"...

***

We rang the doorbell when we arrived, and Steve answered the door with his glowing smile. I again was overcome by warmth and comfort being in his presence. His apartment was beautiful and didn't look like a typical Indian apartment building—it was clean and modern. He had straw mats laid out on the floor in a large circle. Katharina and I both took a spot against the far wall so we would have some back support and I could stretch out my left leg. I wore my favorite long Indian skirt and a tight-fitting tank top; I even had makeup on. It was the most dolled up I had been since my going-away party back in Detroit.

The kirtan was unbelievable. Steve started out with an opening prayer and then a short explanation about the practice of kirtan. He told us each song represents a different God or a specific force in the universe. He told us not to think of the Gods as some outside force that exists up in the clouds, but instead think of each God as one aspect of our inner being. He explained that we were using the kirtan to help strengthen our inner Gods and that kirtan is like a cleansing process to increase our overall vibrational level. He used no instruments, just his powerful and beautiful voice, and it filled the room.

Chapter 12: INDIA, MONTH IN MYSORE — TEACHINGS

The format was call and response—he would sing a line and we would attempt to sing the same line back. We first sang to Lord Ganesha, the familiar Indian God with an elephant head, as all Hindu religious or devotional ceremonies start by paying homage to him. Just like an elephant, he represents the robust force of removing negative obstacles to allow positive forces to prevail.

At first, I was quite shy about singing. I know I have a bad voice and had a policy to not sing in public while sober. After the first couple songs, though, I felt inspired by the energy that was being created in the room and I started to sing. As I sang with my eyes closed, my mind would go into a deep state. It was a joyful experience. At first it felt like I was swirling, then I went into a trance-like state, but I was still singing in complete bliss. Every now and again, my knee would start throbbing and bring my mind back into my body. The 2-hour kirtan seemed like it lasted only 20 minutes.

At the end of the kirtan, Steve said that he was starting a class of reading and understanding one of the foundational books of yoga, the Yoga Sutras by Patanjali. The class would last about a month, but he invited all of us to join the class even if we couldn't complete the entire month. During the ride home, I decided to take his class. It wouldn't hurt my knee, and I was searching to gain insight into yoga philosophy. Also, after that kirtan, I had a major crush on Steve.

The following day, I went to a spiritual bookstore with Sven and bought the book for the class, B.K.S. Iyengar's interpretation of the Yoga Sutras of Patanjali. I tried to start reading it on my own, but it was over my head. I would like to think I am an intelligent person, but between the heavy philosophical concepts and the Sanskrit sutras, it was too advanced for my novice yogic brain.

During Steve's first class we learned the overall history of the text. The Yoga Sutras are an ancient Indian Sanskrit oral tradition; they have been passed along through a very specific way of chanting from gurus to students and through high-ranking spiritual family lines. Patanjali was a member of the royal court. Almost 3000 years ago, he compiled and organized all the chants into the Yoga Sutras to spread the secret knowledge of yoga. The path of yoga is the path to self-realization. To be self-realized means to always be in a place of complete awareness and oneness with all living things in the universe. Some people call this ultimate state of human evolution sainthood, some call it nirvana, and some call it enlightenment. In yoga it is called Samadhi. Once a yogi has stabilized in Samadhi, he lives in a perpetual state of love and bliss for all beings.

During class, Steve went into deep philosophical explanations for each phrase, which in Sanskrit are called sutras. The entire book is comprised of short phrases that pass along the sacred knowledge of how to use the practice of yoga to attain Samadhi. We spent our classes reciting each sutra out loud and then Steve would explain his interpretation and its spiritual message.

I learned that a foundational concept in the Yoga Sutras is lack of attachment. I was familiar with the concept of lack of attachment through the study of Buddhism and my stay at the Buddhist monastery. The yoga concept is similar. Steve taught us about how we are living in the world of duality. Duality is the concept of labeling certain things as 'good,' and other things as 'bad.' Human suffering occurs when we attach to things that are arbitrarily labeled as 'good,' and then crave them. When we are in situations where we no longer have the 'good' things we are attached to, we suffer greatly. The duality of 'good' and 'bad' forms the basis of many of our human attachments, and most of our human suffering.

I immediately understood the many attachments I had in my life and remembered the suffering I had from having lost my attachments. We sat in class and went around the room identifying our attachments. Someone said he had a strong attachment to his career, and when he'd lost his job, he'd experienced great suffering. Most people had attachment to certain religions that caused human suffering and even holy wars. I talked about attachment to boyfriends and lovers, and the intense suffering I felt when relationships ended. Someone spoke of the attachment within our culture to the concept that heterosexuality is right and homosexuality is wrong. We also talked about attachment to our culture and the country we were born in, and the many conflicts that have been fought defending our attachments to our land. All of these were real life examples of how attachment had led to our individual suffering and as a society has led to many wars. Any feeling of being 'right' or 'wrong' and things being 'good' or 'bad' are part of this human condition of duality and at the root of all suffering.

The Yoga Sutras explain that the path to eternal bliss is to let go of all attachments. This comes about from the practice of yoga in a disciplined way. Steve went on to explain that the Yoga Sutras state that the five senses are the main entry points of attachment. The body has a temporary experience of something 'good' through hearing, seeing, tasting, smelling, and touching, and becomes attached to that pleasurable feeling. To reach a state of Samadhi, the yogi should condition the mind to detach from the senses and the temporary pleasure associated with them. Not that you don't hear, but you hear from a sense of centeredness, not experiencing what you are hearing as being 'good' or 'bad' or 'right' or 'wrong.' Next, you detach from seeing. Not that you don't see, but that you see all things as beautiful and a divine expression. Then you detach from tasting, as you give up eating meat and toxic substances and instead fill your body with healing food to purify. A yogi no longer has the deep attachment to the taste of food or the culture of overindulging. Then detach from smell, and lastly detach from touch, which includes giving up sex and living life as a celibate.

We continued to read the sutras and learn that as the yogi continues to detach with a disciplined practice of all eight limbs of yoga, they will start to develop refined perception. Yogis start to experience higher levels of self-awareness and bliss than people who are caught up in the world of attachments can comprehend. At the beginning of trying to learn about the Yoga Sutras, I felt overwhelmed. I would stay up at night reading my book and feel like the entire world as I knew it was an illusion. I was being rocked from my foundation. I started to see the suffering in my life as being a product of my attachment and living so heavily in the world of duality. I started seeing a path out of suffering and a path to a brighter world through the practice of yoga.

It had been almost two weeks, and I was starting to get into a routine in my new yogi life in Mysore. My schedule started to get full. I had pranayama class three days a week in the morning. My asana classes continued six days a week in the evening. Yoga sutras class met three mornings a week at Steve's apartment. The other days in the week I continued going to the kirtans and the pool at the Regency Hotel.

I also started to develop my 'clique.' The members were Elizabeth from Ireland, Madela from Sweden, Sven from Germany, and of course my roommate, Katharina, also from Germany. They all were living in Gokulum, except Katharina and me, who lived in Ballal Circle. These yogis were a courageous bunch. Not only were they here in India, but most of them had rented scooters for the month and were learning how to drive 'Indian style.' Many days one of my friends would come pick me up, and I would ride on the back of their scooter. We would go out to brunch or go to a lake where they would meditate and I would do my pranayama, since I wasn't a regular meditator yet. The common bond we shared is that we all had a history of being heavy drinkers and partiers. I was not really a smoker, but I never passed up an offer to meet up for chai and a beedi. Beedis are small Indian cigarettes; they are actually just one dried tobacco leaf tightly rolled up and held together with a thin string. They look like a small brown joint. I remember my Indian grandpa, while visiting the US, hiding in my bedroom when I was little and smoking these beedis. My parents eventually found out he was smoking in my bedroom when he burned a hole in my bed, and they forbid him from smoking in front of me. Smoking beedis with my friends always reminded me of my Indian grandfather.

Just when my life in India was starting to fall into a nice routine, Katharina's life went into a tailspin. She had just had her initiation ceremony into Transcendental Meditation where she received a mantra. Katharina began meditating twice daily, once in the morning right after she came down from asana class and once in the evening when I went to my asana class. Everything was going smoothly until about the fifth day of her meditation; I came down after my morning pranayama class and found Katharina lying on the floor in a ball, sobbing and

Chapter 12: INDIA, MONTH IN MYSORE — TEACHINGS

screaming. She was yelling out things in German and was hysterical. I asked her what was wrong, but she couldn't speak in English; she just screamed and sobbed in German. I sat on the ground and started stroking her long dark brown hair that was wildly tossed about. I also took out my crystal and placed it on the back of her neck to absorb the negative energy coming out her throat chakra. Her sobbing gradually slowed to a whimpering. Once she had calmed down, I helped her to her bed and made us some chai. It soothed her further until she was slowly able to start speaking in English again. She told me she felt like a prisoner in her life; she spent the next three hours weeping to me about her childhood and sharing with me her previously buried childhood wounds from her parents' separation. That day I spent nursing and caring for Katharina as she relived her painful childhood.

Her emotional rage took a total of five days to clear; for the first three days neither one of us slept. Katharina spent the night frantically writing, sobbing, and screaming. I would try to sleep, but the emotional turmoil in the apartment was too intense to sleep through. It was a time for me to take care of her after she spent those days taking care of me. Katharina was an only child and said she had spent her entire life feeling trapped and controlled by her family. She felt rage, she felt sadness, and that week I witnessed firsthand an emotional meltdown like I had never seen. She didn't leave the apartment; she was even skipping her asana classes. I did all the shopping and had to spoon-feed her to get her to eat. I used all the skills I had acquired in my own experience with counselors and treating patients to get her through her emotional explosion; she had regressed to a childlike state. After about three days of crying, sobbing, and writing, I finally started to seriously worry. I had only known Katharina for two weeks and wasn't sure if this was a 'normal' emotional meltdown or if she was suicidal. I feared she might be having a breakdown that she might never come back from. I convinced her to come to our Yoga Sutras class; maybe talking to Steve would help her.

I helped Katharina get dressed and we went to Steve's apartment. I stopped on the way and bought some flowers to put in her hair. I felt like I was the mother and she was the child;

she had totally regressed and was acting like an eight- or nine-year-old girl. Once we got to Steve's apartment, she started frantically journaling again. About halfway through the class, she lay down right in the middle of the class and fell asleep. She hadn't slept in days, and I hoped that the fact that she'd fallen asleep was a good sign that this mania was passing. After class I talked to Steve shortly before she woke up. I told him what was going on and that I didn't know what to do. Katharina woke up and Steve talked to her for a while. He tried to help her move past her childhood trauma and come back to the present. After we left Steve's apartment, she started acting more like her adult self again. She still spent the next day and a half going back and forth between periods of stability and breakdowns, but she was finally starting to normalize. That was a very exhausting experience; not sleeping for days and seeing her become totally unglued was scary.

As Katharina started to stabilize, I was very eager to get out of the house and see some of my other friends that I hadn't seen during her breakdown. The Mysore Palace was one of the most beautiful in all of India. Every Saturday and Sunday night, they illuminated it for one hour between 6:00 and 7:00 p.m. Sven also wanted to go see the palace, so he came by my apartment and picked me up on his scooter. Riding on the back of a scooter in India became a very spiritual experience for me; I was totally leaving my fate in God's hands. The first couple moments I was in a constant state of anxiety, and my heart raced. I couldn't imagine how we would possibly get downtown to the palace in this heavy traffic without getting in an accident. After a few minutes of panicking, I decided this was the perfect opportunity to practice lack of attachment and the yogic concept of "let go and let God." I closed my eyes and held Sven tightly. Before I could finish my entire set of pranayama, we had made it to downtown Mysore.

It was already 6:30 p.m. so the palace would only be illuminated for another 30 minutes. We turned the corner to the main gate of the palace, and I saw something that looked like it was out of a fairytale. The palace looked spectacular. We parked the bike illegally and quickly walked toward the palace. As soon as we walked up, peddlers trying to sell us souvenirs swarmed

Chapter 12: INDIA, MONTH IN MYSORE — TEACHINGS

us. I could disguise myself as a native Indian woman, but Sven was a tall, bald German man, so we were obviously tourists. We finally pushed our way through the aggressive peddlers, made it inside the gates, and had about fifteen minutes left with the lights on. Inside felt like a magical fairyland; 1 felt like Dorothy after she had gone through the tornado and ended up in Oz. The palace was a splendor with many beautiful arches illuminated in white lights. It was breathtaking. For those fifteen minutes, I left all my yogic teachings behind and longed to be the princess living in that palace.

It was nice to spend time with Sven. After the emotional chaos of the week, it was just what I needed. I had made a policy to not be out in India by myself past 8:00 p.m. unless I was in my neighborhood having dinner within a few blocks of home. This was one of the first nights I was seeing the 'nightlife' of Mysore. Sven wanted to show me the town bazaar, which was walking distance from the palace. The market was lit up with freestanding bulbs hanging off of stolen electrical lines. There were thousands of people pushing and shopkeepers yelling. In the middle of the market chaos was a beautifully calm cow eating a bucket of rotten tomatoes. Sven and I both laughed at the comparison of the calm cow and the chaotic people all around; we decided this is why they must be considered holy. I will never forget the magic I felt at that palace; somewhere hidden within every woman there still lives that dream to be a princess.

The next day was the puja at the shala, a spiritual ceremony to bring good fortune and blessings to Sheshadri's new yoga school. We didn't have asana class on Sundays, and it was one of the first mornings in two weeks I actually "slept in" to about 7:00 a.m. I decided to get dressed up for the puja. I had shopped for a few days to find something, but it is very hard to find anything in India that is not covered in gold sequins and rhinestones. I wanted something plain and nondescript, and after looking at every clothier in town, I finally found a plain royal blue panjabi at Big Bazaar. I decided to wear my hair in two pigtails, and I put on my makeup and jewelry. My social calendar had transformed from the elite fundraising parties of

THE EVOLUTION OF A PARTY GIRL

Detroit to asana class and kirtans in India. Now the big 'gala' was this puja.

The yogis started arriving around a quarter to eight. We all congregated on the roof deck. It was a beautiful sunny morning, everyone was dressed up, and excitement was in the air. Then three Brahman priests arrived to perform the ceremony. They were dressed in white cotton clothes wrapped around them like a sarong and then draped over one shoulder. Their chests were bare, and they were all wearing a piece of string diagonally across their chests like a sash. The priests were scurrying about trying to get everything ready for the puja. By 9:00 a.m., an hour after the puja was supposed to start, they still weren't ready. Sheshadri said since the puja was running so late, they were going to serve us breakfast before it started and hopefully it would be ready to start at 10:00 a.m. Sheshadri's wife had cooked a huge breakfast, and they brought up silver buckets filled with food. There was an Indian style masala cream of wheat called upma, small round spongy rice cakes called idli, and a spicy tomato and lentil soup called sambar to eat with the idli. There was also a spicy potato dish, Indian bread, and a sweet Indian dessert with nuts and coconut in it. The food was an amazing, home-cooked meal, and it only took a group of Ashtangi yogis about fifteen minutes to devour all the food.

At 10:30 a.m., the 8:00 a.m. puja finally started, and we all sat down in the yoga room. The priests had made two beautiful sand art pictures of Indian Gods on the floor of the yoga room, just as you entered. They were ornately beautiful and so precise. The puja started with Sheshadri, his wife, and his son all sitting on the floor in front of the priests. The main priest performing most of the chanting looked to be about 30 years old and was very skinny. He chanted nonstop for about two hours. While he chanted, rituals were performed such as throwing flowers on the statue, putting marks on Sheshadri's forehead, and offering fruit.

I sat with Diego in the back of the room during the puja. Diego was an Italian man who lived in India and was separated from his wife and children who lived in Brazil. Diego was an attorney and was doing legal work for international businesses. He was a true yogi and had basically denounced his previous

Chapter 12: INDIA, MONTH IN MYSORE — TEACHINGS

life and was in the midst of a major identity crisis, along with a divorce. Diego was the local confidant and knew all the yogis' stories and the skeletons in their closets. During the first part of the puja, Diego and I sat in the back of the yoga room, and he told me all the yogi gossip of Mysore. I learned about who was sleeping with whom, and who had someone at home that they were cheating on. He asked me what my story was and what I was doing in India. No one had really asked me that question, and I hadn't come up with a witty response yet. I told him I was there to reconnect with my Indian culture and hoping to discover my purpose in this world. He said he thought it was great I had the courage to do that alone, and he wished he had done it also before he'd gotten married and had three children. He asked me if I had a boyfriend, and I said no. He asked me if I was looking for one and I said not particularly. Then he laughed and told me that if I was looking for a boy toy for the next few weeks, he had the perfect one in mind. I told him I had just had one of those in Japan and didn't think that much of the 'boy toy' dream anymore. After a while, I felt guilty for the conversations we were having during the puja. I had just admitted my sexcapade with Andrew to Diego and in the presence of God—well, I guess God already knew all about it. After Diego had pumped me for info, he said he had to go and clued me in that this puja was still in the beginning stages and was going to last most of the day.

The puja and the chanting went on and on. By 1:00 p.m., most of the yogis including Diego had left. I tried to stick it out. They started a fire and placed a large statue of the God Hanuman in front of the fire. I couldn't imagine how this priest could possibly remember all these Sanskrit chants. For my yoga asana class, we did one chant at the beginning of class, and I still needed the card to recite the chant. By 2:30 p.m. I couldn't last any longer. Buttercup, an eccentric yogi, and I were the only ones left. I was hungry, my knee was hurting and starting to swell, and my brain was on chanting overload. I had to leave. I went to Mahesh Prasad for an afternoon thali. I walked around Ballal Circle for a few hours before returning home at 5:00 p.m. to find the puja was just finishing. From 8:00 a.m. until 5:00 p.m.—it had taken almost nine hours to prepare the room and evoke the presence of the deities. The spiritual path is definitely a path of patience.

I went up to see the room and no one was there, but the floor was still covered in sand art, ashes, rice, and flowers. I sat in the room alone, and although the room appeared empty, it was actually very full of an indescribable energy. An overwhelming wave of silence, joy, and sadness came over my body. The room had a thick stillness, with the smell of fire, incense, and flowers lingering in the air. I sat on a yoga mat and closed my eyes to try to connect to this energy. My mind quickly drifted to a place not in that room, not in India, not even in this worldly human place. My mind and my body filled with emotions, and I felt sadness. Then everything went blank and I sat perfectly still. I had a wonderful and loving companionship swell up from within me. I don't know how long I sat there, but I remembered a few times I would drift back into a present state of consciousness and think I had to leave. Then I would be overcome with a strong yearning to stay and this loving feeling would again fill my body as my thoughts ceased. I lost orientation to time and space when my mind moved into that much deeper state of consciousness.

I could feel that something had changed in that room after the puja. I understood that this is what most people call God. I spent most of my life as an atheist, so to use the word God still sends shivers of rebellion up my spine, but the energetic field I sensed was undeniable. My many years as an atheist were now behind me. I couldn't see or touch this energy field that was permeating my body, but I could tell that God had been in that room and had left behind a beautiful feeling of love. I sat in that room for hours and still didn't want to leave. I felt so nurtured and comforted in there. Everything seemed whole, complete, and beautiful in me and in the world. When I went downstairs, it was past 7:00 p.m.; I had sat there motionless for two hours.

The day after the puja and that deep meditative experience, I had an overwhelming need to be alone. I wasn't feeling lonely; I was just filled up and had no desire for outside influences. I had started my routine week of going to my Yoga Sutras class, my pranayama, and my asana class. My crush on Steve was

Chapter 12: INDIA, MONTH IN MYSORE — TEACHINGS

progressing every day, but I never had the courage to talk to him other than during class about the Yoga Sutras. I wanted to find out more about him, so I asked around to find out the scoop. I finally confessed to Elizabeth about the major crush I had developed. I also shared my guilt for having such impure thoughts about him as he was trying to teach us spirituality. She assured me it was normal and told me that all the girls had a major crush on Steve. Not just all the girls in our class, but all the girls at the kirtans and most of the yogis in Mysore. They all fantasized about making out with Steve.

That night after I confessed to Elizabeth about the fantasy relationship I had been creating with Steve, it got even more intense. I lay in bed and for some reason I could not stop thinking and dreaming about Steve. I don't know if it was a dream or not, but something magical happened that night. As I started to fall asleep, I could feel my mind separating from my body. I wasn't sure what was happening, so I would check if I was asleep and I wasn't, but I also wasn't really present in my body. I was floating around the room, not lying in bed in my body. This went on for hours, and I found it quite exciting that every now and then I would look at the clock and a full hour would have passed and I was still floating around the room. This was the first time in my life that I'd felt like my conscious mind had actually left my physical body. My conscious mind also felt the presence of someone else in my room that night. I sensed someone had come to see me that night while I was in this wakeful dreaming state. I learned that night what astral travel felt like, and by the morning, I felt another dramatic shift in my consciousness. That puja had probably had a profound effect on the energy in our apartment as well, since we were right below where it had taken place. I had experienced some pretty crazy things in my life, but these experiences were all happening to me stone cold sober.

Speaking of stone sober, it had been almost three weeks since I'd had a drop of alcohol when Madela called me. She had been in India almost two months and told me she was feeling more peace and beauty than she had felt in many years back home in Sweden. Madela had been in deep depression and fighting a losing battle with chronic fatigue syndrome when she decided to pack up her life and travel to India for two months. She told me that Sven, Elizabeth, and she were going to the Metropole hotel for a celebration cocktail, and she called to invite Katharina and me to join them. I said yes and asked her what she was celebrating. She said she would tell me over a glass of wine. Wow, a glass of wine. I felt my inner party girl awaken with excitement. I think that elation over a drink was a sign of someone who could possibly become an alcoholic. I asked Katharina, who had been a total homebody since the breakdown, and she said no. She also told me I shouldn't be drinking either. I decide to break my rule and go out alone at night to meet the crew at Metropole.

Metropole was a five-star hotel. It had an elegant décor, with a uniformed doorman, marble floors, and air conditioning. When the rickshaw driver saw where he was dropping me off, he refused to give me any change back from the 100 rupees I gave him, even though we had already agreed it would cost 50 rupees. I wasn't in the mood to get taken advantage of and decided to fight back. It was always the same dilemma. Do you just give in and feel taken advantage of and enable the vicious cycle of rickshaw drivers taking advantage of tourists? Or do you argue and ruin your mood over what amounts to be just over a dollar? Most days I let it go, but eventually I would get fed up with all the cheating and crookery and take a stand; that night I took a stand and fought for ten minutes to get my fifty rupees change. I don't know if it is ever worth it, but that night I fought back and won.

I found my friends outside at a patio table, and I felt embarrassed that they must have heard me fighting with my rickshaw driver. They said they did and were all laughing at another one of those 'only in India' moments. The waiter was wearing a tuxedo and a turban. I asked if they had a wine list, and he said yes. Imagine, a wine list. I was tickled. The wine list was sparse; it had two bottles of Cabernet Sauvignon, one bottle from France and the other from India. There was a huge price difference—the bottle of French Cab was almost $60, the Indian wine was $30. We decided to try the Indian bottle; it was called Sula, which means sun. Elizabeth offered me a cigarette and I took it. We ordered a few plates of paneer Manchurian and in a matter of a few hours, I had gone from a deep spiritual state to drinking wine, smoking cigarettes, and eating fried food as a form of 'celebration.' As we raised our glass for our first toast, Madela made her big announcement in her cute Swedish accent. She had decided to permanently give up her car and apartment in Sweden; she was going to use the money to stay in India another four months. She went on to express her gratitude for us being her friends. She told us how good she had been feeling in the last two months here in India, and how the idea of going back to Sweden was causing her anxiety. She said she was finally happy again after months of being in a depression. We all toasted her and congratulated her on her decision. We all shared ourselves that night over three bottles of wine. I understood why Madela wanted to stay. For all the BS I had to deal with on a daily basis, there was something that was very magical about being in India.

I woke up the next day feeling hungover and disappointed with myself. Even after an intense and amazing three weeks of detoxing and much inner growth, it just took one phone call and I was back in the party scene. I used this opportunity to shed some light on a major dichotomy in my life. I understood that yoga was going to make gradual changes over time, and I forgave myself.

Thursday I looked at the calendar and realized it was Thanksgiving. Katharina and I took a rickshaw down to the Mysore Palace. As soon as we got out of the rickshaw we were again hounded by hundreds of peddlers trying to sell us junk. We made it past the crowd and through the gates. The palace cost two hundred rupees for foreigners and only twenty rupees for Indian citizens. When I saw the palace again, this time during the day, it was almost as beautiful as when it was all lit up. We walked toward the shoe check—in most temples and sacred places in India there are no shoes allowed. We checked in our shoes, almost like a coat check, and then headed to the audio station to get headsets to take the self-guided tour. After the typical Indian hassle of obtaining the headsets, I was excited to finally set foot in the palace. Katharina and I decided we would split up and meet at the end of the palace tour since we would both be listening to headsets and wandering at our own pace.

As I approached the main gate, I was impressed with the huge archways that were painted so brilliantly. We entered the palace and I could see it was even more spectacular inside than it was on the outside. The floors were made of ornately inlaid stone, and the walls were covered with grand paintings and European tapestries. The enormous chandeliers were 24K gold ornately decorated with thousands of crystals. We walked room to room in awe, as each room was grander than the one before.

Then it happened—we entered the grand hall, and I was in the most spectacular 'room' I had ever been in. The floor was white marble, and there were at least 100 perfectly carved bright orange marble pillars. The walls were decorated in bright turquoise and the ceiling was a midnight blue replica of the entire night sky, including the constellations. The room was about the size of a basketball court and only had three walls. The front wall was open and had a row of huge archways that overlooked the gardens and the city of Mysore. I only could imagine the grand galas and weddings that had taken place in that room. I found a corner and sat on the floor and just let the history fill my body. I closed my eyes and tried to connect to the energy.

It wasn't the beautiful stillness that I had felt at the yoga shala or at the temples. It was a more chaotic and powerful force that filled my body. In that moment I understood the enormous responsibility it was to be a maharaja and the power they needed to exert to maintain a kingdom like this. In a country of starvation and poverty, it seemed ridiculous to live so lavishly. My dream of being a princess at that palace quickly faded. It seemed like a life I would have hated, controlled and on display in that beautiful room with no freedom, and totally isolated from life outside of the palace. I remember the feeling of being on display in Japan and how much I'd loathed it. Just as I was starting to feel overwhelmed by the violent energy I could feel, a security guard tapped me on my shoulder and told me I couldn't sit there. I had to move along, thank God. As much as I loved the way the room looked, when I sat in silence I could feel its dark energy. I was glad to be a visitor and return back to my life of freedom, peace, and spirituality in my tiny apartment underneath the yoga room.

Chapter 12: INDIA, MONTH IN MYSORE — TEACHINGS

After asana class I felt thankful for my wonderful Thanksgiving. I talked to Katharina as I lay down in bed, and we discussed our future plans. She was to be leaving soon to an oceanfront town in Kerala, the state to the south of where we currently were. She was going to attend an Ashtanga yoga workshop put on by a famous yogi from Italy. From there she was going to fly to Africa where one of her close friends was going to get married. I was starting to feel sad that our fun and crazy month together was winding down. We had been through so much in the last few weeks, and we both had overcome major obstacles.

Katharina said instead of going to Goa next, I should come meet her in Kovalam Beach. She said she would email Padma, the owner of the guesthouse/yoga studio, in the morning and see if I could come and share her room. I still planned on staying and finishing my entire month in Mysore, but the prospect of spending a week swimming in the ocean before going to Mumbai was sounding pretty delightful.

The next day, as I was leaving my apartment for my Yoga Sutras class at Steve's apartment, a gorgeous Italian guy came up to my apartment and said he was looking for a place to stay and practice yoga for the next two weeks. I was dressed up for Steve's class as usual, so I was looking pretty glamorous for India, and I could tell he was flirting with me. I said Sheshadri usually gets back at about 4:30 p.m. for evening asana class, and I told him to come back then to meet with him. He asked me if I thought this was a good place to practice yoga and how I liked living here. I told him that I loved it, and I had made a great group of friends. I could feel sparks flying between us; I have always had a thing for Italian men...who doesn't?

I went to Steve's class and again spent the two hours lusting over him, but I was starting to feel that the month-long crush I had was not going to amount to anything. Steve was always talking about how yogis need to practice celibacy and show discipline to grow their spiritual practice. I don't know what overcame me, but I raised my hand and asked, "If yogis practice celibacy, then what is tantric yoga?" His face turned red, and I could tell I'd caught him off guard. He sat quiet for a second and the whole room was silent. Finally he said, "That's a good question, Preya. I think I will answer your question at the next class."

After class, Madela and Elizabeth both laughed about my question and how embarrassed he got, saying they were intrigued to hear his answer. We joked about next week being the first class with perfect attendance, as everyone wanted to hear his answer. I said this was probably the only way I was ever going to get Steve to talk about sex! We all had a crush on Steve.

I spent that afternoon contemplating what to do when Katharina left; I had been spending all my time with her and was a little nervous to be in India without her. I headed up to the roof to meet up with my fellow yogis for evening asana class. I looked forward to seeing my classmates every night and sharing stories of our days in India. Many times in Detroit, I would bring a question or problem to my yoga mat and by the end of class I had a clear answer or solution to my problem. I brought my question of what to do after Katharina left to the mat. As I started going through my practice, my mind started to formulate the answer. I realized that Kerala, the state where Kovalam Beach is located, was one of the places I had loved the most while traveling with my family as a child in India. If a beach vacation was what I was looking for, then why not go travel for another ten days with Katharina to Kovalam, instead of going by myself to Goa? I finished my class feeling content with my decision to meet up with Katharina in Kerala at Kovalam Beach. I would complete my full month with Sheshadri, and therefore I would leave about four days after she left. That night I called my family in Mumbai and told them of my change in plans and assured them that I would be to Mumbai in time for Christmas.

Chapter 13
INDIA, A MONTH IN MYSORE — BYLAKUPPE

A screaming baby in the back of the temple quickly took me out of my meditation; at that moment of hearing that crying baby it was a clear reminder that I was not yet ready for motherhood...

***

Dante, the young cute Italian, had moved into the apartment across the hall. He came and knocked on my door after class and asked me if I wanted a glass of chai he had just made. I said yes and told him we could sit out on the roof; it was almost a full moon and the roof was beautiful at night. We climbed up the ladder with chai in one hand. It was a dangerous climb to the roof, let alone with a full cup of hot chai in one hand. Once we got on the roof, Dante pulled out a joint and asked me if I smoke hash. I said I had smoked marijuana, but it had been a while. He asked me if I wanted to try some fresh Indian hashish. The yogi part of my personality wanted to say no, but my party girl crept in and reasoned that part of the experience of India was to smoke some of the infamous ganja, right? He lit up the joint, and I soon learned that smoking weed is like riding a bike; after watching him once, I quickly remembered all my old tricks of how to smoke a joint. Dante was 25 years old and a lifeguard back in Italy. He worked in the summers and saved up enough money to spend his winters in India. He had already been traveling in India for two months and was going to stay three more months. Dante had spent most of his time in north

Chapter 13: INDIA, A MONTH IN MYSORE —BYLAKUPPE

India, and this was his first time studying yoga in the south. He wasn't familiar with Ashtanga yoga. He asked me to tell him about the class. By time he was done talking, I was stoned. I felt my body getting light and full of energy, and my thoughts were getting deeper and slower; I just wanted to giggle and dance.

I had an overwhelming need to stretch and move and was not at all in the mood to talk. So I suggested I show him some asanas up on the roof. I started with my sun salutations and he joined in. Then I told him about the standing series, and he followed my lead. We kept giggling and laughing between all the asanas. We laughed a lot that night. The whole scene was quite surreal—this 25-year-old Italian lifeguard and me on the roof under the full moon stoned and doing asana practice. About one hour into the poses, fireworks started going off, and my buzz was starting to wear off. I told him I couldn't do any more. I'd already completed one asana class that night. We sat down and watched the fireworks, and he asked me a lot of questions about myself. I told him tomorrow was a full moon and there would be no asana class. I was planning to visit a Tibetan refugee camp about two hours away. I asked him to join me and he said yes. We made a plan to leave by 8:00 a.m., but I wasn't sure if it was one of those plans you make under an altered state and then back out of in the morning. I had already decided to go by myself because Katharina didn't want to go; I hoped he would join me, but I was going to Bylakuppe either way.

At 8:00 a.m., I was lying in bed trying to figure out what the hell had happened the previous night. I was tired from my asana marathon and feeling a lot of guilt about smoking hashish on the roof of the shala. I had moved far away from my previous life full of vices and was feeling so grounded in my yoga lifestyle, I couldn't figure out why I'd had such a setback over the last few days. Did it merely take one hot 25-year-old Italian lifeguard to throw my entire new program into a tailspin? Just as I started to question why I was falling back into my old patterns, there was a knock at my door. It was Dante, and he was looking as hot as ever and all packed and ready to go on time—even hotter. I quickly ran around my apartment, got dressed, and packed up for the day. Dante made us some chai while I got ready, and by 8:30 a.m. we were in a rickshaw heading downtown to the public bus station. I had never been on the public bus system in India and was a little nervous about the experience, but I was happy being with Dante. He was well traveled in India and experienced in navigating the totally disorganized Indian public transportation system.

There were mobs of people at the bus station, and everyone seemed to know where they were going but us. I stood in the middle of the chaos looking around at the old busses, the thick hot smell of exhaust, and the crowds of local people. I had a dazed look on my face, and I felt like deer caught in the headlights. What had I gotten myself into? A man in a beige uniform must have seen my look of terror; he approached us and asked in perfect English if he could be of assistance. I said we were trying to get to Bylakuppe. He directed us toward an old, beaten-up red bus and said to take that bus almost to the end of the line and then it is a 20-minute rickshaw drive.

When we got on the bus it was remarkably empty. Dante checked with the bus driver that we were on the right bus, and he assured us we were. Since the bus was so empty, Dante and I each sat in our own row across from each other. The bus left the station and was still mostly empty when we left. I finally relaxed and felt comfortable that we were on the right bus and there were empty seats. Shortly after the bus left the station, however, it made its first stop; tons of people loaded on and quickly, after another stop, the bus was totally overcrowded. I couldn't even see Dante across the aisle. This middle-aged Indian man sat next to me and sat very close. The aisle was filled with people, and then the bus stopped at the market where several men came on the bus with huge baskets of fruits and produce. They loaded their supplies in the storage cabin of the bus. They were using the public bus to transport their goods to sell in the villages. I couldn't believe it. Every time I scooted over, the man next to me scooted closer until he was practically sitting on me. I was crammed between the window and this creepy man who kept trying to rub up against me. I was in public transportation hell, and felt so violated by this man, but I had no choice but to sit there for two more hours. I wrapped my shawl around my head and covered my face, put my head down, and started to do my pranayama. I worked on my deep yogic breathing techniques

135

Chapter 13: INDIA, A MONTH IN MYSORE —BYLAKUPPE

and tried to get my mind to disengage from this mess I was in. Every time I got deep into my pranayama, I could feel this man look over at me with a creepy smile and scoot toward me. After about an hour we had left the city and the bus had started to thin out and I could finally see Dante again. Just as I was about to have a complete breakdown, Dante said, "Hey, Preya, this is our stop." I had to climb over people and try to push my way to the front before the driver pulled away from the stop. I pleaded with the people to let me by as I yelled to the driver not to leave. Dante yelled to me, "Come on, Preya, just shove your way to the front." I cried back, "I am trying, but I am getting manhandled and groped by all the men on the bus." We got off, as tears streamed down my face and Dante was shocked to see how upset I was. I said that was one of the worst experiences of my life. He suggested we get a coconut. So we had a coconut, and he assured me that he would sit with me on the way home.

After about fifteen minutes of hardcore bargaining with the rickshaw drivers, Dante finally got one driver to break the union and drive us for 300 rupees. I have never been so happy to be in a rickshaw and had never before thought of one as being a luxury. We were pretty far into the countryside. The roads were mostly dirt trails, and we passed many tiny villages. Dante opened up his pocket and pulled out another joint to smoke in the rickshaw. He asked me if I wanted some, and after that bus ride I was certainly tempted, but I had already decided that morning that I was not going to make hashish part of my trip to India. Dante inconspicuously smoked in the back and blew all the smoke out the side so the driver hopefully wouldn't notice. We were way off the beaten track, and the last thing we needed was to get kicked out of this rickshaw for Dante's hashish addiction.

I had finally calmed down from the bus ride, and Dante was stoned and starting to crack jokes. We were both laughing when all of a sudden the rickshaw driver stopped. *Oh no*, I thought. *He has smelled Dante's hashish.* But I looked up to see the entire road for about a block covered with hundreds of sheep walking toward us. There was a very skinny man walking with them, wearing a turban and carrying a long stick. The driver turned the rickshaw off, and we sat for about ten minutes as we waited for all the sheep to pass so we could use the single lane 'road.' At the end, the sheepherder was smiling so brightly at me, I pulled out my camera and he proudly posed for a picture. I felt so connected to him during that moment; I had a new understanding and appreciation for his simple life of walking and spending his days with his sheep. I saw brightness and pride in his eyes and his body language, the same brightness I saw in many of the Indian people who lived so simply. I had always thought the more you do, the more you have, the more achievements you attain, the more happiness you would have, but lately I was starting to totally rethink that theory.

The rickshaw dropped us off in front of the large burgundy gates to the refugee compound. They had a large Tibetan flag carved into them. We walked through the gates and were in a large concrete square with dormitory style buildings on three sides. The other side was a long rose garden walkway that led to beautiful temples. Most of the people in the compound were Buddhist monks. They dressed in ankle length burgundy skirts and bright yellow upper cloths. Their heads were shaved bald and some of the older monks had long beards. The main temple was decorated so ornately with gold-embossed woodcarvings. It was a pagoda-style temple, similar to the many I had visited in Japan. There were five levels, and all of the roofs curved up on the edges, but this one was much more colorful than the Buddhist temples in Japan. On top of every building was a gold stupa. Stupas were originally dirt mounds that held the remains of the body of Buddha, but now they have become the typical design of all Buddhist temples. Adorning all the corners of each level of the temple were huge, beautifully carved golden prayer wheels. Front and center in the main temple was an enormous picture of a much younger Dalai Lama. He looked to be in his twenties. We were told that when China invaded Tibet in 1959, the compound of Bylakuppe was established to house 10,000 refugees. Most of the Tibetan refugees were in the north of India in Dharamsala, including the Dalai Lama himself.

We walked toward the entrance of the main temple and passed a small building with walls made from many small windows. Inside were hundreds of small, silver oil lamps in perfect rows. The flames were dancing and flickering about. They all moved similarly, but each one had its own space and special glow. I was mesmerized staring at the flames. While each was unique, I understood how each one represented the commonalities of all people. As we entered, I felt overwhelmed with emotions, first a deep sadness, then joy. Dante and I separated as soon as we walked in; I told him I wanted to stay a while because I could tell this was a special place. The walls were covered with beautiful and vibrant thangka paintings of the stories of Buddha. Each one was about six feet tall and brilliantly colored, with a preponderance of turquoise, blue, and red.

At the front of the temple, there were three enormous golden Buddha statues. The Buddhas all looked slightly different, and each represented a different aspect of the Buddha. The largest statue in the center was the most iconic version, with the crown on his head completely replaced with snails. According to legend, Buddha sat and meditated so long and intensely that his head was covered in snails. This was the second reference I'd experienced to how long it takes to attain enlightenment. In the Jain temple I went to on my last moon day, the statue's legs were covered in vines that had grown on his body during his years of meditation. This Buddha sat naked. All of the jewels were gone, the weapons were replaced with an empty bowl, and he had nothing material left.

I sat down in front of that beautiful golden Buddha and began to meditate. As soon as I closed my eyes, my mind started to swirl, and a blanket of tranquility enveloped my mind. I saw glistening gold light radiating from my heart space. A sense of separation from my body, similar to that feeling I'd had in my bed back in Mysore, also occurred. During this experience of separation from my body, I still had the awareness of being 'Preya,' but my consciousness was vast, enough to fill the entire room. I could have sat there forever. I was alive in the experience of detachment from my physical body, and felt no desire to come back. A screaming baby in the back of the temple quickly took me out of my meditation; it was a clear reminder that I was not yet ready for motherhood.

I walked to the altar to make a donation. There was a sign in front of the center Buddha that said this was the temple of transformation. It stated that this was a place to attain deep

THE EVOLUTION OF A PARTY GIRL

meditative states that allow you to leave your physical body. This confirmed that what I was feeling was real.

After we left the temple, Dante was very antsy, and I could tell he wanted to smoke another joint. He said, "Well, you certainly seemed to like that temple a lot." I agreed and thanked him for being patient with me. I didn't feel any need to share with him what I had just experienced. These experiences were so dramatic that they made me feel insecure. It was hard to explain or convince someone who doesn't believe in the power of the divine what separating from your body feels like.

After lunch we left the compound and walked around the shops that the Tibetan refuges owned. Most of the artifacts they were selling were Tibetan handicrafts that said, "Made in India by a Tibetan refugee." As I walked shop to shop, I felt sorrow among the shop owners. I could see and feel that they were suffering from being forced out of their homeland. I tried to send each one of them love with my thoughts and bought a few souvenirs to show support. I bought a beautiful silver and amethyst beaded necklace, a few of the traditional Buddhist flags, and two very special felt banners that had my favorite quote from the Dalai Lama on them, one for me and one for Katharina.

"A Precious Human life."

"Every day, think as you wake up: Today I am fortunate to have woken up. I am alive, I have a precious human life. I am not going to waste it. I am going to use all my energies to develop myself, to expand my heart out to others, to achieve enlightenment for the benefit of all beings. I am going to have kind thoughts toward others. I am not going to get angry, or think badly about others. I am going to benefit others as much as I can." -H.H. the XIV Dalai Lama

Dante was eager to leave. I wanted to go back into that temple and meditate again, but he refused. So we got a rickshaw and headed back to the bus station. We got on the bus, and I sat at a window seat, and Dante sat next to me. The ride home was much better—it was still as crowded as it was in the morning, but having a hot young Italian rubbing up against me on the bumpy Indian roads was much more tolerable than the earlier

Chapter 13: INDIA, A MONTH IN MYSORE —BYLAKUPPE

situation. On the way home, I realized that Dante was not going to be my Indian romance. I enjoyed his company and his young playful energy, but he was a certified 'pothead.'

When I got home, Katharina had printed out pictures of us and put them up in the living room. One was of me laughing and smiling upside down in a handstand in my T-shirt that says "free yourself, to be yourself." Her picture was of her during her breakdown with this strange look on her face and a small smiley face sticker placed over her third eye. It was so funny to come home to those pictures. I laughed myself to sleep thinking about all the crazy things I had already experienced, and I still had over five months left of my trip.

Katharina had bought her bus ticket and was going to be leaving for Kerala in a few days. That night it sunk in that we only had a few days left together in our small apartment, and had many things we still wanted to do. We sat and talked over chai and decided our plans. She planned to tour the sandalwood factory, and we agreed to spend our last Sunday at the Landmark Hotel pool.

The next day I went to my Yoga Sutras class and was sorry to realize I only had one more class with Steve. His classes and kirtans had been the highlight of my month. He did give a quick answer to my question about what tantra was, but it was definitely not the hot steamy answer that the other girls and I were hoping for. As I sat in class, I had an overwhelming desire to ask him if he wanted to get tea with me after class, but when class ended, I chickened out and quickly left. On my rickshaw ride back home, I promised myself I was going to call up Steve and invite him out to lunch with me before I left Mysore.

Chapter 14
INDIA, A MONTH IN MYSORE — GOODBYE

I forgave myself for my mistakes and tried not to be hard on myself, realizing that these major changes were going to take time...

***

I went to yoga class and saw some new faces. Many of the people I had originally started my month with were gone and new faces were popping up from all over the world. I spent that asana class thinking about Dante, Steve, Andrew and all the other men over the years I have had crushes on. How much time and energy had I wasted in my life pursuing men? How many decisions in my life had I made based on men? In that moment, as I went into my triangle pose, I was overwhelmed with the ridiculousness of this never-ending quest for the next man and started laughing out loud. I kept laughing louder and louder, and I couldn't stop; everyone in class was looking over to see what I was laughing about. Then some other people started laughing, then Sheshadri started laughing, and every time I would try to stop laughing, I would be more overwhelmed with the silliness of my 'dramatic life' and start cracking up again even louder than the bout before. I kept doing my poses through my laughter and couldn't control this powerful release. This laughing yoga went on for about fifteen minutes and at the peak of it, almost everyone in the room was in a full-out belly laugh. After class that day, many of the students came up to me and thanked me for the laughing yoga. One girl in particular, a

Chapter 14: INDIA, A MONTH IN MYSORE —GOODBYE

Russian girl, told me that it was the most blissful yoga experience she had ever had. Blissful, laughing yoga...another reason I had to come to India.

The next day was Katharina's last day and we had been invited to have brunch at Sheshadri's house. After my pranayama class, he called a rickshaw for us. He only rode a bike and told us he would meet us at his house. When we got to Sheshadri's, his wife was waiting at the gate to meet us. He had a modest bungalow style house by American standards, but by Indian standards it was a mansion. Most people live in small two-room apartments where one room is the kitchen and the other room is the living room/bedroom. This house had a beautiful front yard and backyard with a garden, a kitchen, a living room, and two bedrooms. The main sitting room was mostly empty; there was an altar at the northeast part of the room and a large hanging swing in the middle of the room.

There was a display case filled with trophies. I asked Sheshadri what all the trophies were from, and he said they were from his previous career. I could tell he didn't want to talk about it, but I was still curious. After a few more questions, he reluctantly said that he was a professional wrestler before he was a yoga teacher; he had been the lightweight champion. Another strange thing was that he had five cats. It is unusual in India to have any pets, let alone so many.

Sheshadri's wife had prepared a gourmet South Indian breakfast for us. We had upma, idli, sambar, and a sweet cashew honey dessert. I am not a huge fan of sweets, but it was absolutely delicious. We sat for an hour and had breakfast and chai. We talked to Sheshadri about his life, and he shared with us his dream of traveling to America to teach yoga. He told us he was also looking for a wife for his 25-year-old son, and they were looking at girls that were 15 and 16 years old. I almost choked on my tea in disapproval, but he went on to explain his wife was 15 and he was 25 when they got married. Before everyone left, I presented Sheshadri with a gift, a guest book for his new yoga shala. It was an ornate gold notebook in which I had written a sentimental message of gratitude and appreciation. I told him he had so many amazing people come from all over the world that he should keep a book in which his students can write inspirational short stories about their time spent at his shala. I could tell he really liked the idea.

After everyone left, I went into Sheshadri's bedroom and did a craniosacral treatment on him. I told him I wanted to share a special healing technique that I knew in the way that he had shared yoga with all of us. His craniosacral rhythm was very strong, which is a sign of health and vitality. He had some issues in his neck and head from a childhood train accident. When I had finished my treatment, he slowly stood up, and I could tell he was walking on the clouds; he said that it was the most beautiful treatment he had ever received.

Katharina and I went to Steve's house for her final kirtan, and afterward I finally did it! I went up to Steve and said, "A few of us are going to a goodbye dinner for Katharina before I take her to the bus stop tonight, and I was hoping you would be able to join us." He said that night was not a good night for him, but he asked me for my phone number and said if anything changed he would call.

Katharina was all packed up before I went to asana class and said she was going to join me at my evening asana class today. In the entire month we lived together we hadn't practiced yoga together until that night. It was beautiful practicing with Katharina on one side of me and Dante on the other. It had only been four weeks, but I felt surrounded by the love of my new friends.

After class, Madela and Elizabeth were waiting for us outside our apartment. Dante, Katharina, and I quickly got changed and we all walked together to dinner. We spent most of the dinner reminiscing about our month together, then Katharina's phone rang; it was Steve. He called to say he was sorry he was not going to make it to her dinner, but he wanted to say goodbye and wish her luck. Humph, Steve had called Katharina's phone. Out of curiosity, I picked up my phone and I had a missed call—it was Steve. He had called my phone first. I took that as a definite sign. I only had a few days left if I was ever going to get the courage to ask him out.

After dinner, we stopped home and picked up Katharina's bags and headed to the bus stop. It still seemed chaotic even at 9:00 p.m. We said our goodbyes, and I was unhappy as I

Chapter 14: INDIA, A MONTH IN MYSORE —GOODBYE

watched the bus pull away. Just as I was walking to flag a rickshaw home, I saw a neon sign that said "BAR" with an arrow. I followed the arrows and before I had time to decide if this was a safe idea, I was tucked away in a back booth with a bottle of beer in front of me. The bar was a dive, and the only people there were Indian men. There were three rooms in the bar, and I picked the back room that didn't have anyone in it. I also positioned myself with my back facing the door, so nobody would notice me as they walked by. I pulled out my journal and began to write. I had so much to write about. I was afraid with Katharina leaving; she had been my lifeline since I'd arrived in India. I would meet back up with her in five days for our final week together, but for now I was totally on my own.

I finished the first beer in no time and ordered a second. By this time I had been 'discovered.' The room was quickly filling up with Indian men who were staring hungrily at me. I kept my head down and spent that hour journaling about my feelings. I wrote about the realization I'd had in my 'laughing yoga' class about how quickly I became distracted in my life by chasing men. I had clearly decided the goal of my thirties was a path of "health, wealth, love, and adventure," but I still had the party girl inside who loved chasing boys and getting drunk! I needed to refocus and remember the goal of my trip was internal growth and finding my higher purpose. I forgave myself for my mistakes and tried to not be hard on myself, realizing that these major changes were going to take time. By the end of my second beer, the room was filled, and I was the center of every man's attention since I was the only woman in the bar. I needed to get out of there. When I left, I was a little drunk and was craving a five-star hotel and a nice glass of wine. I found one nearby and they said the only bar they had was a nightclub called Opium. I didn't know they had nightclubs in India, so I decided to take a look. It was similar to a cheesy American nightclub, with one major difference—it was filled with only men! I tried to find a table in the corner and ordered a glass of wine. The owner of the club came out and brought five bottles of wine to the table and asked if I wanted to try them all to see which one I wanted. I said yes. I tried all five and none were good, but I chose a French wine. He said he wanted to buy my first drink and when I agreed, he sat down at my table to join me. I didn't realize that in India buying a drink also meant joining me for it. A few minutes into the conversation, I realized this was not a good idea. He was making advances in an aggressive and inappropriate way. I excused myself to the bathroom and made a B-line to the door. I ran to the rickshaw station and jumped in a rickshaw just as I saw him running toward me. I yelled for the rickshaw driver to go, and just as he approached, we quickly drove away. I was so thankful to be in a rickshaw and on my way home. It was my first night without Katharina and I had already managed to get myself into a pickle. Note to self... going to the bar alone in India is very different than going to a bar alone in America!

I woke up the next morning and in the quiet space of my mind I was again making the connection between the problems in my life and drinking. After pranayama class, I decided I would call Steve and ask him to go to lunch with me on Saturday, the day before I left. I called and he picked up on the first ring; he sounded really excited that I'd called him. We small-talked a little bit and I told him about my adventure the night before. I regretted telling him as soon as I started because I knew it was a stupid thing to do. He tried not to sound fatherly but did agree that it wasn't smart to go out by myself to bars in India. Then I went for it and said, "The reason I was calling was that I am going to be leaving Mysore on Sunday and wanted to invite you to go out to lunch with me before I left." He said he was flattered, but since he tried not to eat outside the house, he suggested I come over and he would cook lunch for me instead. I couldn't stop smiling and hoped he couldn't tell I was dancing around my apartment while he was talking. I hung up the phone and called Katharina straight away to share the news about my big date. She answered and said she had been traveling all night and the bus ride was awful. She ended up holding some lady's baby for the entire journey and now she was getting sick, and her back was hurting. She still had some more traveling to get to her new yoga shala. She was excited about my news, but was in a bad mood. I wished her good luck and told her I would be there in a few days to help her.

Chapter 14: INDIA, A MONTH IN MYSORE —GOODBYE

The teenager inside me was so excited for my lunch date with Steve, but I really could see the hypocrisy of myself. I had just spent a night in a bar journaling about remembering the purpose of my trip while I was drinking, and now again I was chasing boys. It's a good thing I still had many months left in India to sort myself out.

Later that day, Elizabeth told me that she had spent every day in the last two weeks with Sven. She was feeling very torn because she had so much more in common with him than her boyfriend back home in Ireland. She told me she was thinking about breaking up with her boyfriend of five years and trying to find someone who was more compatible with her. I listened and empathized with her predicament. Elizabeth was a beautiful girl with an enjoyable personality, and I told her we should all try to find someone who complements us in life, not brings us down. I couldn't help but share my news with her about my big lunch date with Steve. She said she was surprised I actually got the courage up to ask him, and for that she was proud of me; I told her not to talk about it to anyone.

I had spent the month looking up at Chamundi Hill out my balcony window. I had to go down to the bus station to buy my 'luxury' bus ticket to Kovalam and, since I was already at the station and had some free time, it would be the perfect opportunity to take the bus up to Chamundi Hill and visit the temple on top. At the ticket booth I told them I wanted to buy two tickets to Kovalam on the luxury bus. When they asked for the passenger names, I told them both seats were for me. They said I couldn't buy two seats for one person. They were being forceful about their refusal, so told them I was an American woman traveling alone and had already had one bad experience with a man groping me on a bus. I was trying to avoid another negative experience and leave India with good stories that encouraged other Americans to come visit. After my speech they agreed and sold me two tickets. They also gave me the front-row seats so there would be no one sitting in front of me and the bus attendant would be right there to help me if I needed any help. Then I found the bus going to Chamundi Hill—it was a beautiful brand-new Volvo bus—and climbed on.

THE EVOLUTION OF A PARTY GIRL

The bus ride up to Chamundi Hill was quite an exciting one. The bus was driving full speed up the winding mountain road. It was narrow and my heart skipped a beat every time another car passed us. I don't know how we didn't hit each other. I could for sure remove "bus driver in India" off my list of possible new life paths to explore after this trip.

The bus dropped me off, and I was immediately swarmed with vendors trying to sell offerings to take into the temple. I bought a garland of flowers and no sooner had I turned around than a monkey came up and grabbed the garland out of my hand and ran away. I stood there shocked and appalled at the rude behavior of the monkey as all the locals laughed at me. I decided that God was also in the form of that monkey and I was not going to buy another offering. As I walked toward the temple, I saw monkeys everywhere. It was one of the first times I had seen monkeys on this trip and I was so excited. I pulled out my camera and couldn't stop taking pictures—every monkey seemed cuter than the next. Then I saw a group of baby and mama monkeys and I was touched. I felt heartbroken. I don't know if I was lonely and missing my mom, or if it was my deep confusion about having my own baby. My mind wandered back to my childhood and all the love and devotion my parents had shown me. I decided I should go into the temple and pray for my parents and pray to find peace in myself about whether I wanted a baby or not.

The building was a traditional-looking Hindu temple with a tall steeple-like structure of carved marble. I arrived just as a man closed the gate, and he said it was closed until tomorrow. I didn't have it in me to plead, beg, or bribe him, so I just said okay and walked away. I went for a walk exploring the small village located on top of the hill. I was quickly followed by the local village kids all saying, "Hi Miss" and then giggling and running away. I found a spot on a rock just past the village that overlooked Mysore. I could clearly see the palace and the park below. It was nice to sit peacefully and enjoy the quiet on Chamundi Hill. It was the first time I had been away from the rickshaws, the horns, and the peddlers below. A local village girl came up to me with her baby. She said, "Hello, Miss," and I said hello back. She spoke broken English and said, "This is my

Chapter 14: INDIA, A MONTH IN MYSORE —GOODBYE

baby." Babies, babies, and more babies—if there is one thing India is full of, it is babies. Was this some sort of sign from the earlier moment of sadness over my singlehood and childlessness? I said her baby was so beautiful and I asked how old she was—15—and she asked the same of me—34. She asked me if I had any babies, and when I said no, she seemed shocked. I said I was from America and not all women have babies, and many women don't have babies until they were my age. She started to laugh and walked away, like I was telling her a bad joke.

I got up in the morning to get ready for my big lunch date with Steve. I felt butterflies in my stomach. I only had a small bag of clothes, but I still managed to try on every combination. I decided to wear my black and white printed cotton skirt, my black tank top with my white upper cloth that covered my tank top in public. I put on my makeup and headed out. As I passed the lady that I had bought flowers from many times, she said she wanted to give me some. I graciously accepted her gift of flowers, and she helped put them in my hair. They smelled amazing, and I felt beautiful as I flagged a rickshaw to Steve's apartment. When I arrived, I regretted asking him out to lunch, and I was so nervous I wanted to call him and cancel. As soon as he opened the door with his warm smiling face, my anxiety turned to excitement. I felt so lucky to finally be alone in his apartment.

He greeted me with an unsure hug, and I could tell he was a little nervous too. He invited me in and had some mats set out on the floor for us to eat on. He said he was just finishing up cooking something special for us—Asian stir-fry with tofu and soy sauce. I told him I was so excited to eat Japanese food again. I had been sick of Japanese food just a month ago, but now after weeks of straight Indian food, it sounded excellent. He looked like he knew his way around the kitchen pretty well. We talked as he finished cooking and he began to share the unusual path that had led him to India. We sat on the floor and he blessed our food. The tofu wasn't quite up to the standard of fresh homemade Japanese tofu, but it still was a welcome change from my daily meals at Mahesh Prasad restaurant. He told me that he'd left England when he was seventeen years old and had been traveling in Asia for the better part of the last thirteen years. He was 30 years old, and he spent most of his time between Thailand and India with some trips back to Europe to visit his family. He made his money by teaching classes and doing professional editing. He was trying to start his master's degree at the University of Mysore to learn Sanskrit, but the Indian government was causing problems with his visa.

He asked me questions about my life and what had brought me to India. I told him I was searching for a bigger purpose to my life and wanted to reconnect with my roots. He asked me about Japan, and I shared the highlights of my trip—leaving anything about Andrew out, of course. Our conversation switched to yoga, and we talked about our styles of practice. He told me about how he hurt his right knee doing Ashtanga a few years ago and had switched to a slower-paced, gentle style of yoga. I told him about my knee injury earlier in the month, and that I was a craniosacral therapist, and asked him if I could work on him. He said he would love it. I tried to briefly explain about craniosacral therapy, but he seemed excited to have me touch him no matter what kind of treatment I was doing.

We moved to his bedroom. I asked him where his bed was and he said he didn't have one—he slept on his yoga mat. He had done this for thirteen years! He was starting to sound more and more like a hardcore yogi, which probably meant he was a celibate. He laid down on his mat, and I gently placed my hand on his knee and started to tune into his body and his craniosacral rhythm. He had a strong rhythm overall, which was not surprising given his healthy and pure lifestyle, but the rhythm at his right knee was blocked. As I started working, I could feel him relaxing, and his body started to release restrictions. As his craniosacral rhythm returned to his knee, I started to sense that the real problem was coming from his back. I asked him if he had any back problems, and he said lately his back had been aching a little bit. I asked him if I could work on his back. A pelvic diaphragm release was pretty intimate. One of my hands was under his butt and the top hand was over his lower abdominal area. As I started to work on his lower back, I could feel his entire body start to release its restrictions. He said he was feeling amazing things happening in his body. I worked on him for over an hour. When I was done, he said it was remarkable

Chapter 14: INDIA, A MONTH IN MYSORE —GOODBYE

but he needed to lie down for a while. I was tired as well and he asked me if I wanted to lie down next to him. I couldn't help but giggle and smile as I said yes. We lay there next to each other with our bodies side by side talking intimately for about a half an hour. Then his teacher called him and told him he needed him at his house in 30 minutes. He must have sensed a sexy American woman was distracting his star pupil. He said his teacher's house was by Sheshadri's shala, which is how we ran into each other my first night in Mysore. We cleaned up his kitchen and then just before we walked out the door, he grabbed me and gave me the most emotional five-minute hug of my life. He squeezed me so tight it would have been uncomfortable if I didn't love it so much. Then we walked downstairs and took a rickshaw together back to my apartment. We said our goodbyes on the street. I asked him if he was going to the big yogi party that night, and he said it was 5:00 p.m.—our lunch date had lasted almost five hours. I guessed that meant no.

    I dressed in the best clothes I had and headed to Gokulum for the party. I stopped at a liquor shop and bought an expensive bottle of wine. It was my last night in Mysore. The party was fun. Word had spread through the yogi grapevine about my date with Steve, and three or four of the girls asked me how it went. I was embarrassed, but I guess good news travels fast. I had a glass of wine and by the time I got back to my bottle, it was already finished. The sitar was beautiful and the night involved a lot of philosophical yogi conversations on the rooftop. By the time the party wound down, it was almost three in the morning. I was tired, and there were no rickshaws in sight. One of the local Indian yogis offered me a drive home on the back of his scooter. Riding through the empty streets of India at night on a scooter was a thrilling experience.

    I woke up Sunday morning early and did a long session of pranayama. I only slept a few hours, but decided it would helpful to be exceptionally tired for the overnight bus journey to Kovalam Beach. I packed up everything in my backpack and went to have lunch at Mahesh Prasad with some of my remaining yogi friends. It was Sunday, which meant that Steve had kirtan, but I wasn't sure if I should go and say my final goodbye to Steve or leave it as it was, on a positive note. Just as I was figuring out what to do, Steve called me to see how the party went. I was so excited when I saw his name pop up on my caller ID! I had grown accustomed to the American dating 'rule' of waiting three days to call, so I was so glad he wasn't into those stupid rules. We talked for about ten minutes and I expressed my gloom to be leaving Mysore. He said I should come to kirtan before I left so we could say goodbye. Suddenly, I told him I had two bus seats to Kerala and asked if he wanted to join me. He said he had always wanted to go to Kerala, but already had many commitments that week. I agreed to come over early to his house so we could talk before everyone else arrived. Dante stopped by to see what time I was leaving, and I asked him if he would accompany me to the bus stop and get me settled on the bus. He agreed, and I told him I would be back in a few hours so we could have a chai and then head downtown.

I got to Steve's house about 30 minutes before the start of the kirtan. We sat much closer than the day before and shared with each other about our lives. He told me how great his body had been feeling since my treatment and hoped one day soon he would be able to have another treatment with me. I laughed and said he was passing up a week of oceanfront craniosacral treatments. He said he wished he could join me, but it was not possible on such short notice. Everyone was going to be arriving shortly, and he again grabbed me close and gave me an even longer bear hug—no kissing, just a very intimate hug. After our embrace, I looked up at him and we were both looking starry-eyed, just as people started coming for kirtan. I sat directly across the room from him and he started out that afternoon's kirtan with a dedication for me to have a safe journey tonight and for the rest of my stay in India. He said he would be singing for me that day. I saw my new friends one last time, but halfway through the kirtan, I quietly gave one final namaste to Steve, Elizabeth, Sven, and Madela, and I snuck out of his apartment.

I got back to my apartment late and Dante had already made us his famous tea. We drank it quickly and headed down to the bus depot. Dante got on the bus and sat with me until we were ready to leave, then he told the bus conductor that I had two seats. Men only listen to men in India, so the conductor assured him nobody would bother me. I put my backpack on the

Chapter 14: INDIA, A MONTH IN MYSORE —GOODBYE

seat next to me, knowing I would be asleep in a few minutes. As we rolled away, my mind drifted back to all the unique people I had encountered and the amazing things that Mysore had taught me. My heart was full of gratitude. The most important lesson of my month was experiencing the power of yoga and opening myself to experience God.

Chapter 15
INDIA: KOVALAM BEACH

In the past I would have felt lonely being alone, but I could feel that something was starting to change deep inside of me...

***

I spent much of the bus ride reminiscing about my time in Mysore. I could have stayed longer. Previously, when I had visited India, I had counted down the days until I returned to the comforts of my life in America. But this time I was falling in love with the total craziness of India and felt less connected to my life in the US. I had made many international friends and had developed a broader understanding of the world. I had been conditioned to think that everyone's life had to follow the same pattern: finish college, maybe grad school, get a well-paying job, find a husband or wife, buy a big house in the suburbs, have 2.2 children...you know the drill. For many years I had thought this was the 'correct' path to being a productive member of society. After spending just this one month in India, I had learned more acceptance and love, and wondered where this idea came from. I had a lot of time to think about this question, but I still had no answers. It was eye opening to meet so many happy people who traveled an unconventional path.

I was lugging my huge backpack, and I was hot, sweaty, and tired when I finally found the Pink Lotus Guesthouse, where Katharina was staying. Katharina looked terrible; she had been sick for almost five days and was very depressed. She started bawling when she saw me. I bought her some fruit and supplies, but left her alone to rest. I found a cheap hotel room, spent the afternoon on the beach, and enjoyed a relaxing oceanfront dinner in solitude. I felt happy and peaceful in the quiet village of Kovalam.

I woke up early to go to a yoga class taught by my new teacher, a woman named Padma. She was trained in Sivananda yoga, which I was curious to try since I was going to be taking their teacher-training course in a few months. It was just what my body needed—a gentle yoga class. Her rooftop studio was in the middle of the jungle. All the walls were replaced with a mosquito net. The birds were singing, and the lush jungle trees were swaying all around us. While practicing yoga there I could feel the 'prana' permeating my body. I left the class with happiness in my mind and body. The daily practice of Ashtanga over the last month had been so physically grueling that my body was broken down. Padma's gentle yoga was exactly what I needed to recover.

After class I stopped by to see Katharina. She was still sick, and to top it off, her lower back had started hurting worse from spending so many days in bed. Katharina was leaving India in a few days to go to Africa, and decided to see a doctor.

I spent the day exploring the villages around the beach area. In the past I would have felt lonely being alone, but I could feel that something was starting to change deep inside of me. The fact that I was really enjoying being alone was a measurable change.

In the evening I went for a sunset swim. I was relaxed and floated on my back, bobbing in the waves. I looked up and saw this good-looking, dark-haired man swimming toward me, I couldn't help but be curious. I was the only one swimming this far out from shore, so I felt a little concerned seeing him swimming in a full-speed freestyle stroke toward me. He swam out and introduced himself as "G" and said he thought I looked so beautiful swimming in the sunset, he had to come out and join me. It wasn't long before he asked me to dinner. It was the first time in my life I had ever been asked on a date while treading water in the ocean. He was gorgeous and his body was strong and well built, so I agreed, and we decided to meet for dinner at 7:30 p.m. at his favorite restaurant. "G" was a pilot for Air Lebanon, and on a short layover in India. We swam into shore together and said goodbye and that we would see each other at dinner. I went back to my hotel and got ready. I felt a little uneasy because I didn't know him well, but his good looks and my libido overrode my sense of caution.

I showed up at the restaurant about ten minutes late and followed the smell of his strong cologne to our oceanfront table. He had bought me some flowers and incense and he lit a candle and incense at our table. Romance was in the air, and our conversation was pleasant. He was strong and sexy, but I had to keep my reflexes quick to tame his roaming hands. I had a few gin and sodas at dinner, and afterward, he invited me for a nightcap at his hotel. He was staying in the penthouse in the nicest hotel on the beach.

We sat on his oceanfront balcony and talked about life. He told me that his name "G" was actually short for Jihad. As in the Muslim movement that was responsible for many international terrorist attacks—YIKES! I felt nauseous, and decided I was going to quickly have my drink and get out of there. It wasn't long before he was putting the moves on me very aggressively. I flirted a bit as I positioned myself closer to the door. I knew that if I didn't get out of there then, things were going to get dangerous for me. He walked away to make me another drink and I opened the door and ran out. I kept running all the way back to my hotel room. That was my first and last dinner with anyone named Jihad.

I went to Padma's yoga class in the morning. I really enjoyed the change of pace from Ashtanga. Padma, in addition to teaching, also owned the guesthouse. She broke many of the traditional roles of an Indian woman by being a divorced single mother and a business owner. She had been caring for Katharina, buying her fruit, cooking her rice, and nursing her back to health. Katharina was starting to feel better and was eager to get out and explore. She had been in Kovalam for one week but had not left her guesthouse. Katharina and I went out to explore 'the downtown.' We ended up in a Tibetan souvenir shop with many Buddhist religious statues. There was a woman behind the counter with her head down, working on beading necklaces. She didn't say anything to us; she didn't even look up and acknowledge us. We walked around and shopped in peace, which was shocking and refreshing. As we went to check out, I was intrigued by her and wanted to ask her about Buddhism. She asked us if we wanted some chai and sent her son for some. We sat and talked to her for over an hour and found out her name was Karma. She was a Tibetan refugee who had been living in India since her family had been exiled in the 50s.

She showed us many of the Buddhist religious items and explained their meanings. I bought a Buddhist-style mala, which is a necklace, similar to a rosary. She asked me if I knew how to use it and if I had a mantra. She opened a book called *The Secret Symbols of Buddhism* and taught me the most famous Buddhist mantra—"om mani padme hum." She showed it to me in the book and gave its Tibetan translation, which is, "hail to the jewel in the lotus." It is used to heighten your conscious awareness of the divine spark in all human hearts. She explained to me that all malas have 108 beads, which is the most important number in Eastern religions. On each side of the main necklace were two counter chains that each had ten beads. To use the mala, she instructed me: first go around it chanting my mantra 108 times, once with each bead, then move one of the counter beads on the side strand. When all ten counter beads on one side string are moved, then move the ten counter beads on the second side chain. I don't know the exact math, but she instructed me to chant "om mani padme hum" something like 108 X 10 X 10 times every day.

Katharina wanted to go get a drink at a touristy place on the beach called the German Bakery. I think she was feeling homesick and craving anything German. I asked Karma if she wanted to join us, my treat. She left her son in charge of the store and the three of us walked up the beach to the restaurant.

The German Bakery is an overpriced, oceanfront place with a luxurious tropical décor. I had my new favorite cocktail, gin with fresh crushed ginger and soda water, Katharina had a lemon ginger hot tea, and Karma had a bottle of Pepsi. It was a surreal moment—three single women from different corners of the globe, whose lives involved very different paths, sitting at a table together in India. That was one of the beauties of India; it brought together people from many walks of life. It was an intimate exchange. We shared our views on the world, we talked openly about our struggles and triumphs, and we tried to understand each other's unique experiences of life. As I sat with Katharina, who had lived as a child in a divided Germany, and Karma, who had grown up in political exile in India, I felt lucky to have grown up in a country with political and economic stability. Peace and freedom is something that many Americans, me included, take for granted because we have never known anything else. As different as many things were about our lives, there was something that was remarkably the same. I wondered how we still could be so similar when our experiences of life were so different. It was a reminder of our deeper level of human existence.

I asked Karma about what had happened in Tibet. We listened intently as she explained her escape in broken English. In 1959, China invaded and conquered the unarmed government of Buddhist monks. Most people left their homes and all their possessions and were lucky to get out with their lives. The Dalai Lama, along with many Tibetans who chose to leave, accepted political asylum in India. The Buddhists set up in an area called Dharamsala in the northeast part of India. The Dalai Lama and millions of Tibetans still live in India today in political exile. Karma had two sisters. When they fled, they walked for three months through the highest and most dangerous mountains on earth, the Himalayas. They had no maps, there were no trails, and they only used the sun, stars, and God to guide them. The Chinese army was constantly attacking, so they had to hide during the day and walk only at night. Karma's oldest sister died in the cold, thin air of the Himalayas.

I had often seen signs that said "Free Tibet" and had some distant knowledge of the situation, but after meeting Karma and the other Tibetans living in exile in Bylakuppe, my fire was lit. I decided I needed to say something and wrote the first email of my life to the president of the United States. This is what I said: "I can't believe in this day and age of humanitarian projects to ensure basic human rights to all people, that millions of Tibetans including their HIGHEST spiritual leaders are living in exile. The American government has not only turned a blind eye to the inhumane oppressive government of China, we continue to be their largest economic trader, so all of these human rights violations are being funded by our US dollars. We have recently gone to war to supposedly free the people of Iraq, yet we trade freely with the Chinese government, which continues to terrorize the people of Tibet. 'One World, One Dream, Free Tibet!'" I got a form letter response, but I felt like he must have read it. Three weeks later, the president met with the Dalai Lama in the White House for the first time. He had canceled his previous meeting with the Dalai Lama because the Chinese government disapproved.

The next day was Katharina's last day in India, and I would be traveling to Mumbai in two days for Christmas. Katharina and I went to Padma's morning yoga class together and then had lunch at an Ayurvedic restaurant. Ayurveda is the traditional medicine of India; it is over 5000 years old and uses food and lifestyle to balance people's individual constitutions. The food tasted like typical cuisine, but it was all made fresh. It wasn't crazy hot like most Indian food, but instead used many of the medicinal spices of Ayurveda. After lunch we headed back to the beach. We spent our last afternoon together swimming and playing in the Arabian Sea. It was a beautiful beach, with palm trees everywhere and dark lava rock meeting the warm turquoise water. After the beach we went back to our hotels to get dolled up. We met at Karma's shop, and the three of us went back to my favorite restaurant in Kovalam Beach for our farewell dinner. The waiter was a nice guy and pretty cute, and Katharina and I did our best to fix Karma up with him.

Katharina's flight was leaving early in the morning. Saying goodbye to Katharina was easier this time. I now knew I would be okay in India alone. I was very thankful for my time with Katharina. She had been my angel in Mysore, and I knew that without her love and support, I might not had made it this far into my trip. She had been a great teacher and friend, and had really showed me the ropes of getting around India as a woman traveling alone. We both cried a little and planned to meet up in Europe someday for our next adventure. Kovalam had been the perfect rest after the intensity of Mysore. After meeting people from so many countries with political problems, I felt a new appreciation for growing up in the United States.

Chapter 16
INDIA: MY FIRST RETURN TO MUMBAI

It made me realize that all the things I identify with as being Preya— my language, my career, my social life—are all transient...

***

I was enamored by the romantic idea of a train ride up the entire country of India. On this twenty-four-hour ride, I spent a lot of time thinking about how different my life would be if my parents had decided to raise me in India. My brother and sister were both born and spent their early childhood there before moving to the USA. Being raised in India could easily have been my reality, and my life would be completely different. As much love as there was in that country, unfortunately, women in India are not treated as equals. A woman's main value is her ability to give birth to as many baby boys as possible and cook the best Indian food. Some women are now going to college, but their careers are short-lived because once they are married they must stay home and tend to the house. Even in Japan I was told women were not 'allowed' to work once they were married. Most societies in the East have a narrow view of the role of women. Maybe if I had been raised in India I would be traveling and backpacking throughout America, but I doubt I would have had the confidence, courage, or street smarts to be able to take on such an endeavor.

I journaled about what I would be like if I had been raised in India. This is what I wrote on that long train ride:

Chapter 16: INDIA: MY FIRST RETURN TO MUMBAI

If I was raised in India, I would be thinner and smaller;

I would not drink alcohol, and I would not try smoking hashish;

I wouldn't know how to 'shake it' at the best dance clubs;

I would be much more submissive and strictly follow the rules of society;

I would be softer on the inside and harsher on the outside;

I would have never experienced blindly falling in love for the first time;

I would not have the emotional scars from the many loves lost;

I would have never traveled the world alone;

I would be Jain, and I would have been raised a strict vegetarian;

I wouldn't know how to swim and wouldn't even think to wear a bikini;

I would have no male friends;

I would speak Hindi;

I would be married;

I would have several children;

I would have never lived alone;

I would be an excellent cook of only Indian food;

I would be obedient of my parents' wishes;

I would be set in a path with no room for deviations;

I would have stayed a virgin until I was married;

I would not have my master's degree;

I would have never backpacked for days in the wilderness;

I would not know how to drive a car;

I would never be financially independent.

If I had been raised in India, my life would be so different that I wouldn't be recognizable as the same person, but the core of who I am would still be the same being. It made me realize that all the things I identify with as Preya—my language, my career, my social life—are all transient. I was starting to understand the difference between the self I identify with and my true self, which is something deeper than any of my changing labels.

The train pulled into Mumbai 3 hours late, so by the time I arrived, I had been on the train for 27 hours. My cousin Tushar was waiting. I hadn't seen him in almost six years, but he was as pleasant and charming as I remembered. Tushar has always been one of the forward thinkers in our family, and he goes out of his way to please everyone. In a country where everyone is extremely opinionated, to please everyone is a huge feat. For this reason, he is a leader in our family and a successful businessman.

It was nice to see everyone again. I spent two weeks with them and stayed with my Aunt Damayanti and her family. She has two sons: Bharat (who had met me at the airport when I first arrived in India) and Tushar. Both of my cousins are a few years older than me and married with teenage children. They have been successful in the wholesale shoe business and have two large apartments in the same building. During the day everyone stays in the main apartment. They have enough money to each own their own houses and live separately—in fact, they own several vacation homes—but they choose to follow the traditional family structure in India and live together. There are ten people in one apartment during the day and, at night, Bharat's family sleeps in the extra apartment. I stayed in one of the bedrooms in the second apartment.

I arrived on Christmas Eve, and when I woke up Christmas morning, Bharat had a chocolate cake with a candle on it for me. It was a touching moment because they don't even celebrate Christmas. My cousin, Nitin, took me to the Taj Mahal Hotel, a five-star hotel in Mumbai for a special treat. It was decorated extraordinarily for the holiday, and I got to see my first Christmas tree of the season. We had a few drinks at the bar, and he took me out to a Chinese restaurant for dinner. It was a really special day that we shared, and I was able to talk openly about my life, my hopes, and my dreams. He also confided in me, and I could tell he trusted me enough to share his personal stories. The family structure in India leaves little room for people to speak frankly about their true feelings, especially if they fall outside of the strict definition of 'normal and proper.'

Chapter 16: INDIA: MY FIRST RETURN TO MUMBAI

I was able to open up about the things I had been learning in my path of yoga, and the profound changes that were occurring in me.

This was my first time visiting family in India alone. Being an unmarried 34-year-old woman traveling the world alone breaks the traditional rules of my family and of the Indian system. My family went out of their way to be understanding of our vast cultural differences, as did I, but it was a struggle for all of us. At some level, the life I am living represents exactly what they DON'T want for their children. As Western influence spreads through the world, India struggles to maintain its cultural identity. My visit exposed the children in our family to the large differences of being raised in a Western society. I tried to be as conservative as I could, but you can't change a tiger into a rabbit.

Kristina, one of my childhood friends, put me in touch with her friend Rahul, who lived in Mumbai. Rahul and I spent the day at the horseracing track. When the races ended at around 6:00 p.m., he asked me if I wanted to go to the attached social club and get a drink. We had a few drinks and by 9:00 p.m., I was a little buzzed and in a cab back to my aunt's house.

I stopped at a restaurant nearby and Tushar sent his sixteen-year-old son to meet me there. According to my family a woman should not be out alone in the evening. My teenage relative and I shared some appetizers, and he watched me have an alcoholic drink. We got back home at 10:30 p.m., and Tushar's wife was fuming. She doesn't speak much English, but I understood from her firm tone as she yelled at me in Kutchi that she disapproved of me being out so late and drinking alcohol. Drinking is strictly forbidden in Jainism, my family religion. I was shocked. It was only 10:30 p.m., but she felt like I was a misbehaved Indian woman. After spending a month in Japan trying to 'play the role,' I had no intention of pretending to be a subservient woman in India. I said, "Well, I am thirty-four. I am an adult woman, and my staying out until 10:30 p.m. or having a few drinks should not be a concern for you. Your son is a teenager, and if you didn't want him out, YOU shouldn't have sent him up to meet me, but in my view of the world, I have done nothing wrong." At that moment, our dramatic cultural

THE EVOLUTION OF A PARTY GIRL

differences came to a head, and I went to bed with my mind racing. I woke up dreaming of being on my own again in South India and apprehensive of another week in Mumbai.

Despite this clash, it was nice to see my family. I was truly thankful for the support they were showing me, but they didn't understand that I had spent years learning to live my life without the need for anyone's approval. The Indian family structure has no privacy and everything is everyone's business. I needed a day out of the house so I called up Sunita, my second cousin, and we went shopping. She was also struggling with the constraints of the Indian system. Her parents were looking for a husband for her to have an arranged marriage, but she had someone else whom she wanted to marry. Luckily that is one family problem I won't have to face; my parents had disobeyed both of their families to have a 'free love' marriage. I assured Sunita that the other side of the coin, the American dating game, was also difficult. I told her many American women, including myself, after years of heartache, would consider having an arranged marriage to avoid the hassles of dating. I wanted to make her feel better about the situation, but in truth I felt sorry that the current system for women in India does not allow them to choose their own partners.

Time was flying. It was already New Year's Eve, and I was eager to celebrate this amazing year of growth. I made plans to go to a New Year's Eve party at Amber's apartment. She was a friend of a friend I had met in Mysore. Amber was from St. Louis, and she was in Mumbai on a humanitarian mission for one year. She had completed her first month. Her mission was to create legislation to stop the human trafficking of women, which was rampant in India. On our first conversation, I had to swallow my pride and explain to her the situation of my family not approving of me drinking alcohol or staying out past 10:00 p.m. I didn't know her at all, but I asked if could spend the night at her apartment. She said one of her roommates was out of town for New Year's, and I could stay.

I arrived at Amber's apartment at 10:30 p.m. with a bottle of wine and some appetizers. There were about ten people there for the party, and we quietly toasted in the New Year. Just after the toast, Amber came over and said some of her guy friends

Chapter 16: INDIA: MY FIRST RETURN TO MUMBAI

were at a highly exclusive club, and she wanted to know if I wanted to go. I hadn't been out dancing in months, and I couldn't think of a better night than New Year's Eve. We left shortly after midnight; Amber said the club was going to be open until four. Wow, staying out until four in the morning! Lately I had been getting up at four to start my pranayama and yoga practice. It was a stark contrast.

We got to the club to find out there was a 20,000-rupee cover charge—that is 200 US dollars. There was no way either of us, who were both here in India to do volunteer work, would pay what equals a month of expenses while living in India to go into a club for two hours. We were standing outside the velvet rope trying to figure out what to do when a short Indian man came up to us and asked what the problem was. I said we were trying to get into this club but were not going to pay the outrageous cover charge. He introduced himself to me and told me he was the owner; he said it would be a privilege for us to be at his party tonight. He took each one of us by the arm and escorted us in. The bouncers moved aside and opened all the doors and ropes for us. He took us up to his rooftop office and opened a bottle of champagne. The club was right on the beach and overlooked the ocean. They had just set off Chinese lanterns that were floating off above the ocean. I had never seen them before, but Amber told me the heat from the candle fills the lantern and they float like a hot air balloon. It looked so beautiful and elegant, almost like the stars had come down from the sky to celebrate New Year's Eve. Amber and I had a quick glass of champagne with the owner and told him we had to head down and meet up with our friends. We left and quickly found her friends. The club was ultrachic; everything was modern and elegant, just like a lounge in Manhattan. The deck was right on the ocean. I sat alone and watched the Chinese lanterns, listened to the surf, and enjoyed my free cocktails, feeling a lot of gratitude about how well this trip to India was turning out.

Amber's friends were a friendly bunch of good-looking Indian men. One of the guys was from England and had a really sexy English accent. It didn't take long for the owner to come find us, and we all headed to the dance floor. I hadn't felt free enough to dance in a safe place for a long time. I love to dance and once my body starts to move, I can do it for hours. They were playing Bollywood electronic music, and I loved it. I spent the next two hours on the dance floor. It was well after 3:00 a.m. and the party was winding down when Amber came over and asked me if I wanted to go to an after party at this really nice apartment in South Mumbai. I quickly learned that South Mumbai is the equivalent to Park Avenue in NYC.

When we left the nightclub, Etan, the cute guy from England, came up and said, "You guys want to have a rickshaw race to the party?" The teams were Amber and her friend Shard, the guy she was kinda dating, and Etan and I. Then he said, "Ready, set, go!" We all scrambled to get the first rickshaw. Etan got the first one, and he and I jumped in. I looked back, and Amber and Shard had gotten one just after us. We told the rickshaw driver, "Fast, fast!" It was late and the streets were empty. We started talking and laughing, and he told me he thought I was beautiful and that he had wanted to be alone with me since he'd first seen me at the club. He told me I was an excellent dancer and he enjoyed watching me dance. Then he leaned over and kissed me and, wow, what a good kiss it was. It was a celebration. It was my first EVER kiss in India, after seven trips to the country! We quickly forgot about the rickshaw race and became way more interested in making out. Etan told the rickshaw driver to take us to the oceanfront, and we made out the entire way. We stayed at the ocean for about 20 minutes, and then I said I had to get back to meet up with Amber since I was staying at her apartment. We got back to South Mumbai at about 4:30 a.m., and although Etan was crestfallen, Amber and I left right away. What a way to ring in the New Year!

Chapter 17
INDIA: A MONTH IN KUTCH

A beautiful feeling came over my body, and for the first time since leaving America four months ago, I cried tears of joy...

***

On New Year's Day, I took the train from Mumbai to Kutch with my Aunt Damayanti. I again made sure I was good and tired on the train so I could sleep through the chaos of Indian travel. My Aunt Damayanti is a really special woman; she is not only the female leader in our family but also in the community. She barely speaks English, and I barely speak Kutchi, but after so many years, we have learned how to communicate. She and my father were born and raised together in Kutch. I went to Kutch twice as a child to visit my grandparents at our family farm. This area near the border of Pakistan is home to some of my best childhood memories of India

Jaya Rehabilitation Hospital is located in the region of Kutch in the state of Gujarat, which is in the northwest part of India. The climate is mostly arid, and the people live in small, simple villages. The area has only recently received 24-hour electricity. I would be staying here for a month to do medical relief work at Jaya Rehab, and this was the main inspiration for my trip to India. The idea actually started when we came to Kutch and toured the campus while it was still being constructed. Jaya and Arvin Shah are family friends and also live in Detroit, and they are the main donors of Jaya Rehab.

Many years ago, a massive earthquake hit that left the area devastated and caused thousands of fatalities and injuries.

Chapter 17: INDIA: A MONTH IN KUTCH

There were no rehabilitation facilities in this remote part of India. After years of planning and fundraising from abroad, what started as a few therapists working in a tent opened as a full-service rehab hospital that serviced over 1,200 villages. Jaya Rehabilitation Hospital has become a huge success and a tribute to the power of fundraising. They see over 27,000 patients a year in their inpatient and outpatient facilities.

During my previous tour of the facility, I promised myself someday I would come back and volunteer. When I was awarded my Rotary scholarship to Japan and put the dates together, I quickly realized this was the opportunity for me to fulfill my promise.

The journey to Jaya Rehab was physically long and emotionally taxing. It began with an overnight train ride on the far-from-luxury Kutch Express. A family of mice in our compartment kept me sleeping with one eye open. Then we endured a hot and sweaty three-hour drive from the train station at Gandhidham to the village of Bidada. There were eight of us along with half of our luggage crammed into a SUV that was built for six people.

I had emailed and faxed my paperwork in several times, but I had never received confirmation that they knew I was coming. When I arrived, I was pleasantly surprised to see my name on a list of volunteers. I was given a handwritten nametag and told where I would be staying. I loaded my luggage, and my aunt and I took a short rickshaw ride to a complex called Manavmandir. I was happy to see I had a private room, and the driver told me there was a doctor from America staying next door. My room was simple, relatively clean, and sunny. I had a bed and a private bathroom but no hot water. I dropped off most of my luggage, and my aunt and I headed to our neighboring family village of Koday.

The village of Koday is located about three miles away from the hospital on one of the only paved roads in this area. Damayanti is a spiritual woman; she starts every morning by praying at the altar in her kitchen. Her favorite activity is going to the temple, and this was where we first headed. I felt like I was stepping back in time to the days of the Renaissance period as we walked through the village. The tiny streets are dirt, and most buildings are in a state of serious disrepair. They are painted with whitewash and built in simple construction styles. There are many cows, chickens, and very skinny children roaming the dust-filled streets. There are no proper shops, but a few people sell tea or some homemade goods out of their houses. So when I saw the new Jain temple, it looked like it belonged somewhere else. The temple was huge and made of pink and white marble from Italy. Every part of it was carved in immaculate detail, and the statues of the Gods inside were adorned with gold. She showed me around, and then we sat in the temple in silence. It was so special to sit and pray together in a Jain temple in my father's village. This was the first time in my life I had prayed and experienced spirituality with my family.

After we left the temple, we walked to Damayanti's family homes; she has two houses next door to each other, one for each son. The houses were newly built and modern compared to most of the houses in the village. The typical homes in the village had dirt floors, outdoor bathrooms, and sometimes even outdoor kitchens without running water where they build a fire to cook.

We spent the day walking around Koday. Damayanti took me to my grandfather's old farm. It had been sold several years back and now was subdivided into several parcels of land. I met the man who now owns the farm. He invited us in for tea and walked us around the farm. I saw the old irrigation tank that we used to swim in, but most of the land was unrecognizable to me. The main farmhouse had been bulldozed, and the layout of the land had changed so much that it felt unfamiliar to me. As we walked through the area where the farmhouse used to be, I saw my first peacock in India, a vibrantly colored male. I had a lot of emotions running through me, being in such a nostalgic place, and I felt tearful most of the time at the farm. I had so many vivid memories at the *wadi* (the Kutchi word for farm), that I couldn't accept that it was gone. When I saw the peacock, I felt like it was a message from my grandpa to let go of the past and accept the changes of life.

At the farm owner's new house, several ladies were sitting in a row on the front porch, rolling dough and cooking over a fire. They were making an Indian snack food called *kakra*. They were squatting on the hard floor, bent over, working and cooking all day. The physical therapist in me couldn't help but be shocked at the ergonomics. It was a horrific position for your body to be in all day. When my aunt introduced me as a physical therapist that had come from America to volunteer at the hospital, they all lined up. Each lady showed me her aches and pains, and I gave each one of them exercises. Then I convinced them that throughout the day they should get up and do the short stretching routine I showed them. They laughed and giggled with excitement at such simple things. The people in the village were happy and content with very little. Having their basic necessities met was seemingly enough to make them laugh and smile for days, weeks, or even a lifetime. This true appreciation for simplicity made me realize how far away I was from my previous life of complexity.

The last place my aunt took me was to our family home. This was the home that my grandparents had lived in and that my dad had been born and raised in. When I walked into the house, I was so overcome with emotions that I started to cry. I had been holding back tears all day, but as soon as I walked into my grandparents' house, I could feel their presence everywhere. Damayanti was a little shocked when I stated to sob, but she understood what an emotional experience it was for me. My grandpa and I had been very close when I was little. He came to America often and we went on daily walks together, and I spent most of my free time with him. We used to sit in my room and he would tell me all about his life as he smoked beedis. I watched him do yoga every morning, long before I ever knew what yoga was.

The life of the villagers was difficult—they struggled to get clean water, they worked hard to make low wages, and the living conditions were at least 100 years behind America. It was hard for me not to grieve the life of the villagers. It was almost unbelievable that my dad started his life in the tiny village of Koday and made his way to being a successful business owner in America. I had a new understanding of why my dad was a strong and aggressive man. He had developed the personality traits that scared me as a child to overcome the profound adversity of growing up in this indigent village. It had taken strength and perseverance to leave the village and become financially successful living in the US.

I was emotionally worn out. After the train ride, the car ride, and the emotional rollercoaster of trying to understand my difficult relationship with my father, I was ready for sleep. Just before we went to bed, I had my aunt and one of our neighbors help me create a very basic Kutchi dictionary that I would use to communicate with my patients. That night, I slept on the floor next to my aunt. It was a very special day in my life, and I was developing a deeper understanding of my roots and how much impact it had on my current life.

My aunt escorted me to the bus stop the next morning, and the bus dropped me off directly in front of the hospital. I had fear and anxiety, just like my first day of school. I reported to Dr. Samuel, a nice-looking Indian man about my age dressed in a lab coat and Western clothes. I had met him on my last visit there. He welcomed me and said he'd had no idea that I was coming, but he was happy to have me. Then he said that he remembered the promise I'd made to him several years ago to come back and work.

He was professional and sweet-natured. He spent the morning touring me around the facilities. Jaya Rehab had twenty-two inpatient beds. It is impressive to see the grand scale of this facility in such a remote place. The building is shaped like three sides of a square with a large garden in the center courtyard. The patient rooms were divided into different classes. Unfortunately, the system of separating people into classes, which seemed shocking to me in a medical facility, was completely accepted in the Indian culture. The first-class rooms are more expensive and private; the second-class rooms were semi-private rooms; and the third-class was a general ward of six patients. The physical therapy department was situated in the middle of the large building with patient's rooms on either side. The rehab gym was fairly large, but too small for the number of patients. It was always jam-packed with patients who lived in the hospital, outpatients who had come in for their appointments, student PTs from all over India, and TONS of patient family members.

The rehab area was divided into several smaller rooms. The first room had a reception area and the desks for Dr. Samuel and Dr. Loganathan, the head Occupational Therapist (OT). The second room was divided by sliding door partitions into six individual treatment rooms that were mostly used for modalities and manual treatments on outpatients. The third room was the main PT gym. It had two large treatment tables, equipment for hand function exercises, parallel bars, and practice stairs. It was a large area without the typical exercise machines found in physical therapy gyms in the United States. The last room was the pediatric rehab area, which was a small room packed with kids and parents. They had two large treatment tables and exercise balls but very few therapeutic toys. My first impression was positive. It wasn't an American rehab hospital, but compared to most of the other accommodations I had experienced in India, it was relatively modern and clean.

After my tour and a few hours observing Dr. Samuel, it was time for lunch. The lunch area was a large tent that had long tables with local volunteers serving food. I was cautious with my food selection. I avoided eating any of the fresh fruits, veggies, or sauces because the veggies were being served by hand, and most of the sauces were made with water. Drinking the tap water in India is the most common source of sickness in tourists. I had been careful and had made it seven weeks in India without getting sick, which is a big feat, but I could tell this month was going to be more difficult. Dr. Samuel and I talked a little over lunch, but most of the time was spent eating; Indian people don't talk and socialize like Americans during a meal, and they eat FAST! It took us only 20 minutes for lunch, and then he said we had a two-hour break where everyone goes back to their rooms and takes a nap. A nap in the middle of the day—that was always a dream at my old job. I took a rickshaw back to Manavmandir, took a 30-minute nap, and came back to Jaya Rehab at 3:00 p.m. Dr. Samuel spent the afternoon introducing me to all the students and staff. We ended work early that day for the opening ceremonies for the annual charity medical camp of the trust that established Jaya Rehab.

I waited in the crowd of people at the front gates of the hospital compound for the VIPs to arrive from the airport. In the group were my family friends, Arvin and Jaya, who built Jaya Rehab and continue to fund it. There were also represen-

THE EVOLUTION OF A PARTY GIRL

tatives from the US and German embassies. I was so happy to see my first familiar faces from the US. I hugged Arvin and Jaya and we spent time talking; I was thankful they were here. After my last few weeks in Mumbai, I was craving some time with Americans, and the free-flowing conversations that were possible. I sat next to two American guys who were here completing their master's thesis in accounting. They were from Walsh University in Pennsylvania, and their master's project was creating a new system of accounting for the trust. It was their first time in India, and they had a lot of funny stories to share. The opening ceremonies consisted of far too many speeches, which none of us understood because they were speaking in Kutchi. So we joked quietly as we shared 'only in India' stories. They told me about the opening party that night and said I should meet them at the front gate at 7:00 p.m. After the ceremony, I asked Samuel and Loganathan if they were going to the party, and they said they were.

The party was supposed to be formal, and I had not brought any 'formal' clothes to the village. I managed to piece together an outfit and put on the pearl necklace I'd bought from Karma. I met Loganathan and Bhavisha, a PT, at the front gate, and we took a car over to the party. It was in a neighboring village at a farmhouse. The decorations were amazing, and the farmhouse had been converted to a beautiful outdoor reception. The decorations were lavish, and the food was even more so. There was a long buffet-style table with about ten different stations of food from South Indian to Chinese to traditional local food. The servers were all dressed in formal black uniforms and wearing bright red turbans. There was also a live band on a full-sized stage with a large dance floor that was packed. Indians love to dance. I was a bit shocked by the elaborate party and felt socially awkward for the first hour because I didn't know anyone. The party of course had one obvious thing missing…alcohol. I did some mingling and had a chance to talk to Jaya and Arvin, who took me under their wing and introduced me to several people. There was a short presentation where they performed a 'shawl ceremony' on the US and German consuls. Jaya explained to me that in the Kutchi tradition, the highest way to show appreciation and respect to someone is to present them with a locally

Chapter 17: INDIA: A MONTH IN KUTCH

made shawl along with a coconut and some sweets. I made a point to talk to the US consul; he told me that he'd received his bachelor's degree from Michigan State University.

As the party wound down, I was standing alone in the corner next to the tea station and a young guy came up to me and said, "Hi, I am Rohit. I live next door to you in Manavmandir." This was the American doctor I had been told about earlier. We sat and talked for the rest of the party. Rohit was from California and was actually about to start medical school and not a doctor yet. He had the personality of someone who is friends with everyone; he was easy-going and enjoyable to talk with. We took a car back together since we were neighbors. I felt an immediate connection with him and could tell he was going to be my lifeline for the next month.

The first few days of work, I showed up at 8:15 a.m. because the clinic was supposed to open at 8:30 a.m. As I sat around and waited, I quickly realized that 'Indian standard time' even applies to work. After a few days, I got in the swing of things, showing up at 9:00ish and learning to fit in and adapt to a foreign work environment. Physical therapists in India are called doctors, and I started to see why. Dr. Samuel ordered and interpreted X-rays and blood work, and did not work under the prescription of an MD. Patients, some of whom had never seen a doctor in their lives, came in off the street, and he had to diagnose them. I shared with him how restricted things are in the US healthcare system, and how much control physicians, insurance companies, and drug companies have. I told him about the day I got in trouble with my boss at work for "practicing beyond the scope of a physical therapist position" when I advised a patient to lose weight and change their diet to reduce their chronic low back pain. He laughed at the absurdity of it, and he also shared his frustration with the Indian system that lacks organization or efficiency. Dr. Samuel was impressive, professional, and an excellent PT. Since I had a language barrier, he would evaluate patients and hand them off to me to treat. Samuel was interested in learning my treatment techniques since he had very few opportunities to take continuing education courses. I was interested in learning about reading X-rays, so it was a good opportunity for us to share our knowledge.

Though the hospital building was nice, there were no screens in the windows, and I couldn't get used to having houseflies EVERYWHERE inside the treatment areas. The flies were all over the beds, the patients, and me. There were always patients lined up out the door and not enough space or staff to accommodate.

There were ten student PTs who were also there for a month, completing their internships. To my surprise they were all young women. However, they acted quite childish, not as I hoped soon-to-be professionals would act. Women in India live sheltered lives, and they don't develop the street smarts we require in Western cultures. In India physical therapy only requires a bachelor's degree, so most of them were about 21 years old. They were cute, sweet, and eager to help me, but I kept thinking that I *must* have been more mature than that when I was in PT school.

This hospital represented the power of humanity putting their resources together to create something amazingly positive. It was a medical oasis in an undeveloped and impoverished area. It is unbelievable, with so little equipment, how successful the treatment was. The staff was skilled at maximizing outcomes with few resources. The Indian people are strong, and the Kutchi community is woven tightly (which is something I would experience firsthand when I later traveled to Goa and needed help). The community and family support I saw was far beyond anything I had ever worked with before in the United States.

During my first week in Bidada, Loganathan told me he had a scooter and after work he wanted to take me to the new Jain temple they had built a few kilometers away. He said the roads are quiet and 'peaceful' here in the villages. I quickly went home and changed out of my scrubs, and we met up in front of Jaya Rehab. His scooter was old. It reminded me of a scooter from the 1950s, unlike the brand-new Hondas that my friends rented in Mysore. I was filled with childlike excitement; I hadn't been on a scooter in almost a month. The ride to the temple was beautiful. The sun was setting, the skyline was decorated with palm trees and cotton farms, and I felt so free with my hair down and blowing in the air. It was a reality check.

Chapter 17: INDIA: A MONTH IN KUTCH

Was I really in India, traveling alone, on the back of a scooter in Kutch, my dad's childhood home? I was so happy and free! During that ride, my joy confirmed I was exactly where I was supposed to be in my life. After a short tour of the Jinalaya temple, we rode to Mandvi to meet Samuel for dinner. Afterward, we all went to the beach for a 'nightcap' in the form of a fresh cracked coconut. I rode home with Samuel in his car. I was a little nervous being on the scooter at night with no streetlights or traffic lights.

Life at the camp was challenging. I had difficulty with the cleanliness and the limited selection of the food, and my daily interaction with the villagers presented significant language and cultural barriers. I did however, have a sense of freedom being away from my family in Mumbai. I sat down and started to write, and before I knew it I had composed a telling email about the struggle I had living with my family in India. I titled the email "Nurturing Freedom," and I knew from the second I hit the send button that it hadn't been a good idea to share my deepest feelings so publicly.

My time in Mumbai was short and mostly sweet. Seeing my family after so many years was really fun and amazing. The hospitality and concern shown to me was far beyond any hospitality that I have ever received in America. The continued love and support of my family is what allows me to have all of these unbelievable life experiences.

Spending time with my family in Mumbai brings our dramatic cultural differences to the forefront. I have often during this trip thought of who and what I would be if I were raised in India. The role of women in India is still limited. My family in India is traditional. They all continue to have arranged marriages, and dating is strictly prohibited! Very few women in my family are educated beyond high school, and none have a career or work outside of the house, except for me! As understanding as my family tries to be to my American ways, I still feel a level of control that is far different than the life I choose for myself in America.

I AM DEFINITELY AMERICAN! No matter how much my family and others attempt to grant me 'freedom,' the current system in

India is so family controlled and male dominated it is difficult for me to adjust to.

I hope through my short stay in Mumbai that my traditional family could see the possibility of freedom being something beautiful that should be fostered in children and not punished. I have worked hard in my life, especially with my parents, to develop my freedom. It took many years of acting out and rebelling for them to finally accept the fact that I will make my own decisions and choose my own life. We have only ONE life to live, and this precious human life is mine to do with what I choose.

Women in India need more education to promote freedom, equality, and opportunity. I hope during my time in Mumbai I didn't ruffle too many feathers, and instead gave the opportunity to see how amazing freedom is....going to the horse track, high tea at the Wellington club, and a fun-filled New Year's Eve party. I am a 34-year-old, unmarried, assertive, educated Indian/American woman. A woman traveling the world alone, doing charity work in my father's native homeland, climbing mountains, and most of all following my own path. Not a path determined by my religion, my caste, and most of all not a path predetermined because I am a woman. It is ironic that with all of this freedom I have worked so hard to attain that I choose to go back to India and share my education, insight, and physical therapy with the people of India. I hope someday that my path does lead to being married and having a family, but when it happens, it will be something we commit to freely.

My time at the charity camp has been another amazing experience. I still have to be clear and assertive with my communication to get the same level of respect that the men are given, but it's worth it. The people of Kutch are who I am here to serve, and I continue to remind myself of that as I deal with difficult living and working conditions.

After my family received that email, all the calls from my cousins stopped. I could tell I had hurt their feelings and was remorseful. I had been spending most of my time after work with Rohit and when I read him that email he said, "Preya, being tactful is more important than being truthful," and I knew

Chapter 17: INDIA: A MONTH IN KUTCH

he was right. He told me not to beat myself up over it, and that we are all here on earth to learn lessons. Rohit also shared some of the struggles that he had been having with his family. He had converted to Islam the previous year. Most of his family either didn't know about his conversion from Hinduism or strongly disapproved. He told me about the identity crisis he had been having here in India. Rohit's struggle was based on freedom of religion and mine was based on equality of women. Being able to talk to him was helpful during those first few weeks. He was a true diplomat and provided a great space for me to learn to communicate better.

Work started to get busy. Orthopedic camp had arrived. Ortho camp was three long days, and the first day we saw hundreds of patients. Before it started, doctors were sent out into the surrounding villages to screen the villagers and determine which specialist they needed and what day they should report to camp.

Three orthopedic surgeons came from Mumbai to work for free at the camp. Hundreds of local village children with severe orthopedic problems came to receive their annual checkup. If surgery was indicated, they would do it over the next two days. The patients for whom surgery was not indicated would be evaluated in physical therapy. All of the children needed regular PT; however, based on the logistics of getting to us, we had to just show the families a few basic home exercises and hope for the best. There were several times that day that I had to excuse myself and go into the bathroom to regroup. These kids were already facing many obstacles living in this impoverished part of India, and the severity of their deformities was far worse than I could have imagined.

The main surgeon running the pediatric part of the camp was Dr. Tushar. He was a young doctor from Mumbai who had completed his pediatric ortho fellowship in the US. In the morning, he said, "Make sure you go get your camera, Preya, because what you see here today you will never see in the US." He was right; I saw many severely deformed children who had never received any medical care. Dr. Tushar was a compassionate doctor and took extra time to explain each case to me. They only scheduled surgery on the most severe cases, where the patients were in imminent danger. The student PTs, along with the three staff PTs, evaluated, treated, and set up home programs for over 200 patients in that one day!

The next two days I spent in the operating room with the three orthopedic surgeons, and it was mind-blowing. The operating room looked like something out of the 1940s. Although everyone was in scrubs, and they attempted to maintain a sterile field, there were flies in there. In most cases, they used local anesthesia or a nerve block. I was an active participant in the operations. I held clamps and forceps, and was even allowed to assist with some cutting under close supervision. I had taken gross anatomy in grad school and had been a teaching assistant for gross anatomy for two years, so I was skilled at dissection, but these bodies were alive! It was a thrilling day for me because I would never be able to assist in surgery in America. After long hours in the operating room, and the enormous number of surgeries they performed that day, I was an extra pair of skilled hands. After a few hours in the operating room, I was feeling physically and emotionally drained. Then Rohit showed up, and it changed my mood entirely. When I was with him, I was at ease, and it took the edge off some of the heart-wrenching cases we operated on that day.

The first surgery I assisted was a patient with a septic knee that had fused. We opened up the knee, cleaned it out, and sawed away the boney fusion. The most difficult case for me was a nine-year-old boy with a severe scoliosis that was untreated. He'd developed a compensatory limp that eventually led to fusion of his right hip. The surgeon decided the best way to handle the case was to remove the entire femoral head. They sawed off the ball of the ball and socket joint, but there was no prosthetic replacement to implant. In the United States, this patient would have received a total hip replacement, but with the limited resources at the free camp, the goal is to restore function. The end result is that the boy could squat, which is very important in India because most homes have no chairs and everyone sits on the floor.

At the end of the first day, I couldn't help but ask Dr. Tushar about the infection rates. I have observed several orthopedic surgeries in America, and the surgeons are in full space suits with oxygen tanks. The operating room is negatively pressurized and kept at 65 degrees. All these are attempts to minimize infection, yet the infection rate in the US is about 5–10%. This operating room was not even close to the standard of a US one and apparently not even close to modern Indian hospitals. Dr. Tushar told me the infection rate here at the camp is 0%. These patients have such strong immune systems that even with minimal precautions taken and some prophylactic antibiotics, they haven't had any post-op infections to date. This was truly shocking to me. It did resonate with what I was starting to believe from my personal experiences. A person's health is more a reflection of their physical and mental health than what germs they are exposed to. A healthy body can handle most infections, without antibiotics. Unfortunately, I was just one example of how a stress-filled life, combined with a poor diet, results in the chronic diseases that are epidemic in the United States.

I had experienced how difficult it was to have cancer, even with the 'best medical facilities in the world.' These children were facing grave diseases with no medical or financial resources. The future for them was bleak. When ortho camp ended, I needed a mental health day.

Over these first weeks and conversations with the other Indian-Americans, I started to piece together my confused and frustrated feelings. I understood that I was having an identity crisis. I am a child of two vastly different cultures; my dad is Indian and my mom is American. I was NOT a natural at navigating in this foreign culture. I had conflicts because these two cultures are based on entirely different value systems. My mind had been conditioned into an efficient Western mentality. Yet throughout my life, my heart was filled with too much love for the harshness of America. I was just starting to unravel this underlying conflict and attempt to assimilate the best of both cultures. There were many growing pains and tears in this process. I hoped through my time here and the patience and understanding of my family in India that I could integrate myself.

After two weeks of treating patients and getting familiar with the system, I determined how to make my short time in Bidada successful. One night just before I fell asleep, the old proverb about "teaching a man to fish, rather than giving him a fish," came to me. I asked Samuel if I could start teaching classes every day for one hour during our lunch break. I also turned my focus toward an administrative role, trying to integrate some Western concepts into the current system. I put together a budget of departmental needs. I also put together a prospectus of the long-term plan for Jaya Rehab to share with the board members and the physical therapy department.

In order to maximize the impact on the community, we needed more capacity. I started to build momentum around expanding Jaya Rehab, and we discussed building a second floor. After a week of working long hours treating patients, teaching physical therapy classes, and doing research for a department plan, I was feeling optimistic about my impact there. I had successfully taken on new professional roles and was finally earning the respect of the people there. I was being included and consulted in meetings where I was the only woman. I was even asked to write up a capital expenditure report and a newspaper article.

I was excited about my new responsibilities but was feeling drained. Rohit invited me to join the volunteers from the child help program to celebrate Kite Day. I had read *The Kite Runner* and knew about Kite Day. I didn't know that they celebrated it here in Kutch. I told Samuel I was taking a well-deserved day off and joined the group on their Kite Day adventure.

After lunch we headed to Mandvi beach to watch the kite fights. We had one Indian-American man in the group named Kumar. He lived in Boston, but he'd grown up here in the villages. When we said we were going to Mandvi for Kite Day, he became excited and said he hadn't fought kites since he was a boy. We bought three kites and string that was coated with glass. The goal is to use your kite string to cut the strings of the other kites. In the book I read, it was organized in a tournament style, but this was not organized at all. There were thousands of kites fighting on the beach, a kite-fighting free-for-all. After a few attempts we got our first kite up and within seconds a red kite came right over and cut our kite. We looked around and saw a group of teenage Indian boys celebrating their victory. We got our second kite up, only for the same red kite to come over.

181

Chapter 17: INDIA: A MONTH IN KUTCH

Within a minute our kite was falling through the sky with its line cut. Then Kumar stepped up and said he was going to try. He launched the kite on his first try. The red kite quickly came back over to cut our string, but Kumar was an old kite-fighting champion. It must be like riding a bike because with a few very skillful moves he had maneuvered our kite below the red kite and then quickly let out the string and cut the line of the red kite. We all celebrated with a victory dance.

On the way home Rohit and I had a nice conversation about our lives back home in America. I had been traveling for almost four months and being able to talk to about life in the US helped ease some of my homesickness. Rohit and I were developing a true friendship, and I enjoyed every moment I spent with him. I was grateful for the many nights we sat on the roof talking about spirituality and trying to console each other about our struggles of this land. There was no light pollution and the night sky was dramatic.

Rohit was leaving in two days to go see his family in South India. On our last night together on the roof, I told him how much his friendship meant to me and that I hoped we could meet up somewhere in India before he went back to America. He was going to be starting medical school in the Caribbean, and once he got back to America, he said the next four years of his life were booked. Then he asked me what I would do if I met someone in India I was really interested in. I wasn't sure if there was a hidden meaning in his question. I told him my life was in complete transition, and everything I used to be, I no longer was. Then I said, "I think it would take a lot of hard work, and a very special person to start a meaningful relationship in India." There was a long awkward silence as we hugged and said goodnight. I went to say goodbye to Rohit, my kindred spirit, in the morning, and I mourned as his car pulled away.

The day Rohit left, I got sick. I couldn't go to work and spent the day in the bathroom alternating between throwing up and having diarrhea. It felt terrible. I was so tired and nauseated, and my stomach was in a knot. I tried to sleep, but I had the shakes, and my body was so unsettled I kept waking up to go to the bathroom. I took all the vitamins and herbs I had packed with me and tried to sleep it off, but by the second day I gave in and went to the camp doctor and started taking antibiotics. I had to remind myself that this was not America; the bugs in India are different and my system didn't have any immunity against them. Within two hours of taking my first pill, my symptoms had reduced 50%, and by the end of the second day, I was completely better. I stayed on the antibiotics for three days. After being so concerned with the food tents at camp, it was pretty ironic that I had probably gotten sick at a five-star restaurant on our day off. After my illness, I bought an extra stash of antibiotics, and from that day forward, I kept them in my purse at all times. I never wanted go through that misery again! Many of the Americans here were popping antibiotics like they were Tic Tacs. I had been a bit judgmental about what I thought was an abuse of antibiotics, but after two days straight of vomiting and diarrhea, I was in the antibiotic club. It's not an official trip to India unless you get sick, and I had made it almost three months, which is probably a world record!

The second night on antibiotics I was feeling much better, but I had missed two days of work. I was lying in bed reading when Bhavisha knocked at my door and said Vijay wanted me to report to his office immediately. Vijay was the top dog, the man in charge of most of the day-to-day operations throughout the entire complex. I asked her if she knew what it was about, was I in trouble for missing work, and she said she had no idea. My first thought was, *Oh Preya, whose toes have you stepped on?* That walk to Vijay's office was a long one. My heart was racing as I replayed every interaction to figure out whom I could have upset. In my job at the hospital in Detroit, getting summoned into the boss's office only meant one thing: I was in trouble. Could I be getting fired from my charity work? As Vijay sat me down, shut the door, and looked me straight in the eyes, my heart was about to jump out of my scrubs. Then he said he wanted to thank me for the outstanding job I had been doing. I was pleasantly shocked when he asked me if I would do a publicity film for the hospital. He then gave me literally five minutes of instructions before someone came into his office and summoned him to another meeting. He said good luck and shook my hand. He wanted the film to be short and he wanted to put it on the website via YouTube. I was to go to the various

183

Chapter 17: *INDIA: A MONTH IN KUTCH*

areas of the eye camp and show what was happening during each part of the camp. He had already arranged for the film crew and they would meet me at Jaya Rehab at 9:00 a.m. the following morning.

After my meeting with Vijay, I was starving; I hadn't eaten in two days. I missed Rohit, and I wanted to go to dinner with him and tell him all about the meeting. There was only one 'restaurant' in the village, and they only served one item, but it wasn't a good idea for me to walk there alone at night. I had no other choice but to go back to eating the camp food. I forced myself to eat it, which was a true measure of my hunger. I was on my third week of eating *kitchery,* (a bland blend of rice and lentils) every night for dinner.

I lay in bed that evening trying to direct my positive thoughts to imagine the amazing film that I was going to make. I was still recovering and was too tired to do anything else. I had never made a film or been on camera before Japan, and I had limited instructions about what Vijay wanted. I set my alarm early and planned to write my introduction in the morning. When I awoke, I was feeling 100% again. Luckily, my subconscious mind had been busy all night, and I had a vision for what the film would include.

The film crew arrived sharply at 10:30 a.m., which is typical 'Indian standard time'—an hour and a half late. The cameraman's name was Raj, and the lighting man was named Nitin, and of course neither one spoke English. I asked Oggie, a doctor from Canada, if he would meet me and help with the filming. I wanted another set of Western eyes to watch me on camera and give me some guidance. I have always been a good public speaker, but I have never done any work in front of the camera. My job was not only the writer and director, but I also had the starring role.

I spent the day with Raj and Nitin filming the entire eye camp. We learned how to communicate our needs with hand gestures and broken English. It felt like a drunken game of charades, but we made it work. We filmed the patient exams, the laboratory, and the patient's living quarters. The last thing we filmed was the actual eye surgeries. We were able to film a complete cataract surgery. I had never witnessed an eye surgery up close and it was truly amazing. To see such precise and delicate surgery being done successfully in this remote part of India was inspiring. In the four days of camp, they performed over 700 cataract surgeries. Making my first film was a fun and exciting adventure. One thing I learned is that everyone in India loves to be on camera. Wherever I showed up with the camera crew, I was the most popular person in the room. Many people whom I had not talked to in my previous three weeks at the hospital were eager to chat me up.

The next day I went to Mandvi with Devchand, the director of the Natural Cures Hospital. We spent the day in the editing room with Nirav, the cameraman's son. After two intense days of filming and editing, I proudly brought the final product to Vijay's office. We sat in his office with the board members of the hospital, as I nervously watched my first ever documentary. Even though I thought it had turned out well, it was uncomfortable to watch myself on TV. They all loved it! They said they wanted me to spend my last few days here working on two more films, one for the Natural Cures Hospital and one for Jaya Rehab. They told me that they had hired a professional crew from Europe to do publicity films last year, but they were not happy with them. Once again I learned the valuable lesson, "Anything is possible in India!"

Every morning when I walked out of my room, five stray puppies greeted me. Through my month here I had seen them nearly double in size. Many times I snatched a few extra chapattis from the dining tent and hand-fed them to the mother. I fell in love with the adorable dogs. This morning I walked outside and saw the mother lying down and all her puppies nursing off her painfully swollen nipples. I don't know what came over me, but I felt so moved watching that mother in her emaciated state, still giving whatever nutrition she had to her babies. It made me miss my family, which seemed so far away back in the land of overabundance called America. In that moment, I truly understood the enormous sacrifice of motherhood. Through that intense understanding, I questioned if I was on the right path. Is the real purpose of life for a female to have babies and raise a family, as most believed here in India? This stray dog in India with barely enough food for herself, still giving whatever

Chapter 17: INDIA: A MONTH IN KUTCH

she had to raise her puppies, was an ultimate expression of the power of love. I sat on the porch and watched the mother as I prayed for the answer to the purpose of my life. Was I supposed to be finding a husband and getting married, as everyone in my family wanted me to be doing? If so, why, after so many attempts at relationships was I still single and struggling with motherhood, which seemed so natural for this stray dog? It was a reality check that I was still searching for answers in my life. After four months of traveling in Asia mostly alone, I hadn't found the answer. I had learned many lessons, but I was not sure if I was any closer to figuring out my purpose in life. It did, however, make me feel eager to see my mom and dad, who were soon to visit.

Before leaving Bidada, I had to finish all three films. Cutting and editing is a tedious job; you have to be exact down to the millisecond to avoid the film looking choppy and unprofessional. I also had to be decisive, which is difficult for me. Most of what I filmed had to be cut out, but deciding what needed to be cut was challenging for a novice filmmaker. I think if I'd had more time between filming and editing, I would have had a more objective perspective. In the end it was too difficult to get each film down to ten minutes. The films were about 15 minutes long.

I had spent the last few years formulating a vision of the kind of practice I wanted to build. The traditional Western medicine version of a hospital is far from what I now believe health and healing are about. Most of the doctors I worked with in America with were not even taking proper care of themselves. Since my thyroid cancer, I had decided that my answer to health was not in prescription drugs or more surgeries. I created a vision of putting together my specialized training into a holistic wellness center that combined elements of Eastern and Western medicine. I knew that starting my wellness center would be a huge commitment for at least the first five years. I still dreamed that these were the years I was supposed to start a family. Between my fear of the responsibility of being a business owner and my maternal clock, I had put the idea on hold. Coming to India and filming a short movie about the Natural Cures Hospital gave me renewed inspiration to follow my dream. After all, the whole getting married and having a family thing wasn't working out as planned.

It was time to leave the village. I was excited for the next leg of my journey and was sad to say goodbye to this place. As I stepped out of Vijay's office for the last time, all the board of trustee members were lined up in a row along with several of my new international friends and the PTs from Jaya Rehab. I wasn't sure what was happening, and before I could figure it out, Bapu G, the chairman of the trust, stepped in front of me. Bapu G was an old wise man with a gentle presence. He was a man of few words, and when he spoke, everyone listened. He walked me to the center of the line and presented me with a shawl, just like I had seen them do for the US consul general. I felt overwhelmed and honored. I was grateful for the many lessons I had learned, and I guess they felt the same way. A beautiful feeling came over my body, and for the first time since leaving America four months ago, I cried tears of joy. After the ceremony they loaded my bags in a car and I headed back to Mumbai.

Chapter 18
INDIA: BACK TO MUMBAI

At that moment of clarity, I understood that everything in my life had happened in perfect order, and I had no regrets about the 'failures' that had led me there...

***

I flew back to Mumbai, and sitting on a plane again made me feel like a queen. I was thankful to have completed my month at the hospital successfully, and while it was a life-changing experience, it had been difficult. I was dreaming of my first hot shower in a month. I arrived back at Damayanti's and put my shawl on as I walked into the apartment; they all knew what the shawl represented. I received many hugs of congratulations from my family, and they said they had heard through the grapevine that my month at the hospital was successful.

I spent the two 'rest days' I was looking forward to cleaning at my Aunt Shilpa and Uncle Hirala's house. India is a dirty country, and I had become used to overlooking many things that I used to find shocking, but this was my sister-in-law's first trip to India. She is an openhearted woman that is very clean and organized. I hoped to minimize her potential distress, so I spent two days cleaning out years of dirt and grease from the kitchen, bathroom, and guest room. So much for my dream of a day of pampering!

My parents' plane arrived in the afternoon, and a group of us went to the airport to welcome them. My relationship with my parents continued to be bittersweet; we'd had several phone conversations that involved bickering and worry. Still, after

Chapter 18: INDIA: BACK TO MUMBAI

many months of struggling alone, I was overjoyed to see them. My mom and I both had tears in our eyes when we hugged at the airport.

When my brother and his family arrived, I was again excited and filled with love. My brother, Vikram, my sister-in-law, Alisa, and my two nephews ages five and six arrived in the middle of the night. The little boys had grown so much since I'd last seen them, and they looked exhausted; the long flight had been taxing on them. It was an emotional day of reunions, and I couldn't hold back the tears. I was so happy to be around my American family again that I breathed a long sigh of relief! As friendly and helpful as everyone in India had been to me, many things I said and did were easily taken out of context. I remember thinking that this was probably how Hollywood celebrities feel all the time. Being a free spirit and not following the strict rules for women was not something that was taken lightly in Indian culture.

My family in India had arranged a large welcome party for Vik's family on their first trip to India. I enjoyed seeing many members of my extended family that I hadn't seen for years, but after being asked about ten times why I wasn't married yet, it was definitely time to leave for my next party. I changed into my trendy, chic, yet traditional Indian outfit, grabbed a cab, and headed downtown.

I had made it back from the villages and it was time to celebrate. I felt empowered riding around India in cabs alone, especially at night. I took those rare few minutes as another reality check...yes, I was really a 34-year-old, unmarried Preya, taking a cab alone to downtown Mumbai for a party. At that moment of clarity, I understood that everything in my life had happened in perfect order, and I had no regrets about the 'failures' that had led me there.

The Intercontinental Hotel was beautiful and, WOW, was I feeling sexy! I was dressed to the nines, and people were opening doors for me like I was the Indian version of Carrie Bradshaw from *Sex and the City*! I wandered around the hotel for a while taking in all the beautiful Western luxuries that I had been deprived of for quite some time. I eventually found my way to the party, in the basement lounge. "On your mark,

THE EVOLUTION OF A PARTY GIRL

get set, go!" I began to drink....and drink....and drink. I was like a lioness that had been let out of her cage. I floated around, cocktail in hand, and flirted with every single guy at the party. Rahul, the friend I had met at my previous layover in Mumbai, asked me if I wanted to accompany him to the after party. "After party? Heck yeah!" I went with Rahul in his friend's BMW to Almont Avenue, the richest neighborhood in all of Mumbai, and probably all of India. By then it was almost 3:00 a.m. We arrived at his friend's house, went through the security gate, and were greeted by an entire staff who had woken up, dressed in uniforms, and prepared drinks and hors d'oeuvres for us. I was so far away from the village, in this amazing mansion in downtown Mumbai. A poker game started up and I was in. The old 'Party Girl Preya' was out in full swing. I ran the poker table for a couple of hours. I didn't look at the clock until almost 6:00 a.m. and then started to wonder how I was going to get home, and oh my...what was my family going to say now? I snuck in at 7:00 a.m. and climbed into bed. I spent the day recovering, which luckily got me out of a family luncheon. I was glad I had gone to the party as it made me feel free and I was in a mood to celebrate after a month in the villages, but it would come back to bite me later.

That night my American family and Damayanti's family got together at her house. My cousin Tushar had bought beer and everyone was sitting around and drinking, with all the children around. It was a blatant example of the double standard in the treatment of men and women even within my family. I was reprimanded for having a few drinks at a restaurant and coming home at 10:00 p.m., but they'd bought beer for my brother and his family to drink in their house. This sexual bias is taught to children from a young age, and they carry it into their adult and professional interactions. After only a few months, I had become accustomed to it.

I was still in recovery mode and passed up this rare opportunity to drink with my family. I decided it was a good night to show everyone the films I had spent the last few weeks working hard on. About two minutes into the first movie, Bharat started a side conversation with my dad. I asked them if they would not talk and watch the 15-minute movie, but they continued to

Chapter 18: INDIA: BACK TO MUMBAI

talk through my entire film. I was hurt. I'd spent a month doing charity work in my dad's village, and I was excited for them to watch the movie. I left the room and tried to understand why I continued to be haunted by feelings of rejection from my father. In 34 years, my dad had never said he was proud of me. But I still had a little girl inside of me who needed her dad's approval. She was someone I had met many times before, and she had caused me years of emotional turmoil and failed relationships. I understood in my mind that expressing affection and positive reinforcement was not something my father learned growing up in the villages. I understood all of these things about our relationship and myself, but the little girl was still there, still waiting for his approval for the very hard work I had done.

We had a family picnic planned on our last day in Mumbai. We were going to visit Damayanti's family farmhouse about three hours away by bus. The day started out full of excitement, riding in a huge rented bus, the ladies all singing traditional Indian songs and playing games. I sat next to my mom, and we talked and caught up on the last few months. We arrived at the farmhouse at about 10:00 a.m.; it was a beautiful house with a large in-ground swimming pool. I loved to swim and always found water to be the best way for me to nurture myself.

My brother and I sat poolside and cracked a few beers. The conversation started out smoothly, catching up on each other's life for the last few months, then, WHAM, my brother attacked. For the next hour he talked to me about my behavior—staying out late, drinking, and not behaving like an Indian woman 'should.' After months of doing yoga and working so diligently to open my heart, I felt attacked and vulnerable. I became defensive and I tried to explain that the other night was the only time I had stayed out all night and partied in months. My brother and I had been going to parties together since high school. He knew my shenanigans better than anyone else and should have known that this was tame behavior for me. He said that our family had talked to him about my behavior. I told him that being in India for the last few months had caused a complete identity crisis in me. My coping mechanism of going out and having drinks was the first thing I had done in a month that actually gave me a sense of normalcy. I explained that I was

THE EVOLUTION OF A PARTY GIRL

often in violation of Indian norms, just by being me. I did agree that I had a tendency to overdo it. He protested and stated, "Preya, you are not going to change the way women are treated in India by staying out late and coming home drunk. While you are with the family in India, you should behave like an Indian woman." He also requested that I change my ticket and come home with them and not stay in India any longer. I had now become angry and struck back, "I refuse to behave like a submissive Indian woman to please any sexist men!"

I walked to the temple behind the farmhouse and spent the next two hours in a complete meltdown. I was fed up with everything and everyone. What was I doing here? I was so lonely and felt like nobody in the world understood me. I wasn't sure that I even understood who I was anymore. The drama ruined the picnic, which I had looked forward to for weeks. I was mad at my brother, mad at my dad, mad at myself, and sick of India.

I again sat with my mom on the bus ride home; she had no idea what had happened during the picnic. I told her everything Vik had said to me, and she put her arm around me and comforted me in the way only a mother is able to do. She told me that everything was fine, Vik was overreacting, and that my family in India had never said they didn't want me there. Good old Mom, she has always been on my side and had my back. I had been distant with my parents for the last few years, as I tried to work through my childhood issues. Despite my standoffish behavior, she was still the first one to defend me and take my side when I needed support. That love and support on the bus ride home was the only reason I didn't change my ticket and fly home.

Chapter 19
INDIA: THE FAMILY VACATION

As I closed my eyes, my mind began to swirl; I felt like I was floating and my body had lost all sense of direction. The sound of his chanting slowly disappeared, and I was somewhere I had waited many months to experience...

***

We all woke up early the next morning and caught the earliest flight to Jaipur. It was my first family trip in many years, and I was nervous, especially considering how things were going so far. We met our mini-bus driver and went three hours to Ranthambore National Tiger Reserve. We checked into the Jhoomar Baori Castle. Bharat had planned our trip and was given firm orders that our accommodations had to be clean and modern. It was Alisa's and the kids first time in India, and everyone wanted to make sure they were safe and comfortable. She was handling India like a champ and seemed to be having fun trying many new things. Traveling in a third world country with two young children takes a lot of courage and patience. Vik and I had made up and were enjoying our time together, reminiscing about traveling around India together as kids. India is grossly overpopulated and has destroyed most of its natural ecosystems. To finally be surrounded by trees and quiet again, instead of crazy traffic and millions of people, put all of us in a more relaxed mindset. Peace had again found its way to my family and I was truly enjoying the calm after the storm.

The next day we went on a tiger-viewing safari in the morning. Due to human overpopulation, pollution, and poaching, the tiger is almost extinct in India. I have gone on several of these safaris in India, but sadly, I have never seen a tiger. In the afternoon, we visited a 3,000-year-old temple. When we got to the temple, I started wandering on my own. The temples were built into the mountains, along with large concrete pools filled with natural spring water for spiritual cleansing. I kept wandering up the mountain until I found my way to the smallest temple at the top of the complex. A young monk asked me to come in. He showed me the part of the mountain that was supposed to be a natural drawing of Lord Hanuman, the monkey God. Then he invited me to sit down at the altar and meditate with him. He did some chanting and burned incense. As I closed my eyes, my mind began to swirl; I felt like I was floating and my body had lost all sense of direction. The sound of his chanting slowly disappeared, and I was somewhere I had waited many months to experience—a state of complete silence, no thoughts, just absolute nothingness. After some time, I started hearing his chanting again and I remembered I was here in India in a temple and my family was downstairs waiting for me. As I slowly came out of my meditative state, he told me now was a good time to pray for what I wanted in my life. I spent a few minutes praying for safety on the rest of my trip, for my family and I to continue to get along, and my usual prayer to find a soul mate to share a life of health, wealth, love, and adventure with. Then he tied a string around my right wrist to maintain the blessings from this ceremony. I gave him a donation, and he put a garland of flowers around my neck. I felt joyous after that experience. I wasn't sure if that was the state of Samadhi that Steve had taught me about in Mysore, but I was eager to experience it again.

Next stop, The Taj Mahal! It is the greatest iconic landmark in all of India. I went there once as a child and remember it was a mess. Beggars, panhandlers, and hawkers swarmed us, and the grounds were filthy. The once-pristine fountain leading up to the amazing building was filled with squatters sleeping, washing clothes, and bathing. We were all excited to see the Taj especially Alisa and the kids. I hoped it was cleaner than my childhood memory.

We woke up early since the best time to see the Taj is at sunrise. The morning light illuminates the Taj Mahal, and it glows with a pink hue. It has been called one of the most breathtaking views of human creation, and is considered one of the Seven Wonders of the World. We arrived early, trying to beat daybreak, but there was the normal level of Indian chaos outside the gate— lots of tourists and heavy security. It had taken a previous threat of a terrorist attack to clean up the grounds of beggars and squatters. Now, no cars were allowed within a 1 KM circumference, and you needed a ticket to even get close to the Taj. We got through security just as day was breaking, and the first glimpse of the majestic building made me gasp out loud; it was beautiful. The entire Taj was illuminated a glowing pink; it looked like there was a spotlight on the monument. The power of the sun to illuminate the Taj pink, and the power of love to build such a monument created an inner feeling of awe. My mind went silent and my heart felt a surge of energy as we walked up the long walkway to the magnificent white marble domes. We took pictures, and there were many tourists, but I found inner silence again that morning at the Taj Mahal. As I looked around at all the people, hustling and bustling, I felt serenity.

India was starting to wear on Alisa; I could see it in her face. She tried to mask the frustration, but I could feel her tension level rising. I understood how she felt, as I was in the same predicament. The boys were almost on a hunger strike, refusing to eat any more Indian food, and no matter how much Bharat had tried to plan a deluxe vacation; India was not a country for five-star tourism. Family dynamics are complicated, and spending the last few weeks with my family was also wearing me thin.

We arrived at the Delhi airport to fly to Kerala for the final leg of our family vacation. I had never seen a family so excited to see Kentucky Fried Chicken and Pizza Hut. We all indulged—I had never enjoyed a cheese pizza as much as I did that morning at 7:00 a.m. We boarded the plane with all of our bellies full of good old-fashioned American junk food. We flew to Kerala, the tropical paradise of India with oceans, mangoes, and coconuts everywhere.

Chapter 19: INDIA: THE FAMILY VACATION

It had been a big adjustment for me going from traveling alone to being with family and kids 24-7. I was thankful for my family support and for them making a huge sacrifice to come to India to visit me, but I needed some alone time. I decided to forgo the cultural program that my family attended that night. We have always been a family that bickered, but now after opening my heart to vulnerability, I'd had many tearful days since they arrived. I still hadn't achieved my goal of inner strength to stabilize above our family drama. I sat by the pool, wrote in my journal, had a glass of wine, and formulated a plan. I called Rohit, who was still in Bangalore with his family. It was so nice to talk to him again. We exchanged stories of our struggles being back with our families and spent most of the call laughing. It was much-needed therapy for both of us. By the end of the call it was settled—I wasn't going back with my family to Mumbai in a few days. I would instead fly to Goa and meet up with Rohit.

That morning we visited a beautiful tea garden. India became part of the international community in order to trade for spices and tea and is the second largest producer of tea in the world. However, it is such a tea drinking culture that they consume over 70% of their domestic crop. The tea plant is a leafy dark green shrub that grows on the sides of mountains. I found out that the local women handpicked the tea leaves, which was shocking when we saw the thousands of acres of tea gardens. I took some beautiful pictures of the rows of traditionally dressed women with their heads covered in scarfs to shade them from the morning sun, handpicking each tea leaf with love and devotion. After we toured the processing plant and sampled their tea, we took the narrow, winding, and dangerous mountain road to the final destination of our whirlwind family trip across India, a houseboat.

On the drive, I spent a lot of time looking out the window of our luxury bus at the poverty in India. I contemplated the morning at the tea garden and the overall impact of tea in the Indian culture. I wrote a journal entry and later, after we concluded our time on the houseboat and my brother's family had returned to the U.S., I decided to send it to everyone on my email list.

Indian Tea

The price of tea in India is three rupees on the street and seventy rupees at the Taj Hotel. That is a pretty accurate representation of the dichotomy of the social classes in India. Tea is the main drink of all Indians, the richest and the poorest, so the price of tea is a good way to understand the society.

Traveling with my family we have played the role of rich American tourists: staying at the best hotels, never carrying our own luggage, eating massive amounts of food in private dining rooms, and having a 'party bus' with a full-time driver. We see the poverty of India, but only through the tinted windows of our air-conditioned luxury cab. The previous months on my own, I tried to live more at the level of the common man, taking a train or bus versus flying. Staying at basic accommodations without hot water and living a simpler life. Even in my attempt to live as an Indian, I still lived at a higher standard of living than most people in this country.

India has a dramatic split between classes. There is the elite class of India that lives a Western-style life. I spent some time with the elites at the horse track and club. I also went to an after party at someone's house in Mumbai where there was a private waitstaff who woke up, dressed in uniforms, and served us drinks and snacks. Then there are the patients I treated at the hospital who live in small one-room buildings with dirt floors. This room is the room where they socialize during the day, sit on the floor to eat meals, and pull out mats to sleep on the floor at night. There is usually a small kitchen that is either indoor or outdoor. The basic bathroom consists of a porcelain hole in the ground, and a faucet used to fill a bucket to bathe with and do laundry. The patients at the hospital, whose houses I just described, live the way the LARGE majority of Indian families live.

India is very overpopulated, and the poverty is more severe than almost anywhere the world. A large part of this meager lifestyle is ingrained in Indian culture and traditions. There is a large class in India of 'New Money.' In America when we think of new money, we think of the flashy 'look what I've got' mentality where they show off with their over-the-top excessiveness. In India, new money is a class of merchants who have become wealthy in business but still choose to live a simple and traditional Indian life. They grew up with a mentality of saving and frugality that lives deep within them. Seeing the pervasive poverty does reinforce the attitude of frugality as in, "I don't ever want to have to live like that!" After all, the Dharavi slum in the middle of Mumbai, where Slumdog Millionaire was filmed, is the largest slum in Asia. The area has a population similar to that of Detroit all living in huts held together by strings and sheets. People who live in these have a lot of sickness attributed to bathing, cooking, and cleaning from the same contaminated water supply.

Don't get me wrong, the good life in India is very good! But you leave these fancy parties and luxury boats to get approached by beggars and have to drive home past the slums. The split between the classes has been a long part of Indian history. With my family, we were toured many of the famous palaces of the Indian Maharajahs (kings). Each state in India had a ruling family, and they ruled until just about 60 years ago. These palaces, including the magnificent Taj Mahal, represent some of the most ornate and lavish buildings in the world. The elite class of India, which represents 0.5% of India and still includes the families of the maharajahs, contains most of the wealth. India has a small middle class and is a country of 'Haves' and 'Have-nots.' The 'Haves' of the elite struggle to keep in place the system that maintains their status, and the 'Have-nots' fight and struggle to survive and break the system. This basic struggle between the classes leads to deep layers of political corruption in India and a defined class-based system. Hence the price of tea is 3 rupees on the street and seventy rupees at the Taj Hotel.

Vik, Alisa, and their children have left and are back safe in Detroit. It was a nice family vacation that gave us an opportunity to spend more time together than we have in years and share many exciting adventures together.

I am now in the hedonistic paradise of Goa for carnival. My new friend from the hospital, Rohit, met me here for a few days to sow some wild oats before Lent. Day two post-carnival...doing good still!

I hope all my loved ones are well and I think of you often.

Peace and Love,

Preya

Chapter 20
INDIA: CALANGUTE BEACH, GOA

Hanging out with Rohit, dancing, feeling total safety and freedom with a few cocktails pumping through my veins—I was in Goa heaven...

***

I took the overnight train from Kerala to Goa. Since I'd first planned this trip, the only consistent thing my dad said is that whatever I did, I shouldn't go to Goa. Like every other time in my life my dad begged me NOT to do something, it made me want to go there. What Las Vegas is to the US, Goa is to India, a hedonistic paradise. I was so excited to experience the 'party scene' of Goa and see Rohit again. I had one week there, then one week back with my parents in Mumbai, and then I would immerse myself in yogi life at the ashram in Vrindavan.

On the train, I had met a helpful gay couple from Amsterdam and they gave me a ride to Calangute Beach in the state of Goa. I checked into the Osborne Resort and waited poolside with a fruity cocktail for Rohit. The resort was filled with sunburned and drunk Russian tourists.

Rohit's plane arrived about three hours late. I was excited to see him, but it took some time to get acquainted again. He unpacked in our room while I got 'dressed up' in a black tank top, jeans, and my sparkly flip fops. Goa was so Western that I could finally wear a tank top out in public without covering up. I felt happy and safe to be hanging out with my dear friend, and it wasn't long before there was a natural flow between us again. It was a Thursday night and there was supposed to be a great nighttime hippy market in town. Hippies from around the world who had transplanted themselves to Goa came out to peddle their goods to the new 'hippy tourists.' We walked around the market and enjoyed the best people-watching thus far in India. This place was a magnet for all of the strange, freaky types that go to India to 'find themselves.' Yogis, spiritual seekers, potheads, hippies, conspiracy theorists, and any other off-the-wall tourists, all thrown together in one huge street market with the common goal of nonconformity.

We walked to the amphitheater where there was a kirtan being performed. I hadn't been to a kirtan since Steve's apartment. This wasn't nearly as good as Steve's, but it felt really good to be back with yogis and singing devotional music. We ate at a nice restaurant by the beach, and we were both eager to blow off some steam in the famous nightlife of Goa.

Rohit had done some research and had the names and addresses of all the best dance clubs in Goa. We got in a rickshaw and headed to Mambos; we paid the only-tourists-could-afford-it cover charge and headed in. The club was hopping. The music took me back to my party days living in NYC. It was mostly electronic but mixed with Indian classical instruments, and we both loved it! I beelined for the bar, ordered a stiff drink, and slammed it. Rohit waited for me, since he does not drink, and then we headed to the dance floor. We started to dance, and it was pure ecstasy. Hanging out with Rohit, dancing, feeling total safety and freedom with a few cocktails pumping through my veins—I was in Goa heaven. We danced and danced until almost 5:00 a.m., barely noticing the hours as they passed. We danced fast, we danced close, we clowned around on the dance floor, and by the end of the night when the lights came on, we both agreed it was the most fun we'd had dancing in years. Luckily Rohit was sober, because I needed an escort back to the hotel.

As expected, I woke up my first morning in Goa with a hangover. I was still blissed-out from the feeling of freedom I'd experienced on the dance floor the night before. Since I'd left America almost six month ago, it was the first night I'd felt like I had my guard down and was totally carefree.

It was Valentine's Day, and I asked Rohit if he wanted to do yoga with me. I was so excited when he agreed. We spent an hour doing yoga together, then we spent the rest of the morning swimming and sitting poolside. Our cheesy resort had put up red hearts all over the hotel and these especially corny bright red glowing hearts were hanging above the pool. We both felt a little awkward because we were on vacation together in Goa on Valentine's Day, yet we were only platonic friends...bummer!

I told Rohit I wanted to go to a nice oceanfront restaurant for lunch, so he rented a scooter from the hotel and we drove to one. I needed a drink after the waiter asked if we were on our honeymoon, so I ordered my first shot of Fenny, the strong local liquor of Goa made from distilled fennel seeds. After lunch, Rohit and I spent our day touring around Goa on his rented scooter and then took a walk on the beach.

It was one of the best Valentine's Days I had enjoyed in years. Rohit and I sat on the beach and talked; he really opened up emotionally to me that day. It became clear that he was not interested in a casual make-out like I had been considering. He said he really hadn't found anyone that he wanted to seriously date in a long time, and he wasn't interested in casual dating. He also said the next four years were going to be the hardest years of his life in medical school, and he had no plans to get distracted by a girlfriend. I understood that my relationship with Rohit would continue to remain platonic, but it was still one of the most romantic Valentine's Days of my life.

After dinner, we headed back to our resort. We had a late-night swim alone in our pool under the red neon hearts. Valentine's Day fell on a new moon, and I asked Rohit if he would perform a new moon ceremony with me. I explained it to him, and he agreed it was the perfect way to spend our last night together. We stayed up late that night, both of us savoring our final night and knowing that we only had a few hours left together.

Chapter 20: INDIA: CALANGUTE BEACH, GOA

******NEW MOON MANIFESTATIONS******

Feb, 14th, 2010 Goa, India

I bring these things into my life now for the greatest good of all concerned:

I hope to continue to grow personally and professionally, as I continue forward on this amazing, life-defining trip!

<u>**NEEDS**</u>: *Carpets for my car back in the "D," and resolution of my sunroof leak.*

*CLEAN BEDS, CLEAN WATER, AND CLEAN FOOD!

*Political stability and a healthy economy in a peaceful country

*Healing of myself, as needed: **spiritually**, **chemically** *(my past of too much alcohol),* **my body, emotionally**.

*Mount Everest to be magnificent!

<u>**WANTS**</u>: *ABUNDANCE OF ALL MY WANTS*

*Pearl earrings, emerald earrings, and good gifts to take home

*$200,000 YEARLY income working 55 HRS/wk

*A career with professional freedom, autonomy, ethics, equality, and in alignment with a higher life plan

*A magnetic personality, with unlimited access to life

*My beautiful cats to have a good life always, with me or without me

*An emotionally healthy, stable, and loving relationship

<u>**DESIRES**</u>: *safe, orgasmic, and fulfilling sex life*

*A LIFE OF HEALTH, WEALTH, LOVE, ADVENTURE, and SPIRITUALITY with my SOULMATE!

<u>**DREAMS**</u>: *A clear path to emerge to lead me to follow my dreams, allowing me to live wherever I want and work is fun*

<u>**Healing of One = Healing of all = PEACE**</u>

***

We woke up on our final morning and practiced yoga together. Rohit was NOT a yoga superstar, but I was happy that he was willing to practice with me. We had connected on so many levels over that past few days, and sharing yoga is my highest way of connecting with another person. I had gifted Rohit a certificate for a craniosacral treatment from me for Valentine's Day, so after yoga, we spent our last hours together nurturing each other, platonically. I gave him a two-hour craniosacral treatment, and he gave me an hour-long oil massage with my Ayurvedic oil from Kerala. I felt so close and intimate with him, but we had never even kissed. I asked if he could stay a few days longer and travel with me to the south of Goa, but he said he had to get back to Bangalore. I felt deep sadness when I watched his cab pull away.

I stayed one more day in our resort as I finalized plans to head to a small village in the south of Goa to practice yoga. There was a shift that occurred when Rohit left. I had felt so carefree and safe for the past three days. I could let my hair down and not cover up. As soon as he left however, I had to completely change back to covering up, never making eye contact, and being hyper-aware of everyone around me...yuck!

After investigating several options, including this strange Bonnie-and-Clyde-type couple trying to get me to go with them in a car, I decided paying for a private car and driver was my best option. I still could hear my dad's plea for me to not go to Goa and how unsafe it was for foreign women. I had no idea really what that meant.

Chapter 21
INDIA: ESCAPING GOA

I had my backpack on and was running down the crowded main street of Chaudi looking for a church while being chased by ten motorcycles...

***

It was about an hour-and-a-half drive to Palolem Beach; I was in a new SUV and had a nice, safe driver. I sat quietly in the car looking out at the beautiful countryside and every now and then I could see some views of the ocean. I didn't have a place to stay, but an oceanfront beach shack and yoga would be the main focal points in finding a hotel. The driver agreed to stay with me and help me find a hotel before he left. He first took me to his friend's dirty hotel for 800 rupees a night. I said no thank you and we walked down the beach to the Big Fish Resort. It only cost 500 rupees a night and was much nicer, but no yoga.

There was a large sign at the end of the beach that said YOGA. It was a beautiful hotel called the Endless Sun Beach Resort, which took up the entire peninsula. It had the traditional palm leaf beach shacks, but these were up on the cliff overlooking the ocean. I walked down the beach with my driver to check it out. Manish, a very hot young Indian man who said he was the owner greeted my driver and me. He said they didn't have any cottages tonight, but if I came back in the morning there would be a vacancy. I asked him about the yoga, and he said they teach Kundalini-style yoga, which was something I had heard a lot of people talk about and wanted to try. He showed me a private cottage with balcony that overlooked the

Chapter 21: INDIA: ESCAPING GOA

ocean in all directions. I could imagine myself sitting, reading, journaling, and watching the waves crash onto the rocky cliffside. It was perfect. I decided I would stay one night at the Big Fish Resort and come back at 11:00 a.m. the next day to check in.

I walked back to the Big Fish, had a quiet dinner, and was in bed by 8:00 p.m. I woke up early the next morning and had breakfast at my resort. I started with a pot of my favorite masala chai, a perfect start to a day in India. It was early so the hotel restaurant was still empty, and I had the same waiter that I'd had the night before. He was a nice middle-aged Indian man who was wearing a bright yellow shirt. He tried to make small talk, but I had my guard up pretty high and tried to deflect any personal questions, including everyone's favorite question: "Madam, what country are you from?" I made my first new friend in Palolem Beach—a beautiful cow. It came up the beach and stood in front of me at my table. It just stood there for about ten minutes staring at me! I finally started talking with the cow, asking him what he wanted, how his day was, and the typical questions you would ask a new friend. His sweet stare worked because he ended up getting half of my breakfast before the waiter scolded me for feeding the cow.

I packed up and as I walked down the beach and up the winding trail with my overstuffed backpack, I was surprised to see the same cow I had made friends with that morning. He was standing firmly, blocking my path. I tried to talk to him again and coax him out of my way, but he was standing with determination blocking the path to my new hotel. A local man had to come and pull the cow out of the way for me to pass. As I look back now, that cow had good reason for blocking my path.

When I got to the resort, Manish greeted me. He told me it would still be a few minutes until my cottage was ready and he made me a glass of fresh squeezed OJ. I drank it, and we small-talked and laughed. He was flirting with me, but this time, I was flirting back. By noon, I was in my cottage and on my own for the first time since my family had arrived. It had been a while since I'd had a whole day free. I decided to go back to the reception desk/tiki bar and ask the guys that worked there what there is to do in this area.

I sat there and had a chai. Manish was leaving with another young guy just as I came down. The tiki bar overlooked an amazing rocky beach, and between it and the ocean there was a large sandy beach. The private beach had couches and tables and a large black metal structure that I quickly realized was a DJ booth. It didn't take me long to recognize the familiar structures of a nightclub on the beach. I had spent most of the weekends of my 20s in nightclubs, so I was no stranger to that scene, but I had only been to two nightclubs in the last many months. Had my search for a quiet yoga resort taken me to another infamous nightclub in Goa? I talked to my bartender, Ace, and he assured me they only have parties once a week, and the rest of the time it is very quiet here. He also said many times they have to cancel the parties because of problems with the local police. Yikes...my first red flag.

After the late night of dancing on Valentine's Day, I was desperately in need of my yoga mat and looking forward to the 5:00 p.m. yoga class. The yoga area was amazing. It was at the highest peak of the resort, and I could feel strong energy fill my body when I walked onto the pure white platform. It was a cement floor with cement pillars at the four corners and tall palm trees all around. We were on a peninsula so there were amazing views of the ocean. The breeze was strong, and I felt like I was in heaven. As I started practicing, I felt happy and free, and I decided that coming to Palolem Beach to practice yoga was the right decision. I closed my eyes during my sun salutations and could feel the energy flowing through my body and radiating out. I felt like a brilliant lighthouse with beams of light shining in every direction.

When I opened my eyes after we were done with our sun salutations, I was surprised to see Manish sitting on a rock not that far in the distance staring at me doing yoga. It was a little creepy. He pretended to be 'supervising' some of his guys doing some work, but it was clear he was there to watch me do yoga. Raja's class was a little strange and unlike any yoga I had done before. He did some of these funny exercises and breathing techniques. I was just so happy to be doing yoga in this divine space that nothing else mattered—not the weird Kundalini yoga or Manish watching me through almost my entire practice.

Chapter 21: INDIA: ESCAPING GOA

After yoga, I was hot and sweaty, and the ocean was calling me. I changed into my bikini and went to the beach. I got there just in time to swim in the warm water while watching the sunset. After yoga, all of my senses were heightened. Swimming in the Arabian Sea felt so good....ahhhhh

I went back to my room, showered, and changed; I was starving since I hadn't eaten lunch. I went down to the tiki bar and ordered a glass of wine, and Manish came over and sat down next to me. We talked and got to know each other. I asked him if they served dinner here, and he said he would go into the kitchen and cook something up for us. I sat at the bar and played rummy with Ace and about fifteen minutes later, Manish came out with dinner for us both. He had prepared pomfret for me and dal fry for himself. We sat at one of the beachfront tables and had a private dinner. I tried to find out more about him, but he was very short and elusive with his answers. I did most of the talking, and he did most of the listening. After dinner and another glass of wine, he asked me if I wanted to go for a walk on the beach. I didn't know him well, but I assumed since he was the owner of the resort it would be fine. We went for a romantic evening stroll with the moon high above us and the sound and smell of the ocean all around. After our walk, we sat on one of the outdoor couches and had a good old-fashioned make-out session. Another first—my first ever make-out with a man born and living in India. It was late and I said I had to get to bed, and just as I was walking up to my cottage he said, "Preya, do you want to spend the day at the beach with me tomorrow?"

Friday I woke up excited to spend the day with Manish. I had developed a crush on him. I went to Big Fish for breakfast and when I returned, Manish was sitting at the reception bar talking to yet another Indian man. Manish casually asked me what my plans were for the day and asked if I still wanted to go to the beach with him. I said yes, and I would be ready in an hour.

We walked the back way out of the resort to his new white car with dark black tinted windows. As we drove out the narrow beach roads, everyone on the street stopped and waved at him;

it was like he was the mayor or something. We headed to Baga Beach, a few miles down the shore from Palolem Beach.

We parked the car in front of a small resort called The Tiger Den. The owner of the resort came out and introduced himself to me and shook Manish's hand and gave him a half hug as if they were good friends. The resort was on a beautiful white sand beach; it was pretty empty and the ocean was calling me. I asked Manish if he was going to swim, and he said no. I had my bikini on under my sundress but wasn't sure if that would be acceptable. I asked Manish if girls swam in their bikinis there, and he said it was fine.

I took off my sundress and headed to the ocean. The sand was hot on my feet, and I was so excited to go swimming; the waves were huge! I dove in and swam out far past the surf. I floated on my back and felt so happy. Life was good! I went in and out of the ocean a few times. I would sit with Manish and his friend for a while, have a glass of white wine, and then I would go out and swim again. They talked mostly in Goan and seemed like they mostly were talking business. We played poker and drank wine for about an hour and I won fifty rupees. Manish leaned over and whispered in my ear that I looked really good in my bikini. We flirted a lot that day, some winking and smirking, a few stolen kisses, and lots of compliments. I tried to convince him to go kayaking with me, but I could tell he didn't know how to swim. Most Indians don't know how to swim. He said maybe tomorrow he would go kayaking.

After a few hours at the beach, I was feeling really happy about my new friend Manish. We had just finished a delicious lunch of palak paneer and fresh-caught ocean fish when things got strange. These four hoodlums came over to our table. They were tall and overweight and none of them were dressed in beach clothes. As soon as they came over to our table, my hair stood up on end. I could tell something was off with these guys; they made me feel scared and uncomfortable. Then one of the waitstaff came over with a cordless phone and handed it to the owner, who immediately handed the phone to Manish. They were all taking in Goan, and I was feeling something in the pit of my stomach. I excused myself and went for a swim. When I came back from swimming, Manish was sitting at a back table

Chapter 21: INDIA: ESCAPING GOA

with the four hoodlums. There was also a new table of young hippies from Israel. They were smoking weed and one of the girls was playing the guitar. Manish asked me if I wanted to sit with them in the back, but I said I wanted to sit with the hippies and listen to the girl play the guitar. I had a nice conversation with the Israeli hippies. I passed on the weed, but took her up on her offer to teach me how to play a little guitar. After a few minutes, Manish came over to my table and said we had to go; he had a few hours of business to take care of. I said goodbye to the owner and the Israeli hippies and we left.

The four hoodlums followed us in a car all the way back to the resort. Just as I was getting out of the car, Manish asked me if I wanted to meet him for dinner. I said yes and he said he had some things to take care of and would meet me at the bar at 7:30 p.m. I went to my cottage to rest for a while before dinner. I was half-asleep and felt startled by the sound of a loud 'pop.' Was I dreaming or was it real? I grew up in Detroit and went to school in Flint. I knew that sound. It was a gunshot.

I went down to the reception tiki bar at 7:30 p.m. and didn't see Manish anywhere. I sat with Ace and he schooled me in rummy again. By 8:30 p.m. my stomach was growling, and I asked Ace where Manish was. He said he was right outside of the back gate taking care of some business. A few minutes later, Manish appeared, and he looked awful. He looked sweaty and stressed, and his heart seemed like it was beating a mile a minute. He apologized and said something had come up and he had to cancel our dinner plans. I said okay, but I felt like something was really wrong. As he was walking toward the back gate, I called out to him and asked him if everything was okay. He assured me he was fine and that he just had some unexpected business to take care of. As I left the resort from the front entrance, I swore I heard the sound of someone getting beat up. Things were starting to get weird. I wondered if this was what my dad had been talking about.

Once I left, things went from weird to weirder. I found what a thought was a remote, off-the-beaten-path resort and went upstairs to have a quiet dinner alone. I asked for a corner table and carefully positioned myself so nobody could see me and I could still look out at the ocean in the distance. The waiter came over to me, and he was shirtless, which is pretty unusual in India. His body was covered with lash marks and scars. He seemed like he was strung out on drugs. I ordered a stiff drink and tried to piece together the events of the day. After a few minutes at the table, it started—the distinct sound of sex! Not just any sex, but totally crazy whips-and-chains sex. The restaurant was empty except for me, and the owner, Suresh, came over and asked if he could sit down. I said yes; I was starting to feel afraid to be alone in Goa and was happy to have someone sitting with me. Near the end of our dinner, the waiter came back and seemed even more strung out. He was yelling and carrying on, saying he was a "Jesus freak"; he had a huge tattoo of Jesus on the right side of his chest. I tried to talk to the waiter about Lent, which had just started a few days prior, but he said he didn't know what Lent was. That seemed pretty strange for a self-professed "Jesus freak." Then he told me he was from Iran and was in the war. It was a strange conversation and not much of what he said made sense. Then he left and I again heard the sounds of crazy sex from behind the wall. Suresh said it wasn't safe for me to be out this late by myself and he would walk me back to my resort. I felt comfortable with him and also was starting to wonder how safe Palolem Beach was. Suresh walked me to the main gate of the Endless Sun Beach Resort and said goodnight.

I was concerned about everything that had happened earlier in the day and called Manish to make sure he was okay. He answered on the first ring and told me to wait at the reception area for him. He came over shortly and poured me a glass of wine. It wasn't long before we were kissing again, and he offered to escort me up to my cabin. We sat on my balcony and I drank my wine.

We made out a little more, and then the party moved inside to my bed.

I made it clear I wasn't interested in having sex with him, and he agreed. He said we were just going to "play around a little." And play we did—for the next hour we kissed, giggled, and caressed each other. Then he quickly got dressed and said goodnight.

The next morning I woke up feeling awful, which was surprising because I'd only had two drinks the night before,

Chapter 21: INDIA: ESCAPING GOA

although I'd had a few glasses of wine in the afternoon. I wasn't sure if it was a hangover, I'd eaten some bad fish, or I had been drugged. I went to Bridge and Tunnel, the next resort over, and ordered breakfast, but I was so sick I had to pack it up and take it to go. I had cold sweats, I was nauseous, and I felt like I was about to faint. This European guy named Steven came and sat at the table next to mine. He said I looked green, and he thought I should go back to my hotel room, put on the fan, and rest in bed all day. I agreed, and spent the day nursing my illness. I sent Manish a text since we had talked about kayaking at 10:00 a.m. and said, "I am not feeling well. I am in my room." He didn't respond.

By 3:00 p.m. I was feeling better and went down to the reception area. In the upstairs area above the reception bar, Manish was sitting with a bunch of other young Indian men. As I walked up the ladder to the roof, Manish said from across the room, "So was it good?" I knew he was talking about our hookup last night but I ignored his comment, which he'd inappropriately made in front of ten guys. He then asked what I had been doing all day; I said resting, relaxing, and praying. I told him I was sick and something inside of me wasn't feeling settled here anymore. He introduced me to his friends who were all in red shirts, but he only introduced them by their nicknames (aliases): Elvis Presley, Albert Einstein, Abraham Lincoln, etc. It was strange. They were all drunk, except for Manish, who doesn't drink. It was now 3:00 p.m., and I could tell they had been drinking for hours. They talked mostly in Goan, and I could understand they were listing cities in Goa and then giving numbers after each city. Manish said they were all in the shipping business. I wasn't sure what kind of 'business' they were in, but I could tell that Manish was the leader. He had a magnetic personality, he was good looking, and his presence commanded authority.

I went back to my room and got ready for yoga at 5:00 p.m. On the way, I walked by Manish, and we exchanged greetings. I told him I was going to go to the small beach by the hotel to swim after yoga if he wanted to join me. I had a good yoga practice despite all the crazy things that were happening around me. I was becoming better at finding my center despite the chaos.

After yoga I changed into my bathing suit and headed to the small lagoon beach by the hotel. I loved swimming at sunset and had a sense of inner peace that was hard to find in the heat of the day. Manish was sitting on the rocks of the lagoon fishing when I came down. He was looking especially hot against the rocks, wearing a tight red shirt. He seemed to really like red—since my first encounter with him, I had only seen him in red shirts. I swam out deep beyond the rock, and he watched me the entire time. I also couldn't help but watch him. I had a crush on Manish.

After my swim, I saw Manish behind the bar. I sat down, and Manish poured me a glass of Indian wine. Saturday night was the night the club was supposed to come alive with a big party. I thought it was going to be an interesting night, and I would finally learn more about Manish. However, a week before there had been a bombing at the German Bakery in a city called Pune. Manish told me the police had ordered the closing of all nightclubs and public gatherings until further notice. I was surprised to hear that, because Rohit and I had just been to a nightclub a few nights ago. As I sat at the bar and had my glass of wine, a group of two guys and three girls came and sat at the bar also. One of the guys told me they had come from the south of India to come to this night club, but now the night club was not open so they were going to have dinner at a nearby beach and go to a bar there. He said they had a van and asked me if I wanted to join them. We talked a bit more. They were all computer programmers and lived in Bangalore, which is the Silicon Valley of India. They were a friendly group and the fact that there were three girls in the group made me feel safe. I asked Manish if he knew anything about this group and he said no. I said I was going to go out to dinner with them and have a drink. His mood changed, and I could tell he was not so happy about me going out with this group. I said, "Don't worry, I am a big girl and can take care of myself." He told me to be safe and to call him later.

We all squeezed in to their van and headed out to have dinner. We sat right on the beach with our feet in the sand and ordered up a feast. I talked mostly to the guy who had invited me along. His brother lived in West Virginia, and he wanted

Chapter 21: INDIA: ESCAPING GOA

to know all about America; he said he planned to go there in the next few years to visit. I had spent some time white-water rafting in West Virginia, and I shared the stories I had from that area. Our conversation was easy, and we both were happy to talk about America.

I couldn't help but notice these two sketchy looking guys at the table next to us. They had been staring at me the entire time I had been sitting there. In India, lots of people stare, but these guys were trying to act like they weren't staring at me, which was very unusual. I tried to ignore it, but it was bothering me. I also couldn't help but notice that both of these guys were wearing red shirts. I was getting really tired after dinner, and my group was getting ready to go to another bar, so I had them drop me back at my hotel. I lay in bed and tried to understand all these weird things that had been happening around me since I'd arrived in Palolem Beach just three days before.

I called my cousin Bharat in the morning and said I was ready to go back to Mumbai. He booked the earliest train on Thursday for me. It was Sunday morning, and I had four more days in 'paradise.' I sat on my balcony for a few hours and couldn't help but notice two ships that had been there all week. It was weird that these ships seemed like they were anchored around the resort. My gut was talking to me, and I decided I needed a day away from this place and all its madness. I was happy to not see Manish in the morning as I left. I went to Big Fish and had my normal breakfast. After my third glass of chai, I got up to go to the bathroom in the back of the restaurant and saw two hoodlum-type Indian guys there. They quickly looked away and tried to look busy when I made eye contact with them. I felt a sickening pain in my stomach; they were both wearing red shirts! I paid my bill and left quickly. I went for a walk along the beach. I decided I would venture to the north side of the bay, as far away from my hotel as possible. I walked on the beach and sat in the sand at the far end of the bay. It was a remote area without hotels, and the shoreline was mostly trees and natural beauty. I built a sand castle that looked like the Taj Mahal. I made friends with little crabs that buried themselves in the sand, and we played a game of hide and seek. I was fully involved in my childlike activities when I looked up and saw a

THE EVOLUTION OF A PARTY GIRL

young Indian man quickly approaching. When he got to me, I felt annoyed and tried to make it obvious I didn't want to talk to him. He was overly persistent. He kept asking if I spoke Hindi, but when I told him no, he didn't seem satisfied with my answer and asked me about five more times. He would speak in English and switch to Hindi, almost like he was testing me to make sure I really didn't speak Hindi. It was weird but fit a pattern. I had been afraid to think about it, but I was becoming sure that Manish was heavily involved in organized crime. After about ten minutes of interrogation, he finally left. I was feeling a deep sense of uneasiness growing inside of me, as he too was wearing a bright red shirt!

I walked to a restaurant on the north side of the bay and sat down to have lunch. A few minutes later, Steven, the man I had met a few days ago when I was sick at Bridge and Tunnel, came in to the restaurant and asked if I was eating alone. I said yes and he asked if he could join me. I was happy to have lunch with a foreigner. All of these crazy Indians in red shirts were starting to create a lot of stress and paranoia in my mind. I was happy to see Steven was wearing a blue shirt. We had the normal get-to-know-you conversation over lunch. He said he was a flight attendant and lived in England. I asked him if he came to India a lot, and he said this was about his 28th trip there. Wow! I asked where he travels in India, and he said mostly here to Palolem Beach. What? After only three days I was going out of my mind, and he had come here that often!

I decided he would be a good person to ask about some of the things that had been happening around me. I didn't get into all the details, but I asked him what he knew about Manish and the Endless Sun Beach Resort. He said he knew very little because he mostly stayed on the north side of the bay. As he was talking I couldn't help but notice his English accent seemed a little off, but I hadn't spent that much time in England, and maybe after so many years of traveling for work his accent had started to fade. He asked me if I had been around to any places on the street side, away from the beach, and I said no. He asked me if I wanted to go with him; he was going to check his email and maybe do a little shopping. I wasn't sure about anyone or anything anymore, and even this simple request made me think

217

Chapter 21: INDIA: ESCAPING GOA

twice. Was I becoming paranoid? Just then I looked out the restaurant to the beach and was surprised to see four men in red shirts waiting on the beach, smoking cigarettes and drinking beer—and watching me. Without a second thought, I said yes. I was happy to be with someone.

When we left the restaurant, the men followed us, but I didn't say anything to Steven. He said he knew a shortcut, and we quickly turned down a small path that led to a luxury hotel. The walkway led us right to the reception desk and he asked to see their nicest room. They walked us on a little path to a beautiful bungalow that was decorated with teak furniture. The bed was amazing with a huge canopy and mosquito net. It cost 3000 rupees a night. Steven said thanks, but not tonight, and we walked back through the hotel to the street side. His shortcut worked; I was happy to see we were no longer being followed. Had he seen those guys following us?

The street was a typical Indian street, but less crowded than most. We went to an Internet shop, and I sent a quick email to my parents telling them I was fine and that I loved them. I also sent an email to Rohit. I told him a little about the craziness since he'd left but tried to downplay it. I told him I wished he was there with me. Then I sent an email to Cassie and told her everything: my hookup with Manish, some of the weirdness happening around me, and about being followed everywhere by slimy Indian guys dressed in red shirts. We walked around the town a little and went in a few shops, but I wasn't really in the mood for shopping. Then he suggested we get a chai. We walked a few blocks to a bar right on the street and sat at a front table next to the road. After a few minutes, a fancy 'crotch rocket' motorcycle pulled up in front of the bar. It was Ace, my rummy partner from the hotel and another guy from my hotel. They were carrying a large brown bag. They went into a private room in the back of the bar with the bartender; after a few minutes, Ace and the other guy walked back out. He stopped when he saw me and greeted me. He seemed very surprised and nervous to see me. He glared at Steven who pleasantly greeted him. Within ten minutes, about ten guys in red shirts walked into the bar and stared at us. Steven said, "Let's go," and we left quickly.

He invited me to his hotel, and we sat in his room and talked for about an hour about our families and life back in our hometowns. I finally said something to him about the guys in red shirts who had been following me for a day and half now. I suggested we sit on the porch, and when I opened the door to his front porch, I saw three guys in red shirts standing in front of his beach shack. I went back in his room, shut the door, and started to cry. For the first time since I had gotten to India, I was scared—really scared.

I decided being with Steven and getting him involved in this situation wasn't going to help anything. I needed to talk to Manish. I left Steven and walked on the beach back to my hotel. Five guys in red shirts followed me, along with a police officer now. In India the police are so corrupt there was no use telling him about the men following me; he was obviously in on it all. I got back to my hotel and found the tiki bar empty. Manish and the staff were nowhere to be found. I went to my room and took a nap, thinking after sleeping I would feel better and have an idea how to handle this situation. When I woke up, I got dressed to go out to dinner. Ace was at the bar, and I asked him where Manish was. He said he wasn't at the hotel today and as I was walking away, he said, "Preya, I heard you have been asking around town about Manish. That's not a good idea, and I suggest you don't ask any more questions." I said I wasn't sure what he was talking about, but if he was trying to intimidate me, it wouldn't work. Then he said, "I know you are starting to understand what is going on around here; be careful who you are making friends with."

I had made a habit of not going out in India alone at night, but I wasn't feeling safe at my resort, and a public place seemed better. I walked the beach until I found a busy restaurant. It was an upscale place with lots of tourists—perfect. I chose a table in the back looking out to the ocean. I had lost my appetite after my unpleasant conversation with Ace, who basically confirmed that I wasn't being paranoid, and I was really in a mess. I felt scared and uneasy and not sure who to talk to. I decided to call Steve from Mysore. I needed some prayers and advice and he was the perfect person for both. He answered my call right away and told me he was at the airport. He was leaving

Chapter 21: INDIA: ESCAPING GOA

India and going to Thailand for a few months; he was surprised to hear from me after so long. I summarized what was happening to me and asked him for advice. He said, "If you really feel afraid, get out of there!" I knew he was right.

I called my cousin Bharat. I didn't want to make them afraid, so I didn't tell him about all the men following me, just that I wanted to leave earlier. He said there was no earlier train tickets and the planes were really expensive. It was only a matter of a few days, and he said I should just wait it out. I asked my waiter for my bill, and he said, "You should wait here, the big boss is coming to see you." Oh, shit! The big boss! Then he said, "You know who I am talking about?" Oh yes, did I ever know. Manish was the last person I felt like talking to then. I paid my bill and left. As I walked back to the hotel, a parade of men in red shirts and now also men in blue shirts followed me!

I woke up early the next day and went to Big Fish. It was early so the restaurant should have been empty, but within a few minutes, it was filled with five guys in red shirts and five white guys in blue shirts. I grew up in the suburbs of Detroit, and while my neighborhood was hardly gang-infested, I watched the news and I knew about gang colors. I ordered my usual breakfast, and my waiter was acting afraid; it was clear what was going on. After breakfast, I went to the Internet café, followed by the men in the red and blue shirts. I Googled gangs in Goa, and the page lit up with story after story about the Indian and Russian mafias that run Goa. I learned about drug trafficking and weapons trading; I also read stories of many foreign tourist women who had turned up missing in Goa. I had to get out of there. There was an overnight bus leaving at 4:00 p.m., but a bus didn't seem safe enough. I walked out of the café, and my unwelcome shadows were all waiting for me, this time with two corrupt police officers who were likely also part of the gangs. I tried to use my phone to call my cousin, but there was no signal. I tried turning it off and on, and still it was not working. Were they jamming my phone?

I went back to my hotel, and Manish was nowhere to be seen. I hadn't seen him in days now. I went to the tiki bar and asked Ace where Manish was; he told me he was not here. I went to my 'perfect cliffside beach shack' and packed up everything, and put on my gym shoes in case I had to run. When I came down the stairs with my backpack, Manish was sitting at the bar. I asked if I could talk to him, and we walked away and sat on the couches...the same couches we had made out on! I asked him what was going on; he of course played dumb, and said, "What do you mean, Preya? I haven't seen you in days." I told him these men were following me—first the men in the red shirts and then men in red shirts and blue shirts. He said in a very coy voice, "Oh, my staff, are they bothering you? I had my staff taking care of you since I was busy and not able to be with you." I said, "Your staff? Yes, they are bothering me, and they are following me everywhere." My eyes were filled with tears; I was trying so hard not to cry but I was scared, hurt, and filled with anxiety. I said, "Manish, I can't live like this. I like you, but this life that you live, it's not for me, and never will be a lifestyle I can live with." He looked very sad. He looked down, no longer able to make eye contact with me, and said, "Preya, I like you a lot, and I had hoped that we would be able to share our future together." I understood that this was a very delicate situation—rejecting him at this moment could produce catastrophic results.

Marriage comes quickly in India, and I understood that he wanted me to be his wife. I spoke softly and gently held his hand. "I am a physical therapist from Detroit; I am here in India doing medical relief work in my village. I am not going to live in India, and I could never live this fast lifestyle that you live. You are a hot, sexy, and passionate man who could have any woman you want; please understand I am not going to be happy here in Goa, and you are not going to be happy with me being unhappy. I am begging you to tell your staff to stop following me and let us end this little romance as a positive memory for both of us." Then he said, "It's not just about my staff, they are protecting you." I told him I didn't need protection and gave him the money for the room and checked out. I kissed him on the cheek, got up, and walked away.

I went to the street and tried to get a rickshaw to take me out of there. I asked all the rickshaws on the street. I offered them thousands of rupees, and they all said no. They had orders—orders from Manish to not let me leave! It was getting late in the

Chapter 21: INDIA: ESCAPING GOA

day. I was scared, hot, carrying my heavy backpack, and still being followed. I tried to use my phone, and it still was being jammed. I had nowhere to sleep, and I was physically and emotionally drained. Why were they all still following me? I went back to my breakfast restaurant and talked to my waiter; I told him I was in trouble, and he said he knew. Then I realized he always wore a yellow shirt to show he was neutral, that he wasn't part of this gang war that was going on in Palolem Beach. I asked if I could talk to the owner. I told the owner I was in trouble and needed a place to stay that night. He told me I could stay at his family bungalow near the edge of the hotel. He told me he sleeps right next door with his family and would ensure I was safe for the night. I had no other options; he seemed like a genuine man, although at this point I was seriously questioning everything and everyone, especially my own judgments. I took the room and lay in bed trying to piece everything together. I understood that I was a pawn in a dangerous game of gang warfare. The missing piece was Steven; I needed to talk to him. He was part of all this, and I needed to make it clear to him that I would NEVER be Manish's wife. Steven was part of the Russian mafia, and he was using me also in their game.

I went to the Fox Den, the restaurant that Steven and I had had lunch at and now understood it was the Russian gang's hangout. Steven was sitting at a table with a woman. I asked if I could talk to him, alone. We sat at a corner table and all the eyes on the restaurant were on us. I saw a man with a gun standing close to Steven. I started by telling Steven that I was not there to cause any problems; I was a simple physical therapist from Detroit who was here in Palolem Beach for a week to practice yoga. There were men all around me and many had guns. I was a nervous wreck, but I had to stay cool. Steven pulled out his marijuana and stated to roll a joint. I explained to him as sincerely as I could that the reasons I was in India were to do charity work and to develop my spirituality, and I had no interest in getting involved in or creating problems for anyone. I told him the only reason I had stayed at the Endless Sun Beach Resort was to have privacy and to practice yoga, and that I had never heard of the place before I arrived here a few days ago. Then I told him that I was not and would never be Manish's girlfriend.

He lit up his joint and listened to my pleas without saying anything. Steven had a very different air about him now. Everything he did was very calculated. I begged him to stop having his men follow me, and I told him I'd checked out of Manish's hotel. Steven never admitted or denied anything I said, but at the end he told me I was a sweet girl, but I was in way over my head. He offered to help me, but I told him I didn't want any help. I just wanted him to clearly understand that I wasn't involved with Manish and to have his men stop following me. I said goodbye to Steven and I gave him hug. I joked with him and asked him if he ever checked into that penthouse we used as our shortcut, and he laughed back.

The next morning I went to breakfast and thought that things were over; I'd talked to Manish and I'd talked to Steven, and hopefully I could finally have a day of peace to relax on the beach and do yoga. Within ten minutes of sitting down, the entire restaurant was filled up with creepy men dressed in blue and red shirts; it wasn't over. I realized the only way it would be was to get the hell out of there. I needed help, but not from either side of this war. I had put it off long enough—I needed my family to help me.

My phone was still being jammed, so I went to a payphone and called my cousin Tushar. I had ten guys and two police officers sitting outside the phone booth. I told my cousin I was in trouble, and I needed to get out of Goa today. I didn't give him too many details, and he didn't ask questions. He said he would make some calls for me and to call him back in ten minutes. When I called him back, he told me to get to the nearby village of Chaudi and go to the tailor's shop. He said the tailor was Kutchi, part of our community in India, and he would ensure I was safe until he made more arrangements. I told him that none of the rickshaws would take me out of Palolem Beach. He suggested I tell them I was going shopping and pay them whatever they wanted.

I went back to my room at the bungalow and packed up my bag. I was shaking as I put my money belt on with my passport, cash, and credit cards tucked safely inside. I dressed in my sweat suit with my running shoes and sports bra...and put a pocketknife in my bra. I hadn't dressed like this in the five months I'd been in India, but I felt like I was preparing for battle. I had everything on my body that I would need to get back to the USA in case I had to drop my bag and run. I left money for my room on the bed. I didn't tell anyone, even the owner of the bungalow, that I was leaving.

I tried to hire two taxis, but they continued to refuse to drive me. As I approached the third taxi driver, I had tears in my eyes. He seemed empathetic toward me. I told him I was going shopping in Chaudi, and I wanted to go to the tailor. After a long pause, he said 1,000 rupees, and I readily said yes. The other taxi drivers had all picked up their phones, made a call, and then said no. This guy didn't make the call, thank God! I got in the cab and we started to drive; behind us was a row of motorcycles. The cab driver was nervous, and as we left the beach area, my phone rang. I almost didn't recognize it was my phone, because I hadn't heard it ring in days—my phone was working again! It was Tushar, and I told him I was on my way to the tailor. I told the cab driver to pull over, and all the motorcycles pulled over with us. I whispered to Tushar in an attempt to not scare the driver, that there were about ten motorcycles following us. It was probably only a few miles, but it seemed like the longest cab ride of my life. My driver kept looking in his rearview mirror and then looking back at me, rarely watching the road in front of him. We approached the town and all I knew was that the tailor was across from the church. The driver was getting more and more nervous and told me to get out of the cab, so I put him on the phone with Tushar. Tushar is a great talker and if anyone could convince this cab driver to help me, he could. The cab driver kept driving for a few more minutes, and then he stopped the cab and told me I had to get out. I grabbed my bag, paid him the money, and started to run.

I had my backpack on and was running down the crowded main street of Chaudi, looking for a church while being chased by ten motorcycles. I was dripping with sweat and panting when I saw a steeple. I had never been so happy to see a Catholic church in my life, and as I approached the church, I saw the tailor's shop across the street and I ran in. They were expecting me; the entire shop was filled with Kutchi men. They took my backpack and put it outside, as if to say, "If you want this, take it, but you can't have her." They took me to the back of the shop and the Kutchi men crowded in, creating a human shield. Outside, the motorcycles lined up in a row. It was a tense few minutes. The phone at the shop rang, and it was Tushar. I was so happy to hear his voice, I could have cried. He was straight to business, talking very quick, clear, and concise. He said the highest local politician was coming in 20 minutes to take me to the airport. I told him all the motorcycles were waiting outside for me. He said this politician had a lot of power and they would leave me alone once they saw him. He said his brother Bharat had booked me on the next flight to Mumbai, leaving in a few hours.

It was a long, tense 20 minutes to say the least. My heart was pumping out of my chest, and the owner of the tailor shop was scolding me about being a woman traveling in India alone. It was the last thing I wanted to hear, but I sat and listened to him go on with his sexist lecture. Then I saw a black sedan pull up. A tall and overweight Indian man dressed in professional clothes got out of the car and came into the shop. He introduced himself to me and said he was going to take me to the airport. He loaded my bag in the trunk of his sedan and then came back and we walked out together. I tried not to look, but there were all the same guys who had been following me for the last three days on their motorcycles staring at me.

We drove off and all the motorcycles followed us. We were driving away from the beach through small villages and rice fields. The roads were mostly empty except for the parade of motorcycles following us. Then I saw them one by one answer their phones and pull to the side of the road. Slowly, there were fewer and fewer motorcycles until finally there was only one red shirt, one blue shirt, and one small white car. As I looked more carefully, I recognized the car; it was Manish. Within fifteen more minutes, all the motorcycles were gone. I wanted to scream with joy and cry with sorrow. The politician looked in the mirror at me and said, "Are they gone?" I said, "Yes, the motorcycles are all gone, but there is still one car." He said, "If the motorcycles are gone, then you are safe." Within a few more miles, Manish also pulled aside—my first and last fling with an Indian mobster.

Chapter 22
INDIA, SAFE AND SOUND IN MUMBAI

I felt tears streaming down my face, and I realized I had passed a big test of letting go of the party girl and was ready to move forward to a more spiritual chapter of my life...

***

It took me days to stabilize once I got to Mumbai. I spent the first two days in posttraumatic shock. I still felt like I was being followed; I hid down low and looked out the window every hour to see if the men in red or blue shirts had found me. My cousin Tushar, who had arranged my escape, was the only one I told the entire story to. I left out the most traumatic part—that I actually really liked Manish. I felt ashamed for unknowingly getting involved with a gangster when I was supposed to be focusing on my spiritual growth.

My mind was so unsettled during this time. I tried to piece things together, but my mind was already starting to block out the details. I went to my journal and started to write. This was one of the first times I seriously considered writing this book. I felt healed after writing and understood that sharing my story authentically was part of my purpose.

I was thankful that my parents were still in India to help me through that dark chapter. I spared them the scariest details of the story, but they understood the gist of the trauma I had just been through. Being around my parents helped me to recover. I spent a day on the computer Googling Manish and the Endless Sun Beach Resort and trying to find out as much as I could about the situation. I shared my feelings honestly with my mom

Chapter 22: INDIA, SAFE AND SOUND IN MUMBAI

about the 'crush' I had on Manish. I was sad for him, and I was scared for him. I still had so many questions in my head and he was the only one who could give me the honest answers. My mom empathized with my feelings and understood why I wanted to talk to him. I knew it was totally crazy to call him after I'd almost lost my life because of him. What confused me even more were the feelings of compassion I had for him, not the anger I would have felt in the past. My mom listened to me without lecturing or unleashing her anxiety. She gracefully made me realize that Manish chose to live that lifestyle, and that if he wanted to leave the gangster life, he would have acted differently during that situation. She reminded me that the life he lives now would make me profoundly unhappy.

After that emotional conversation with my mom, I took a big step forward in my healing process. I had nightmares for many nights about those few days in Goa. My dad pleaded with me to leave India and come back to the USA with them, and for a day I seriously considered going back. But I had two big adventures ahead of me, and I would not get derailed from finding my life's purpose. We all cried as I said goodbye to my parents at the airport.

I had been afraid to leave the house since narrowly escaping from Goa, and the next day my cousin Bharat decided it was time for me to start venturing back out. He convinced me to go with him and his family to downtown Mumbai to an area called Whirly Sea Face to watch the sunset. It was my first time out in public in several days. I sat with my cousins on the concrete ledge overlooking the ocean and felt peace for the first time in more than a week. My heart rate was slow, my mind was clear, and I had a deep sense of love and gratitude for my family in India for saving my life. I started to understand why families protected Indian women. Goa changed my entire perspective, and I was actually thankful for my family's watchful eye. I felt the dark cloud I had been living in since arriving at Palolem Beach lift off of me. I forgave myself for getting in the entire mess. I began to feel compassion toward the men who had followed me; they were just as lost in their lives as I was in mine. A strong shift in the perception of my Goa experience occurred during that sunset. In that peaceful moment of pure awareness,

I understood the Goa situation from a place of pure gratitude and love. I felt tears streaming down my face, and I realized I had passed a big test of letting go of the party girl and was ready to move forward to a more spiritual chapter of my life.

Chapter 23
INDIA: SIVANANDA YOGA TEACHER TRAINING

March 10th was the day that changed my life; I had my spiritual awakening. From that day forward my relationship to life was never the same...

***

I met up with the other participants for the one-month yoga teacher-training course in the lobby of Hotel Shanti in Delhi. We sat anxiously in silence awaiting the arrival of the charter bus that would take us to the ashram. At 10:00 a.m. a man dressed fully in orange came down to the lobby; he was a middle-aged white man with grey hair. It was hard for me to explain, but he was radiant. It was like there was a spotlight on him, and he was glowing with life. His name was Swami Atmanramananda, and he started to organize our departure. It was the first time I had ever talked to a real swami. All the other participants were also foreigners; most of them were from Europe. We loaded into two busses and set off on the four-hour journey to Vrindavan. I would be living in an ashram built over 500 years ago and studying to become a yoga teacher.

The journey was long, the bus was hot, and the roads were so narrow and crowded the bus could barely fit through the streets. Vrindavan was one of the most ancient cities in India, and the roads were not meant for cars, let alone a full-size bus. The bus went as far into the city as it was able to, and then we had to get off and walk through the streets. We created a total spectacle:

Chapter 23: INDIA: SIVANANDA YOGA TEACHER TRAINING

over 100 tourists walking to the ashram, ironically overloaded with stuff. Many of the others had just arrived in India that day and were shocked by what they were seeing. I was at the point that nothing shocked me anymore, but Vrindavan was really dirty, and the crowded streets had open sewers on both sides, with wild pigs and rats eating from them!

The ashram was a gated compound. Upon arrival we sat in the main hall and waited for our room assignments. I had registered to stay in the women's dormitory; it was the cheapest accommodation, but it still cost about $3000 for the one-month training, which was a lot of money for anything in India.

The women's dorm was located just off the main hall; it was a huge room with four rows of single beds. Many women were scurrying for the 'best' bed when I first arrived, but it made little difference to me at this point, and I ended up with a bed in the middle of the room. The girl who had the bed at the foot of mine was eager to talk to me. She was raised in South Africa but lived with her boyfriend in London. She already had a long list of complaints about the Sivananda organization, the ashram, and India in general. I let her vent but immediately decided this was not a woman I wanted to spend time with. We had a few hours to get settled, and then our first yoga asana class was at 4:00 p.m.

I walked around and explored a little. The ashram was beautiful. I had done very little research before registering or arriving for this course. Like most of my travels so far, they were spur of the moment, fly by the seat of my pants, or half-ass planned (as my dad like to remind me). From the moment I arrived, I knew this was going to be amazing. The course had people from all over the world and was being taught in four languages. Everywhere I walked there were conversations going on in different languages, and the ashram was filled with excitement. I was in the English group, and our yoga class was on the roof. I found out the ashram used to be the summer home for one of the royal families of India. A palace—what girl hasn't dreamed of living in a royal estate? And now I was living in a palace and doing yoga; I was in heaven!

There are seven spiritual rivers in India that are blessed with divine nectar. The Ganges is the most famous. The ashram was situated right on the Yamuna River which is also on the list. I rolled out my yoga mat at the corner of the fourth floor roof and had a great view of it all. Finally, I was feeling joy flowing inside my veins again. It was my first formal Sivananda yoga class. I felt a little awkward because most of the people in my class had been practicing at Sivananda centers in Europe for years and now were taking the teacher-training program. I, on the other hand, had never taken a Sivananda class. I had been practicing yoga for about five years, but mostly Ashtanga Vinyasa style.

The class was simple—too simple. We spent most of the class on breathing exercises, eye exercises, and simple range of motion exercises. I really liked the breathing exercises; it took me back to my pranayama classes with Sheshadri. I was surprised that with such simple exercises I could still feel the energy flowing in my body, further proof that yoga always gives me exactly what I need. I had been practicing Ashtanga and Kundalini yoga, two of the most aggressive physical yoga practices and that first class left me mistakenly thinking that this month was going to be 'easy.'

That evening we had our first ritual, an initiation into the Sivananda yoga teacher-training course. It was one of the first proper rituals that I'd been an active participant in. As part of the ritual I had to get on my knees and bow to the pictures of the gurus. I had never bowed on my knees before anyone before. I wasn't even sure who I was bowing to, but I let go of the protest my self-pride was putting forth and performed an insincere bow. I was then given a manual, a uniform, and a red dot on my forehead between my eyebrows.

"Om Namah Shivaya, it's 5:30!" I felt startled and confused as the morning bell was rung and the swamis took me out of my deep sleep. *"Om Namah Shivaya, it's 5:30!"* What does that mean? Where am I? I sprung out of bed, rushing to get to the bathroom that twenty women had to share. I sat for my first morning meditation—it was the longest 30 minutes of my life. Every cell in my body wanted to climb back into bed and sleep, but my stubbornness made me stay and sit...and sit...and sit. I will never forget how painful those first few days of meditation were. Every minute felt like an hour, every inch of my skin was itching, and every muscle in my body was hurting. After medi-

tation we went right into a kirtan; ahh, I was so happy to move. Six swamis sat on stage and played instruments and led us, and we sat on the floor and sang with them. My mind wandered and I envisioned being back at Steve's house. After kirtan, the swamis read some teachings from Swami Sivananda, and then they gave us our schedule for the day. Oh my God...day one of yoga teacher training!

The first few days I felt like hell. I was beyond tired, beyond sore, and felt fed up with the minute-by-minute militant schedule. After the wake up at 5:30 a.m., we had an hour and a half of morning meditation and chanting. After a cup of masala chai, we had our yoga asana class for another hour and a half. At 10:00 a.m. we FINALLY got to eat! We sat on the floor and ate a very basic Indian vegetarian yogic meal with our hands. At 10:45 a.m., I had karma yoga. Karma yoga is doing good deeds in your life to neutralize the bad karma you have developed. My karma yoga was cleaning the bathroom of the women's dorm.

After I cleaned the bathroom, we had a noon lecture to study the Bhagavad Gita (the main Hindu spiritual text), chai break at 1:00 p.m., and main lecture from 2:00 to 3:30 p.m. At 4:00 p.m. we had our second yoga asana class until 5:30 p.m. Dinner was at 6:00 p.m., followed by meditation and chanting from 8:00 to 9:30 p.m. We had a little time to study and do our homework and laundry (in a bucket) before lights out at 10:00 p.m.

Over time, my body became stronger, my mind calmed its protest, and I started getting into a rhythm. The dorm added to the chaos of it all, but it was fun to live with twenty women from all over the world. Five days into the course, I had already made a good friend. Her name was Meliza, and she was from Guadeloupe, a French island in the Caribbean. Meli and I had a lot in common—she was thirty-three and single, she collected crystals, and she was a reiki master. Meli had beautiful dark brown hair, a smile that lit up the room, and was an eternal optimist. We talked and shared a lot about our lives and our common interests. Having someone to share this experience with brought a sense of fun to everything we did together. It was Meli's first time in India, so just as Katharina had done for me, I showed her the ropes on how to dress, how to bargain, and how to manage as a single woman in India. Meli slept in the bed next to me in the dorm. We saw each other a lot on breaks, but she was in the French-speaking group and I was in the English-speaking group during our classes.

Meditation was something I had already wrestled with several times in my life, first at the Buddhist monastery in California and again at a six-week mindful meditation class I took through my hospital. This was for sure my most dramatic experience with meditation. We did it twice a day, sitting on the hard marble floor, being swarmed by mosquitos, during the wee hours of the morning and late into the evening. We were using the sound "OM" as our mantra. As I sat with my eyes closed and repeated "OM," it usually only took a minute for my mind to start to go crazy! Most of my 'meditation' time was spent thinking about men and my many failed relationships. From time to time my mind would get tired over obsessing about men and would change gears to analyze how I was being perceived by everyone: the other yoga students, the swamis, my family in India, my family in America, the people at Jaya Rehab, and even the man I was buying my fruit from!

After about a week of this nonsense, I had my first moment of clarity. During meditation, I felt my mind go still and the focus between my eyebrows became very concentrated, deep, and strong. It only lasted a few moments, but it was beautiful, pure silence. After that brief experience of silence, I had gained some wisdom. It is hard to put into words, but this wisdom came from a much deeper place than understanding how to solve a math problem or a superficial understanding of my life. It was an experience of insight into my overall relationship with the world. With this wisdom, it was undeniable how egotistical, self-critical, and selfish my current thoughts and actions were. My entire relationship with society and with the universe was based on self-serving ideas with a strong flavor of negativity. This was my first experience with the truth, and it was very difficult to accept.

I decided that month I wanted to spend my time alone doing deep work on myself. I carried on some small talk, but I could only repeat and hear the same stories so many times. Aside from my time with Meli, I minimized my conversations.

Chapter 23: INDIA: SIVANANDA YOGA TEACHER TRAINING

About a week into my teacher training, my mom and I finally talked on the phone. After our beautiful reconnection in India, we were back to our same old bickering. We had a fight—not a tear-up, knock-down fight, just another exchange of the same lectures that we have been giving each other for the last ten years. She unloaded her anxiety on me about how I would get raped and robbed or die while traveling, and I just couldn't hear it. I was physically and mentally exhausted trying to keep up with this course and I couldn't deal with trying to reassure her. I told her that her negativity made it difficult to talk to her. Then I went on a rant! I explained that the constant stream of unsolicited advice she gave had pushed me away from her and made me not want to share the events of my life with her. I hung up the phone feeling frustrated with her and myself. I was at my wits' end with our relationship. Before coming to India, I had barely talked to my mom for a year. I had tried to speak to her more positively, but many times I found myself giving her unsolicited advice too. I had tried so many ways to make her understand that this bickering was destroying our relationship.

As I sat on the banks of the Yamuna River lamenting my relationship with my mom, I had another moment of clarity. Everything I had tried so far to solve the issues with our relationship had failed. I had to bring God into my relationship with my mom. This whole concept of God still seemed a little scary to me since I had grown up with Western religions that still use the concept of God to instill fear. Now I understood God to be the highest form of love—a beautiful, powerful force that can solve anything. I still didn't completely understand the message I had received, but it was clear to me that the way to solve this long frustrating fight was to bring God into our relationship.

March 10th was the day that changed my life; I had my spiritual awakening. It was the most powerful, scariest, and most beautiful experience of my life. From that day forward, my relationship to life was never the same. We had completed our first week of the yoga teacher-training course. It was a week of profound internal cleansing in my mind and body, and this was an intensive final purification before God revealed itself to me.

THE EVOLUTION OF A PARTY GIRL

A priest had come from Karnataka, South India, near Mysore. He was from a long line of Brahman priests, and his family was one of the lineages responsible for passing down the Rig Veda. The Vedas are the holiest texts in all of India and the foundation of the teachings in Hinduism. There are four 'books' in the Vedas, and the Rig Veda is the first and most important. The teachings were only compiled into written books in the last 1,000 years. Before that, they were passed down in secret through an oral tradition in the highest Brahman families.

The main lecture hall was set up for the puja, a traditional Vedic religious ceremony, similar to the puja I attended at Sheshadri's yoga shala. The Brahman priest was a clean-cut, middle-aged Indian man. He was wearing no shirt and was draped in a yellowish-orange robe. He had three white lines going across his forehead and three lines on each of his arms. The puja was to honor Lord Ganesha. There was a large black stone statue of Ganesha in the center of the hall next to the priest. The priest explained that he was going to chant in Sanskrit, the ancient Indian language that he called "the language of the Gods." The verses he was going to chant were thousands of years old. He would accompany his chanting with *mudras* (hand signals) to invite divine energy into our space. Once the energy was present he would direct the energy into the statue of Ganesha.

I arrived at the puja late, so I sat near the back of the hall. Once the chanting started, I felt a dramatic shift in the room. The air became still and everyone in the room became silent. It wasn't just that no one was talking—I could feel everyone's *mental* silence. The chanting went on for about 30 minutes, and I was sitting motionless in meditation. Then the priest invited the swamis and students one at a time to come up and make an offering by pouring milk over the statue of Ganesha.

I debated for a long time if I should go up and participate in the ritual, but finally my curiosity took over and I lined up in the queue to walk up to the altar. I put my shawl over my head, like I saw the women in my family do. As I got closer, I felt a powerful energy filling my body; it was a mix of anxiety and pure excitement but stronger than anything I had ever experienced. I had my Ganesha silver coin in my pocket, and I was

Chapter 23: INDIA: SIVANANDA YOGA TEACHER TRAINING

going to also pour milk over my coin. These feelings continued to get stronger the closer I got to the statue. The air around the altar was different than anything I had known; it seemed like I was walking through a force field, and inside it a thick stillness consumed me. As I poured milk on Ganesha, I felt like a train was traveling inside of me—the amount of energy in my body was incredible. I heard a loud sound in my mind. I was having difficulty pouring the milk, and my entire body was shaking. I wanted to scream louder than I had ever screamed and to dance around like a crazed lunatic. Just as I finished pouring the milk on my coin, everything went silent.

I was no longer in my body. I could see myself walking back to my seat. I still felt connected to that body walking in the hall, but it was only a tiny part of me. I was an infinite web of energy that was in everything and part of everyone. The world looked gold and shimmery, and the feeling of silence and complete joy was far beyond even the best orgasm of my life. In some ways it felt like it lasted forever and in others it passed in the blink of an eye. I was completely absorbed into my surroundings and had the experience of jubilation. I had achieved a state of complete Samadhi. Then something shifted in my mind and reminded me that I was still Preya—I was not the perfectly beautiful field of gold shimmering light. As soon as that awareness of my identity came back, fear flooded my body; I wanted out of this trance state, I wanted to feel 'normal' again. I begged to just be Preya. I wanted to have my life back and to see my family and friends. After a few moments of experiencing the totality of the universe, it transitioned into total fear and surrender, and then ended. I squeezed back into my body just as quickly as I had come out of it.

When I came back to my body, I was sitting back in the lecture hall, singing my heart out with everyone else. I was hot and sweaty and shaking. For the first time ever, I'd felt the awesomeness of God, and it was coming from inside of me! I understood the interconnectedness of the universe and now knew the true purpose of being human. In Samadhi, I was alive and completely detached from my worldly existence. After I came out of that experience of unity, I was overwhelmed with sadness.

My perspective on everything about my life was rocked to the core. I still felt like Preya, but everything was lighter, more insignificant, and I experienced that sense of detachment that Steve had taught me in Mysore.

The days continued to pass on my strict schedule. Another week had gone by, and I still felt like I was floating and disconnected from the human plane. All this drama, all this bickering, all this trying to be someone—it felt like a total waste of my life! I looked at my calendar and realized that the next day was St. Patrick's Day. For a moment I tried to visualize what I would be doing if I were back home. I saw myself drinking green beer at a local pub while laughing and dancing to the typical St. Patrick's Day sing-a-longs. I felt nauseated and appalled at the idea of that life. I thought about the many nights of my life I could barely remember, the money I had wasted at clubs, pubs, and parties, and the health problems I had created in my body trying to maintain that toxic lifestyle. It all seemed like a cosmic joke. Now, after experiencing the totality of the universe and the absolute beauty and peace that is possible, I could barely wrap my head around how I could have been so enamored by that lifestyle for so many years! Above all this, I felt grateful to be at an ashram in India finding God and myself.

It had only been a few weeks but everything in my mind was feeling turned upside down. After my experience in the puja, and this intense yogic lifestyle, I developed respect for the swamis who were guiding us in the path of yoga. In one moment, my entire understanding of the universe had changed. However, I feared the return of my old demons. I needed to talk to someone.

That night I talked to Swami Atman, my teacher for yoga asana and the class on the Bhagavad Gita. He was the one I connected with the most. I told him about my difficult relationship with my mom. I was considering telling him what happened to me in the puja, but it seemed too fresh and personal at that point to share. I thought there was no way anyone could understand; I actually still didn't understand it myself. I told him about Goa and how I had come close to being kidnapped and killed. He instructed me to really think about what had happened in Goa. He told me that situation had not happened by

Chapter 23: INDIA: SIVANANDA YOGA TEACHER TRAINING

chance, and I must fully learn the lesson I was supposed to learn there to avoid being in the same situation again. He told me that experience in Goa was a long karmic lesson that I had to live through. He was saying what I had already begun to understand on my own.

Then he talked to me about my relationship with my mom. He told me I had to be the one to be yogic and peaceful in the relationship, regardless of how confrontational my parents were toward me. He said my mom was never going to change and the only thing I had control over was changing myself. He told me to change the thoughts I was projecting in the world about my mom and my relationship with her. If my thoughts toward my mom were compassionate and loving, my entire relationship with her would change quickly. He also said to continue to minimize contact with my parents until I was in a balanced mindset. Then he ended by saying that if I continued to do yoga, especially yoga in my relationship with my parents, things would evolve. His final words were, "Preya, this is definitely something you can handle. You have overly attached parents. This is not a major obstacle, and you have the power to fix this." Somehow being yogic, compassionate, and peaceful with my parents still seemed almost impossible...he had never met them!

My marathon schedule at the ashram continued with waking before dawn, and eating only two basic meals a day. It was exhausting, and then everyone started getting sick. Not just a cold, but full-blown diarrhea. On the third day of cleaning the bathroom I had an emotional breakdown. The bathroom was disgusting and the drain became clogged. There was diarrhea on the floor. They had taught me to wash the floor by flooding it with soapy water and then squeegeeing it dry. But the drain was clogged, so after I flooded the floor, I was standing in a pool of diarrhea. I could deal with a lot of things after so many months in India, but this was more than I could handle.

I left the bathroom crying. I found Swami Atman and told him I couldn't clean the bathroom anymore. I explained to him how the drain had become clogged, and with so many girls sick in the dorm, it was the most disgusting thing I had ever had to do in my life. He told me to take a shower and he sent one of the local Indian servants in to unclog the drain and clean the bathroom. I took a shower and found Meliza and told her I needed to get out of the ashram for a few hours. We went shopping at Yogesh's shop, our favorite shopkeeper in Vrindavan. His shop was filled with yoga clothes and he was a playful Indian man. The retail therapy helped me to decompress from the bathroom trauma. I bought a bright orange outfit to wear on our next free day.

Later that evening Swami Atman called me over and said, "Preya, I want to tell you a story." He explained that when Mahatma Gandhi was becoming well known, people were coming from all over India to see him and talk to him. Gandhi lived in a small, simple ashram that couldn't handle the massive amounts of people who were coming. They didn't have indoor plumbing, and everyone, including Gandhi, used outdoor portable style toilets. Gandhi implemented a rule. Anyone who wanted to meet with him had to live at the ashram for one week and clean the toilets every day; at the end of the week he would meet with them. Most people left the ashram after the first day and never met with him. Swami Atman said the spiritual path is also like this—after a month of hard work and purifying, you may get a few moments to meet with God. That put it back in perspective; I'd had the opportunity to meet God and for that I had to prove myself worthy. The next day I was back to cleaning the bathroom with a sense of gratitude for the lessons I was being taught.

One of the things I looked forward to the most was Meliza and I trading reiki and craniosacral treatments. I worked mostly on her hips and back, and she worked mostly on my neck and my heart. She told me my heart was blocked and had been for several years. Traveling alone around India was a double-edged sword; in some ways it made me more guarded and in other ways it made me more trusting and openhearted. During one reiki treatment, I felt an intense physical pain in my chest along with emotional sadness. After the sensations subsided, I felt a wave of joy. She'd helped me unblock my heart chakra, but there still were layers to peel away before I would truly be capable of unconditional love.

Chapter 23: INDIA: SIVANANDA YOGA TEACHER TRAINING

I sat and talked to Swami Atman again that night right after my reiki treatment. I was a chatterbox—my heart was open, but I was like a dam that had just opened. I talked continuously and am sure most of it was nonsensical. After a few moments, he said, "Preya, you need to calm down. Most of your issues in life are because you are not calm and patient." Even though I justified my excitement because of just finishing an amazing reiki treatment, I knew he was right. I am a person who gets bored quickly, and I don't do tasks thoroughly because I just want to move on to the next thing. There has been a thread of impatience and boredom in all aspects of my life. To stay home alone for one night and do nothing was a rare event for the old Preya. Swami Atman told me that meditation would help me to live life from a stable foundation rather than being here, there, and everywhere.

We talked about my mantra, which I was supposed to be choosing that week. I explained to him that I had chosen the mantra I liked, but after a few minutes of meditation, my mind would start repeating a different mantra. He explained to me that these mantras are thousands of years old, and that I had probably used this other mantra in a past life, so my mind keeps going back to it. He said that I should use the mantra my mind is choosing during meditation. He says sometimes we choose a mantra, and sometimes it chooses us. I asked him if he would be the swami initiating me. He said, "God chooses these things, not me."

It had been another strenuous week, and I awoke excited for our day off. I needed to come up for air. I had arranged with Yogesh, our local shop owner, for two cars. We were going to the Taj Mahal. Most people are lucky to see the Taj Mahal once in their life, and I was getting to see it twice in a matter of two months! Before we could leave, we still had a morning meditation and chanting followed by a quick lecture. Asana class was optional that day, and I was happily opting out. I could barely sit through my meditation. My mind roamed the entire thirty minutes, never once actually going into a place of 'meditation.'

I ran out of the main hall to be the first one in the shower. I dressed in the brand-new bright orange half sari I had bought from Yogesh's shop. I had never worn a sari, and had made an agreement with myself to never wear one, as I saw it as the outward expression of the repression of women. I had seen the ladies in my family wrap themselves up in saris since I was little, and I'd loved to watch them put them on, but I had no interest in wearing one myself. Today, I was experimenting with a half sari. I tucked the corner in to my back right hip and draped the fabric around my body and threw it across my left shoulder. Once I put my makeup on and looked in the mirror, I was stunned—I felt beautiful and, wow, I looked more Indian than I had ever seen myself look.

I went back to the main meditation hall and waited in line to get my brown bag lunch to take with me. I gathered Meliza, who was dressed in bright blue, and her friends from the French group, and we walked to Yogesh's shop to meet up with our cars. When Meliza first contemplated coming to India, she said she had a vision of herself in a bright blue outfit standing in front of the Taj Mahal. She was filled with pure excitement as we got into our SUV. The roads were clear early in the morning, and we were enthusiastic to be out of the ashram; driving in a car seemed like such a luxury. The driver took us as close as he could, then he dropped us off at the security barricades. We bought our tickets, went through security, and began the long walk to the Taj.

As soon as we turned the corner and passed through the gate, it happened again—the Taj Mahal took my breath away. It was later in the day and there were lots of people everywhere, but its beauty overshadowed all of these details. Meli and I took lots of pictures, smiled, and giggled a lot that day. I already knew the ropes since I had recently visited with my family, so I served as the tour guide for the other yogis who came from our ashram. Inside the Taj Mahal, I again experienced the power of divine grace. I was filled with that familiar feeling of God while I sat quietly in the hustle and bustle of the crowds. Initially, I felt a heavy sadness, and then as it passed, my mind felt covered with a heavy blanket. Finally, out of that silent space, my heart started to swell with love. I again was lighthearted and airy on the drive back to the ashram.

The next morning, waking up was difficult. After just a few hours away, it was tough to get back into the swing of ashram

Chapter 23: INDIA: SIVANANDA YOGA TEACHER TRAINING

life. I struggled through asana class and my meditations. It took a day or two of the hardcore schedule until I was focused again. The life of a yogi is the most disciplined experience of my life so far. My month training was winding down, and I knew after I left I would miss how strong my body was feeling. But for now, I couldn't wait for this grueling month to end.

I spent the few days before my initiation really trying to understand what was going on with this mantra 'choosing me.' Is this concept of reincarnation really possible? Had I already had many lives on earth repeating this other mantra? During my meditation I tried to grasp this concept and had many questions, the biggest one being how could I not remember any of my previous lives? As I started to analyze this, I remembered that throughout my life I'd had many 'visions' of an ancient brick wall situated next to a river. It had come up in dreams, in a state of hypnosis, and I had seen it during meditation. As I tried to wrap my head around the concept of reincarnation, the wall came to me again. It was a strong image in my subconscious, however clearly not from my childhood. I concluded that this ancient wall vision must be some form of past life memory.

The spiritual path does take trust; it has taken me opening my mind to things beyond what my five senses are able to perceive. I've had to trust Vishnudevananda, the yogi that started the Sivananda organization, and many other yoga masters, who have dedicated their lives in search of God and had experienced these sacred truths. It was only after I opened my mind and let go of my dangerously over-analytical approach to understanding life that I was truly able to experience my own inner wisdom. Once I was open to accepting that higher states of existence were possible, I had my own powerful experience of the 'oneness' that exists in this universe. I decided that I must honor these many past lives I spent in India by being initiated into the mantra that chose me.

Our last week at the ashram was spent completing a Bhagavata Saptaham, which is a seven-day spiritual teaching with live music. After dinner, the owner of the ashram performed the reading of the spiritual scriptures in Sanskrit, with a small Indian band playing music. It lasted about three hours each night and it was beautiful. The nightly ritual began with a procession that was led by the swami carrying the sacred golden book that he teaches from. The purpose of this seven-day ritual was to clear our energetic bodies to prepare us to take initiation. I was happy to have a break from our evening meditation, although listening to his chanting put me into a meditative state.

The morning of initiation I woke up excited for many reasons. I had considered taking initiation many times before in my life, but something always held me back. Now, I knew I was finally ready. Initiation represents taking birth in the spiritual world, and while I don't think I really understood the totality of what that meant, I was thirsty for anything that would bring me closer to God.

I awoke at 4:30 a.m., before the wake-up bell, and went to take a shower. I knew from my previous experiences of Indian rituals that taking a shower and putting on clean clothes was the first step to preparing myself. I sat up in bed journaling, waiting for meditation to start. My meditations continued to be all over the place. Some days the thirty minutes felt like it was over in five, but most days it seemed like it lasted two hours. I spent many of my meditations still obsessing about men and my failed attempts at love. The day of initiation was yet another difficult meditation. My right hip and my left knee were painful, and I spent most of the time trying to overcome the pains in my body. Finally, the end of our morning meditation and chanting had come, and I had a deep sense of excitement as though this initiation was something I had been waiting for my entire life.

They had chosen our initiation day carefully, and it was supposed to be the most auspicious day of the month according to Vedic astrology. I quickly dressed in an all-white outfit I had bought the day before. I prepared my offerings on a platter. I offered lots of mangos, because I knew it was Swami Atman's favorite fruit, and I was hoping he was the swami who would initiate me. I also put 500 rupees ($10) as a symbolic monetary offering in a small envelope nestled between the roses and jasmines. We were divided into groups based on the mantra we chose. There was no specific order in which the four swamis were initiating the different mantra groups. When it came time for the group of us yogis that had chosen the Ganesha Mantra, Swami Atman came up and said to follow him. There

Chapter 23: INDIA: SIVANANDA YOGA TEACHER TRAINING

were twelve of us taking initiation at the same time, and just as I was about to sit down in the back of the group, he called my name and said, "I want you to sit right here in front of me." The ritual was short. There was a small fire, we chanted, and then he did a short teaching. During the chanting I felt that train sensation again, but it wasn't as powerful as the first time and I didn't feel the anxiety I felt that day. I felt a huge surge about to explode inside of me. It lasted only a few moments and stopped as soon as I opened my eyes and Swami Atman started to speak. He told us we had just been initiated into the Shakaracharya lineage. He also explained that the mantra had now been passed as a divine spark inside of us, but we had to feed that spark. He explained that it was like a fire had been started, but I needed to put wood on it daily by meditating. He explained that the Ganesha Mantra represents supporting the positive forces in the universe and removing all the obstacles to the positive aspects of reality. He said this mantra would give us strength and fortitude, and that it was the bestower of success.

After the initiation ceremony I sat alone in the temple and began to meditate. It was amazing. There were no distracted thoughts, no obsessing, just my mantra for a few minutes and then a deep, pure silence that lasted for a long time. I sat in meditation for about an hour without once feeling my hip or knee pain, obsessing about men, or dreaming about food. I couldn't believe how quickly my meditation had completely changed. When I left the temple, I saw one of our new swamis. She had been assisting the entire month, carrying the title of a Bramacharya (a celibate). After the swamis finished initiating all of us with our mantras, they performed an initiation on her to make her a full swami, which translates as a priest or "knower of the ultimate truth." She was beaming when she walked out of the ritual. I was shocked when she took her final vows and become a swami. I feel a deep respect for the disciplined lives these swamis live, but I couldn't help but feel sadness that she had left her worldly life.

The final step to become a certified yoga teacher was a long examination. I quickly understood that for me this month was about finally connecting with God. Experiencing the divine presence that was within me was my life's purpose. I felt a new level of inner strength, peace, and balance in my life. By experiencing my spiritual center, I had already passed 'my examination.' The divine spark had definitely been ignited within me, but the question remained how to integrate it without renouncing my entire life.

My yoga poses had become more advanced; I had mastered many poses I never knew I could. My headstand was rock solid and many days I was able to push-up into scorpion from headstand. I had also mastered my side-balancing crow. My body had become fluid and supple again, and my flexibility and endurance were better than they had been in years. I still had some aches and pains that I nursed through my poses, but overall my body was feeling strong. Something inside of me had changed since initiation and now silencing my mind was completely effortless.

That evening at satsang, Swami Atman announced he was leaving in a few hours and flying back to Germany. He shared some compelling stories of his time with Swami Vishnudevananda. He told us a story of a time when he was totally fed up after months of advanced spiritual work and traveling around India; I was familiar with that feeling. The lesson he was teaching us is that it takes months of hard work to have a five-minute taste of the divine, but without the work, spiritual progress is hard to achieve. After satsang, I waited in line to say goodbye. I gave him a thank-you note and expressed humble respect for him. I turned to walk away and the final thing he said to me was, "Preya, really work on your communication with your parents. It will help you greatly in your life."

There have been so many teachers and friends that have come into my life, taught me a great lesson, shared love and experiences, and then gone on their way. I was starting to see life as an interconnected web of people, experiences, and lessons with the bond of love holding this divine matrix together. This is the lesson that I have struggled with so much during my life, the ability to enjoy and share with someone and not attach to them being 'mine.'

Later that day I sent another mass email home. It was titled "A Spiritual Journey."

Chapter 23: INDIA: SIVANANDA YOGA TEACHER TRAINING

I started practicing yoga about five years ago. It was a difficult chapter of my life; I was not well physically, emotionally, or mentally. I was starting to question the bigger purpose of my existence and the big question of who I am. I began reading many philosophical, scientific, and spiritual books about different theories of the universe. I made friends with Cassie, my first spiritual teacher. I gave up eating meat, started practicing yoga regularly, and really worked on improving myself. This journey has led me around the world alone in search of knowledge, hoping other cultures had a better answer to the question of "who am I?" After many months of learning and struggling through difficult situations, the answer still seems to be somewhere inside of me, not in a book or a country.

I have given up most of what I considered my identity. I have given up my house, my career, my friends and family, my country, my language, my culture, my cats, and all my normal day-to-day happenings. However, even after letting go of all of these identifying factors, the strong core within me feels much the same.

During times of sickness I learn I am not my body;
During times of heartbreak and anger I learn I am not my emotions;
During this time of homelessness I learn I am not my house;
During this time of joblessness I learn I am not my career;
During this time of living without my friends or family I learn I am not them;
During this time of living abroad I learn I am not my country;
During this time of international communication I learn that I am not my language;

Who then am I?

This month at the yoga ashram has been difficult. I have completed sixty yoga classes in 30 days! My different life paths have all led me here; to be back in India has been quite an experience. To be with many other people who are physical therapists or healers from around the world has been beautiful. Most of my so-called 'new age concepts' all are firmly planted in the oldest Vedantic Sanskrit scriptures from 5,000 BC. Many of the beliefs I have gained in the last five years all are coming together in this deep study of yoga. The practice of nonviolence, the law of attraction, truth in all religions, and finding the answers deep within myself are at the heart of yoga.

Living this spiritual life has been really great! It has been detoxifying, and has allowed me much more inner peace than the fast life I have always lived. This month of cleaning my body and mind from the chemicals and destructive thoughts I have filled myself up with has allowed me to finally understand the true essence of who I am. To find my inner spirit that exists deep below my identifying factors has left me humble.

I have had the gift of old Indian spiritual teachers and European swamis to guide me on this long-awaited journey inward. Tomorrow I have my three-hour exam to be a certified yoga teacher. The real achievement of this journey was finally feeling the power of God and being in the presence of inspiring spiritual teachers. Finding my inner source has been more of an accomplishment than any certificate I can hang on my office wall.

I will be climbing MT. EVEREST in two days!

Peace and Love,

Preya

That night we had a puja to the Hindu Goddess Durga. Durga represents the part of God that is the powerful divine feminine. She is beautiful and calm but rides a fierce-looking tiger. The tiger represents the woman's ability to be a fierce protector of her children. During the puja we each had a small light in front of us and made offerings of rice. I became sad about my relationship with my mom, and my uncertainty about becoming a mother. I realized that for me to become a good mother, I first had to master the relationship with my own mother.

When I turned in my exam, I was ecstatic; I wanted to go out into the streets of Vrindavan and jump for joy. This had been the most difficult experience of my life on so many levels—physically, emotionally, and spiritually—and I had done it! And through that work, I had gained pure wisdom.

That afternoon we had our certification ceremony. Swami Sivadas, who is the same swami who initiated me into the teacher-training program and was now giving me my certification of completion. I prostrated to the pictures of Swami Vishnudevananda and Swami Sivananda, and this time it felt so natural. I was sincere in bowing down to their spiritual life

Chapter 23: INDIA: SIVANANDA YOGA TEACHER TRAINING

and the gift of yoga that they had passed on to me. We all spent our final evening in massive celebration in the temple where we offered tens of thousands of flowers to the Gods, followed up by a huge flower fight. Every inch of the temple floor was cover with five inches of flowers; we all hugged and threw flowers at each other, then we danced and we threw more flowers. It was pure ecstasy and we all glowed with health and happiness.

I spent my final hours at the ashram alone on the roof. It was a full moon. I performed a full moon ceremony in solitude that night, feeling a mix of many emotions about it being my last night in India. I released all the negativity in my life that had been holding me back. I released all the nights of drinking and partying, and I looked forward to a fresh start when I returned back to America. Meli woke up early with me on the final morning and walked me to the ashram gates. We hugged and kissed and said our final goodbyes. I took my cab to Delhi and hopped on a plane to Kathmandu.

Chapter 24
NEPAL, CHAOS IN KATHMANDU

After living a quiet and secluded life at the ashram for the last month, this whole scene looked shockingly alien to me…

***

It was Easter Sunday when I arrived into the hustle and bustle of the largest city in Nepal. I knew very little about Kathmandu. I was surprised to see how much better organized and clean the roads were, and there were tourists everywhere. I already could tell that I was no longer in India.

I took a cab from the airport and the driver dropped me off in the middle of Thamel, the busiest part of the busiest section of the largest city in Nepal, telling me my hostel was somewhere in this area. I loaded up my heavy backpack and began to wander. I decided I would walk around for a little bit before asking for directions.

"Preya, PREYA!" I heard a beautiful American accent calling my name. It was Amelia! I ran up to her and gave her the biggest bear hug I could while not toppling her and her tiny body over. At the going-away-to-India party that Cassie had thrown me, I had talked to Amelia about my plan to climb Mount Everest. She had been intrigued, and I spent some time during the party convincing her to come join me. She said she wouldn't have to worry about dying on Mount Everest because her parents would kill her first! A few months before my expedition to Everest, I had gotten a random email from Amelia telling me she was "bungee jumping with her life" and that she

Chapter 24: NEPAL, CHAOS IN KATHMANDU

had made the reservation to join me amidst a flurry of controversy with her parents.

Amelia had arrived a few days earlier and was out on a tour of the area with her new man friend from Nepal. She directed me to the hostel. I told her I was exhausted and needed to rest. I was arriving late to the tour; our group had already had their first meeting that afternoon. She told me we were checking out and heading to the airport at 5:30 a.m. We made plans to meet up in a few hours for Easter dinner. We were supposed to have another meeting with the group at 7:00 p.m., but we both decided we would skip it and have a nice dinner instead. I was unfortunately not making a good first impression by missing the first two meetings, but after a month at the ashram, food was my top priority.

The Kathmandu Guesthouse was an iconic hostel in Nepal. It was one of the original guesthouses in Nepal and a long list of celebrities had stayed there over the years. When I walked in, I felt like I had been transported to Europe. Everyone was sitting at these fancy little wicker tables drinking coffee, smoking cigarettes, and talking very LOUDLY. After living a quiet and secluded life at the ashram for the last month, this whole scene looked shockingly alien to me. I felt a wave of anxiety come over me and quickly picked up my key at the reception desk and escaped to my room. I slept for an hour then did my evening meditation and some yoga and took a long hot shower before Amelia came back. I got dressed up and put on some lipgloss—my first attempt at beauty in over a month. Amelia came back, we talked for a bit, and I told her I had been dreaming of Italian food for many months. Amelia is Sicilian, so Italian food was the perfect choice for her also.

We found 'the best' Italian restaurant in Thamel, called La Dolce Vita; it was a small, quaint restaurant with red-and-white checkered tablecloths, candles on the tables, and MUSIC. Thamel caters to Western tourists, but everything Western seemed so foreign and strange to me. I was giggling like a schoolgirl about sitting on a proper chair, the sound of American music, and especially using silverware again—I had been eating with only my hands for the last month. I studied the menu with total delight, looking at all the beautiful entrees, but

I had known what I wanted to eat for many months already... gnocchi with palomino sauce. We started our meal with Chianti, and I could feel the heat of the first sip of wine drain down my throat, all the way into my stomach. It had been a month since I'd had a glass of red wine. Then came the bread—hot fresh bread covered in butter—which I saturated even further in olive oil and parmesan cheese. It was light and flakey and I couldn't eat it fast enough. Then we indulged in an appetizer of fresh mozzarella with basil and tomatoes. It was unbelievable. They have cheese in India, but it is mostly cottage cheese-style, nothing like authentic fresh mozzarella. I thought I could live on just cheese for the next few days. Amelia and I continued talking and I caught up on some of the Detroit gossip, but I was focused on the food. For the last six months, with the exception of a few meals, I had eaten Indian food twice a day. I wanted to savor every morsel because I knew it would be a few weeks before I would be eating such an extravagant meal again. The gnocchi was just as I imagined it, homemade and thick, drowned in an extra rich palomino sauce, with tomatoes and lots of cream. My senses were so heighted after being in the ashram. The background noise seemed so loud, the flavors seemed so strong, even my fingers had a heighted ability to feel. We ended our Easter dinner with tiramisu and a final toast to this amazing adventure we were about to start.

    I woke up at 4:00 a.m., meditated for 30 minutes, did yoga for 30 minutes, and then took another long hot shower, not sure when I would have that luxury again. And for the first time since Goa, I shaved my legs and my bikini line...just in case. I was the last one to check out and get on the small bus waiting for us to head back to the airport. The tour guide, Sameer, came over to me on the bus and introduced himself. I apologized for being late and missing both the meetings yesterday, and assured him I was eager to trek Mount Everest. Sameer was a nice-looking Nepali man about my age; he was friendly and made me feel welcome.

    We boarded our tiny little 12-seater Tara Air plane. I was sure to wear the necklace that my friend Annette had given me the day before I left the US. She told me it was an ancient artifact that was to protect me whenever I wore it. After seeing the

Chapter 24: NEPAL, CHAOS IN KATHMANDU

size and condition of this plane, I was glad I had it on. Andrew had told me many months ago in Japan that Lukla airport has the most plane crashes of any airport in the entire world. It was a quick flight, about an hour long, and the landing was dramatic! We landed on the side of a very steep mountain. The landing strip was short and steep, and at the end was the side of a mountain. We landed going uphill to slow the plane down quickly. When planes take off from here, they go downhill to gain speed quickly before literally falling off the mountain.

We got our bags and set off to have lunch and meet our local porters and guides. Our expedition group consisted of twelve members: eight English, two Australian, and two American. We would have Sameer as our main guide, and three assistant guides: Emraj, Ram, and Peakos. We had about eight porters who would carry our bags. I had left a suitcase in storage back at the hostel, but still my large backpack was loaded with gear. I also had a small daypack, which I would carry. Once I left my large backpack with the porters in the mornings, I didn't have access to it until the evening. In my daypack I carried my water, snack food, survival gear, and a few layers of warm clothes. Lukla is the last town we would be at—the rest of the trek was through small mountain villages. I didn't have a parka; I had a soft shell jacket and a thin down coat. Sameer said I should definitely have a parka because it gets very cold and there could easily be a blizzard that we would have to hike through. It was hard for me to think about snowstorms when I had been in 100-degree heat in Delhi for the last month. I followed his advice and rented a parka for the trip. I would leave it in my big backpack until we ascended into the frigid mountain air.

I no longer had a cellphone; in India I had used my phone for my alarm clock. I was now traveling with Westerners, no longer working on 'Indian standard time.' I looked in the shops for a watch but didn't see any digital wristwatches with an alarm clock; well, I did see one...on the shop owner's wrist. I worked my bargaining magic, and by the time I walked out the door, I had bought the storeowner's watch!

Chapter 25
NEPAL: MOUNT EVEREST

My eyes filled with tears again, but tears of joy as I experienced a deep sense of knowing that God was with me in my life and I could now ask for help in dark moments...

***

All of the final preparations in Lukala were complete, and the time arrived for us to start our trek to Mount Everest! Pasang Lhamu memorial gate, marked the beginning of our 'long walk.' It was late in the afternoon, and the sun was strong. There were amazing views of the snow-covered Himalayas in the distance. It was springtime; the trees were budding and small wildflowers were in bloom all around. I especially enjoyed the large rhododendron flowers. Rhododendrons are the national flower of Nepal. They are striking with their brilliant fuchsias and pinks against dark green leaves. My nose had its first beautiful smells in months—clean mountain air mixed with the fragrance of wild flowers. The trail was a very wide dirt path. We were in Buddhist country, and there were traditional carved stones with Tibetan mantras and many large prayer wheels along the trail. I spun as many of them as I could as I passed by and recited my mantra. This was going to be the most physically demanding experience of my life. Although my body was strong from yoga, after six months in India I felt worn down before even starting. The prayer wheels were amazingly beautiful; some were small, carved brass, some were large and colorfully painted, and some were so enormous they took two to three people to spin. They were all barrel shaped and filled with tiny pieces of paper with the foundational Buddhist mantra "om mani padme hum," the same mantra that Karma gave me to recite with the mala I had bought from her shop in Kerala. Spinning the prayer wheel is equal to the merit of reciting all the mantras written inside it. By the end of my first two hours of hiking and spinning prayer wheels, I had hopefully accumulated enough merit to survive this experience.

Our first few hours of hiking were remarkably scenic, yet hot and sweaty as we hiked high above a raging river. It was called the Milk River because of its white foamy color. India is incredible for many reasons, but not its pristine beauty. Massive overpopulation and pollution have destroyed most of India's natural ecosystems. To experience pristine beauty again gave me much joy and reestablished the strong connection that I have had my whole life to the natural world.

By the end of the day we had descended down to the Milk River. I had been in awe of its beauty all day and couldn't resist taking off my boots and walking in. It was probably the coldest water I had ever been in. I couldn't believe it wasn't frozen. After about 30 seconds in the glacial meltwater, my legs were numb. I thought it would be beneficial to my swollen feet as they adjusted to this new lifestyle of long hikes for the next twelve days. I lingered in the river just long enough for Amelia to snap a picture of me then hobbled back to shore. We stayed that night at a teahouse right on the Milk River's banks.

Amelia and I would be sharing a room every night. The rooms were simple with two single beds and a table between with a small light on it. After living in the ashram dormitory, the teahouses almost seemed extravagant. I meditated for 30 minutes while Amelia lay down. My meditations were still going great since my initiation. For the first ten minutes, my mind was usually busy, almost like it had to empty out all the information of the day. Then something magical started to happen. My mantra started to repeat itself on its own, while the rest of my mind ventured into silence. I finished meditating and did a few sun salutations before they called us to dinner.

It was delicious; I was happy to have anything other than the 'ashram slop' I had been eating for the last month. At the time, the ashram food was fine because I was so hungry with my metabolism in overdrive. Now, to order off a menu and eat meals that weren't all running together on my plate gave me a renewed appreciation for food.

I continued to feel overwhelmed with integration back into the Western culture of my group in Nepal. I interacted very little with the rest of the group except for Amelia. The truth was I didn't feel comfortable around Westerners these days. At this point I felt like I could relate so much more to Asians. The conversations were simple and direct, without the overly sugary English way of speaking. Amelia was coming from the US, and therefore was much more social with the group than I. She created a bridge between my isolated ashram mentality and everyone else. Most of the group stayed up late into the night and played games, but I went back to my room to do a little journaling and spent my time alone before going to bed.

I woke up at 5:00 a.m. and it was absolutely silent. It had been many months since I'd actually heard silence. In India, no matter what time of day or night, there was always noise. During the day street venders yelled, cars honked, and people chanted prayers on megaphones, then at night the dogs barked endlessly. To finally hear silence was worth waking up for, and it led me right into beautiful meditations. In my periods of empty thoughts, a whole new world was revealing itself to me. I wanted to be isolated under that blanket of silence the entire trip. But as Amelia awoke each day, I was pulled back into Western small talk. I had undergone major changes in the last months, and my perspective on life had shifted such that I found my conversations to be strained.

We had to be packed with our bags in front of the teahouses we slept at before breakfast each day. My body was adjusting to the new demands of hiking, and I had done virtually no cardiovascular training for this trip. The others in the group talked about their months of intense cardio training, and I had done only yoga.

Our hike the second day started with a steep incline for about two hours to the first bridge of the trip. It was one lane and was made of steel held up by suspension wires. Every step that I took made the entire bridge shake, rattle, and roll. Below us was the Milk River, and we would soon be saying goodbye to

257

Chapter 25: NEPAL: MOUNT EVEREST

it as we moved deeper into the Himalayas. Just after we crossed the bridge, a team of four large male oxen with long curly horns approached the bridge. They hesitated, but with some coercion and butt slapping, they also crossed, burdened with enormous loads. They must have weighed over a thousand pounds each! I was in disbelief while admiring the courage and power of these animals.

We took a chai break after a few hours and then set off again. About one hour later, I realized my camera was gone. I told Sameer that I thought I'd left my camera at the rest stop. I was really embarrassed to tell him and risk holding up the group, but I couldn't imagine hiking the rest of Mount Everest without a camera. Without a second thought, Ram, one of the guides, volunteered to run back and check if I'd left it there. He left his pack and took off running. I said a prayer and asked Ganesha to please return my camera. Ram was back in about fifteen minutes. It was unbelievable! It had taken us an hour to walk that distance! He was smiling ear to ear as he approached and holding up my camera. Thank you, Ram, and thank you, Ganesha!

As we hiked on, the terrain changed quickly. The air was getting cold and thin. I needed to put my jacket on whenever we stopped to rest. The jagged peaks of the Himalayas were now approaching. The hiking became much more difficult; our dirt trail became a mix of dirt and rock, and I had to stay focused on each step so I wouldn't tweak my already fragile knee. We took breaks every 30 to 45 minutes, but it wasn't enough for me; I was huffing and puffing to keep up with the group. As I panted for air, the Nepali porters would pass us walking quickly; they usually traveled in groups of three to five, ranging in age from young children to old men. They carried goods in tattered, handwoven wicker baskets held together with a collection of random ropes and strings. The baskets sat on their backs and the main handle looped over their heads. They were loaded with heavy boxes of bottled water, beer, and other tourist-friendly supplies. There were no roads, so these porters walked for weeks carrying these heavy loads. As soon as they arrived at their destination, they would drop off the delivery and then walk back to the airport at Lukla to get another load—

this was their life. Many of the porters had on flip-flop type shoes. Others had full shoes that were falling apart and taped together. It was an unbelievable sight. Every day I handed out 30–40 pieces of candy to the porters as they passed us. I felt sadness for their difficult life. My heart was more open than it had ever been, and although I felt separated from the superficiality of the Westerners in my group, I felt deeply connected to the authenticity of the Nepali people. I was struggling, and every inch of my body was sore; every time I felt exhausted, I gained inspiration from these amazing people.

After lunch we began our hellacious ascent to Namche Bazaar. There were hundreds of switchbacks as far as I could see. I looked up the trail, feeling overwhelmed, and remembered Andrew telling me about the climb to Namche Bazaar. I started off tired and by the third switchback, I needed a break. I could no longer keep up with the group, and they hiked on. I was struggling all the way around. Emotionally, I was trying to get used to the small talk about English football (soccer) teams, drinking, and gossip about British celebrities. Now I was also physically struggling to keep up, so I decided to separate from the group. Ram stayed back with me. After many rests we made it to the teahouse about an hour behind the rest of the group. I had already given Amelia my dinner order, so my food was ready when I arrived.

By the end of that hike, I was starving. I ordered two meals: vegetable momos and vegetable noodles. I split my food on two plates and gave Ram the other half as a thank you. After dinner, I ordered a hot lemon ginger tea and sat and talked to our head guide, Sameer. I was developing feelings somewhere between admiration and a crush on him. I asked him about his life in Nepal, and he asked me about what life was like in America. We both felt a little nervous talking; I think he was developing a crush on me too. We sat by the wood-burning stove. It was a cozy place, and he made it even cozier.

The third day was what I thought was a rest day—NOT. It's actually called an acclimation and rest day. What that means is that we get up just as early, hike straight uphill for three hours, and then hike back down for lunch. I did the best I could but again fell behind the rest of the group and only made it about

Chapter 25: NEPAL: MOUNT EVEREST

2/3 of the way up and then joined them on the hike down. This time Emraj stayed back and hiked with me. I liked hiking in silence and repeating my mantra; it was a spiritual experience. I decided that if Sameer would let me, I would stay back and use the rest of the trip as a walking meditation.

After lunch I shopped around Namche Bazaar; it is the last big village to buy gear in on the way to Mount Everest. I was still obsessed by the simple pleasure of food as Amelia and I shared a pizza. I began to accept how intense the next week of my life was going to be.

Even after our 'rest day,' I felt exhausted. It was a no-win situation. I was short of breath as we hiked for hours up the endless switchbacks, and my knee hurt when we hiked the short downhills. The panoramic views were spectacular, but most of the time my head was focused on my feet. I enjoyed the rests not only to catch my breath, but also to actually look around at the highest mountains in the world.

The weather also changed and became bitterly cold; I dripped with sweat when I hiked and then was shivering cold as soon as we stopped to rest. It was an intense experience on all levels. I spent most of the next day hiking alone with Ram, about thirty minutes to an hour behind the group. They took my food order, and I caught back up with them at lunch. I kept up with the group for a few hours after lunch, and then I started taking breaks. In truth I probably could have hiked with them, but at their speed it was miserable for me. I didn't come to the Himalayas to be miserable; I wanted to take in the amazing scenery and breathe deeply! Everything in my life had slowed down since coming to Asia. My mind and body moved with more awareness. As I saw everyone rushing to keep up with the group, I remembered the old 'party girl' always trying to keep up with others. Now I was happy to walk slowly alone behind the group and just experience the moment.

We ended day four at a remote village called Phorse. I looked around at the women who ran the teahouses and tried to understand what their lives must be like. Most of their husbands are porters or Sherpas, and many of these women are alone for days or weeks at a time. They have to work hard—they collect wood, cook food for the guests, clean the rooms, and run the businesses. They looked tired, and this life on Mount Everest is the most difficult I have ever seen humans endure.

The altitude was starting to set in, and I was so tired and freezing at the end of the day that I started to sleep in my clothes. The temperature dropped far below freezing at night, and our rooms were not heated. It took all my energy to take off my boots, go to the bathroom, and unpack my sleeping bag; I couldn't imagine how much energy it would take to actually strip my layers off to change my underwear, and I felt I would freeze in the process. Cleanliness became a small detail I was no longer concerned with.

I woke up early the next day and meditated. I knew if I was going to make it to my goal of reaching Base Camp, I needed divine guidance. I learned I should ask God for exactly what I wanted, so I prayed for inspiration to help me finish my ascent and return to Kathmandu safely. I was freezing, aching, and I had blisters on my feet. For one of the first times in my life, I surrendered to God and begged for help. The morning hike was the hardest because my body was cold and stiff. Every step hurt until I warmed up. I hiked with the group until the first rest stop, where I had some ginger lemon tea. I wasn't interested in food at all anymore; I just wanted the heat from the drink. Even though my metabolism was on overdrive, I had nausea that stayed with me most of the day and didn't feel like eating.

After the break, I started to fall behind the group. Sameer came back to check on me, gave me encouragement, and then ran and caught back up with the group. The air was thin and I was panting with every step. In true Nepali form, he ran up the trail and I was impressed with him. He assigned Emraj to walk with me until we met up at lunch. Some of the group members were getting altitude sickness. It started out as nausea and a headache, and then progressed to severe vomiting. I had a small headache and some background nausea, but mostly I was just exhausted. I walked for hours and questioned why I had a need to put myself through such strenuous activities. What aspect of my personality needed to push myself beyond my limits? In yoga, we spend time trying to understand the human ego. The ego that drove me to achieve successes also caused me to suffer with feelings of inadequacy. I reasoned that I was climbing Mount Everest simply to strengthen my ego, and I was no longer interested in living with it dictating my future. I walked silently reciting my mantra and ignored my labored breathing. After hours of hardship I hit rock bottom and was about to give up. I prayed and told God I was about to quit and head back down the mountain. I needed a sign if I was to finish these last few days to get to Base Camp.

Within minutes, the path turned a corner and there was a beautiful herd of wild mountain goats. I was elated. It was the first wildlife I had seen in days, and I felt like my prayers had instantly been answered. There must have been about twenty of them; males, females and babies. They were dark brown and had huge curly antlers. They were a little startled by Emraj and I, but they were also curious. They were so agile and playful in the way they jumped onto rocks and interacted with each other. As I sat there and watched them, I thought back to my friend Karma from Kovalam beach. I gained strength thinking of her tragic journey through these same mountains while fleeing from Chinese soldiers. I decided that even if my ego had brought me here, I was thankful for the insights I had gained.

My eyes filled with tears again, but tears of joy as I experienced a deep sense of knowing that God was with me in my life and I could now ask for help in dark moments. I felt full of a deep peace that I was coming to know as bliss. My soul was nurtured and my mind was clear. I can't describe it in words, but although my body was just as exhausted, and my breathing just as labored, I found a sense of joy in the experience rather than my previous misery. God had shared grace with me, and I knew the rest of this trip would be divine.

That afternoon, we passed an old Nepali man sitting on a rock facing Mount Everest. He was holding his mala and chanting while rocking back and forth. I was drawn to him. His skin was brown and leathery and his fingers were thick and heavily calloused. It was obvious his body had worked hard during his life. I sat on the ground next to him, took the mala off my neck, and began chanting with him. He kept pointing up to Mount Everest with tears in his eyes and saying, "Sagarmāthā." Emraj told me that it was the Nepali name for the mountain. It meant Holy Mountain. Most of the locals believe Sagarmāthā to be a

God, and they have a profound love for her. I sat for about ten minutes chanting with the old Nepali man. I was now able to appreciate all the beauty on my journey.

The next day was an acclimation day. I no longer called them 'rest days!' We woke up early at Dingboche, had breakfast, and set out for a three-hour climb. Dingboche was at 4,440 meters, almost 14,600ft. I was now at the highest altitude I had ever been in my life, and higher than any mountain in the contiguous US. The terrain was tundra-like. There were a few small and windblown trees. The ground was covered with several species of lichen in many colors, but they were primarily greenish grey and added to the overall grey color scheme. Grey rocks, grey lichen—even the plants and trees had a greyish hue.

I spent the afternoon resting. I slept for a few hours, and it felt glorious. When I woke up, it was cold, but bright and sunny. For the first time in several days, I did yoga, and as always, I felt much better. I was still riding high from my divine intervention. The days continued to be difficult, but my relationship to the pain in my body had shifted dramatically.

After yoga I sat with Amelia on the balcony of the teahouse and we watched an older couple plow a field with a yak and plant potatoes. Potatoes were the staple food at this high altitude, and I had been eating them for many days now. The old Nepali couple worked hard on the land. I understood that their relationship was not just a marriage but also a partnership. As Amelia and I sat and talked, I told her I dreamed of a loving partnership. I prayed that I too would find my soul mate.

The next day, I woke up excited; we were getting close. I knew we had a few more intense days, but I was starting to feel a sense of peace as we climbed higher up the mountain. Maybe I was getting delirious from the low oxygen levels, but I was feeling significantly less stressed about the struggle. As we hiked to Lobuche, the land became more desolate, and only tall and jagged peaks now surrounded us. We passed a frigid rushing river and had to carefully climb boulders to cross. I was happy that Amelia had brought me hiking poles because the trail was becoming treacherous, more like rock climbing than hiking. The people in our expedition that were experiencing altitude sickness looked ghostly white. I was thankful that the

Chapter 25: NEPAL: MOUNT EVEREST

group was hiking slower and I was able to keep up. I hiked with Sameer. He asked a lot of questions about my life, and I could tell he was interested in knowing more about me.

That afternoon as we trekked along a steep cliff, I looked down over the edge and there was a tiny little speck…it was a helicopter, and a clear indication of how high we were! I kept up with the group the entire day. It reminded me of the childhood story of the turtle and the hare—I was the turtle who was now keeping up and even passing some of the group members. In many aspects of my life, I had been a late bloomer, and this trip around the world at age 34 signified my blossoming as a human being. Ever since I'd had my rock-bottom experience of almost giving up on this mountain, things had become much easier. The realization of the power to truly surrender and ask God for what I wanted was now a new way of living that I would continue to develop.

At dinner, a Sherpa asked me for a donation. One of the Sherpa's had died that day at Base Camp during a training exercise. I had seen the group earlier in the day, running with a basket carrying a limp body. I gave him money and sent him love, and as he walked away, my eyes filled with tears. The life on this mountain is the hardest I had ever seen: no roads, few supplies, and the nearest hospital was a two-day walk down the mountain.

We woke up early at Lobuche and set off with our day packs to hike to Base Camp. I wore my hair in two braids; it had been about ten days since I'd washed my hair and about a week since I'd showered. My skin was suntanned, and my face had developed harshness from the hours of being out in the cold, windy Himalayan air. The trail was now only jagged boulders. Everest loomed above us, but was hard to see. Every once and a while I would get a glimpse of the peak from behind the clouds. All the mountains in this area are so high that the mountains in the forefront looked taller. As we climbed up one of our final ascents, I became exhilarated at the prospect of accomplishing my goal. I still remember sitting on my red leather couch back in Ferndale, Michigan, and imagining what it would be like to climb Mount Everest. That 'party girl' seemed so far away physically and spiritually from where I was now. The last stretch was atop a steep rocky ridge. The wind was blowing very strong, and every step needed to be carefully placed and the trekking poles planted to help stabilize me. I looked down the other side of the ridge and saw a glacier. Just beyond was Mount Everest Base Camp!

It was a village of about fifty teams from all over the world. The climbers would live at Base Camp and train at that high altitude in preparation for their ascents to the summit. A post was decorated in Buddhist prayer flags and a small aluminum sign with "Everest Base Camp" handwritten with a black marker. This is the email I wrote that day to share the good news with my friends and family around the world.

Butterflies at Base Camp

Well, this is probably one of the few emails you will receive in your life from 5,140 meters (17,000ft). I am emailing you from a satellite connection at the highest Internet cafe in the world! Gorkashep, Nepal.

I climbed to Everest Base Camp yesterday, another very strenuous nine-hour hike.

My time at Base Camp was short but sweet; after the necessary photo shoot, I found a nice rock away from my group and sat in a meditative pose. I sat quietly and gazed at the amazing Everest glacier all around me. And there with me was a butterfly. I have no idea what a butterfly was doing in such extreme conditions, but it stayed fluttering around me the entire ten minutes I sat on the rock as I contemplated my goals, my purpose, and my future. The terrain is almost like a desert with high winds, and very dry, and there are large glaciers everywhere. The glacier ice is bright blue and jagged; it looks like a mountain range with many sharp peaks. As I sat with the butterfly, I felt overwhelmed that my homecoming was less than two weeks away. I heard a large booming sound; as I scanned the mountainside I heard the thunder of an avalanche, the first one of my life! It was luckily small but still a powerful force.

The actual Base Camp is a group of 50-100 tents. One in particular caught my eye, a white dome tent covered in solar panels. The tents are only allowed for people who have permits to summit Mount

Chapter 25: NEPAL: MOUNT EVEREST

Everest. *They live at Base Camp for a few weeks and train and acclimate to the high altitude. When they begin their ascent, they spend many days at each camp until they hopefully summit. It takes one to two months to reach the summit. There are many memorials along the way dedicated to those who have died attempting to summit Mount Everest.*

This last nine days have been the most physically challenging of my life. I am down to basic survival; trying to eat enough calories to sustain me, trying to breathe deeply while gasping to get enough oxygen to alleviate my headache. Safe and sound decisions are all the Himalayan mountains allow for, and even then, one avalanche or landslide can bring about an unmanageable situation.

This has been an amazing journey, and I am once again humbled by the greatness and vast diversity of our planet. Today I begin my four-day walk back to Lukla and say my final goodbyes to Mount Everest, for I don't think I will ever be back.

Peace and Love,

Preya

The hike back was kind of a blur; I felt proud, the anxiety had lifted, and my body was feeling strong. I was on 'cloud Everest.' I spent most of the time talking with Amelia and Sameer. We took a different route on the descent, and had a free day in Temboche, an amazing Buddhist monastery. The current monastery was built in the early 1900s, but the spot had been a secret Buddhist retreat for thousands of years. We visited the temple when the monks were chanting. The monastery was cold, and I kept thinking about the monks only wearing robes to cover; I was freezing in all my high-tech gear, and I felt a bit embarrassed for my softness. I sat in meditation as the monks chanted. In that temple I had a profound spiritual experience. In my third eye, I saw a light, brighter than a thousand suns, and then the chakra at the top of my head opened. Brilliant rays of light filled my hollow body as I experienced forceful waves of energy. When I came out of my mediation, everyone was gone. I had attained new wisdom: the more light I saw in others, the more divine light I would possess.

As I got back to our cute teahouse, the fire was burning, the room was filled with warmth, and I was content. I ordered a dinner of hot-and-sour soup and french fries. With my renewed sense of needing to connect with other people's divine light, I decided to join my group for dinner. The English guys continued to talk about beer and football, but also about a website where you can rate the prostitutes in London! I kept trying to see the light and shine without judgments. I stayed up with my group later than normal; we taught Sameer how to play spoons. It was fun! I kept seeing that amazing light; I will never forget it.

I woke up early to see the most spectacular sunrise of my life. It was so beautiful I had to wake up Amelia. It had snowed overnight and everything was covered. The sun was rising from behind Mount Everest, and the mountains and valley were ablaze in a beautiful hue of pink. I did a full yoga practice, and finished my meditation. Then I sat and prayed and started learning how to have an ongoing conversation with God.

Every day it was getting warmer and we descended about 3,000 feet a day. As we dropped below the tree line, I was happy to see that the rhododendrons were now in full bloom. I picked a rhododendron flower every day and put it in my hair. I felt like a Nepali princess as I flirted with Sameer. I handed out all the remaining candies we had, and I made a point to smile and send love to every person we passed on the path. The Nepali mountain people are the strongest and most courageous people I have ever had the privilege of knowing, a true testament to the strength that we ALL possess as humans.

Our final night in Lukla was the Nepali New Year, and Sameer had arranged a feast for dinner. Everyone was happy and playful. The porters were all singing Nepali songs, and we even had a mini dance party. Amelia and I left the party fired up and decided to go bar hopping in Lukla. There were several tourist bars in town, and I was ready to have an 'I survived Everest beer.' We met up with several people we had seen along the way, and it was a celebration; we all bonded for achieving this huge feat. In the morning we loaded up on our green Tara plane and had an unforgettable takeoff right off the edge of the mountain. I experienced the thrill of why this is called the most dangerous airport in the world.

We got back to the Kathmandu Guesthouse in the afternoon. Amelia and I were excited to eat Western food again. We went out for a long lunch, looked at some of our pictures, and congratulated ourselves on this unbelievable accomplishment. It felt weird to be back in the chaos of Kathmandu. It was loud, and the air was so dirty, but none of it mattered as I was still feeling a natural high. It took weeks of intense yoga at the ashram to achieve a state of Samadhi, and it took weeks of climbing Mount Everest to experience a 'climbers high.' I walked tall and my stride felt strong as I walked the streets—I almost felt superhuman. This time it did not take blue streaks in my hair to make feel like Wonder Woman, and for days after I returned I felt like I had superpowers. We got back to the hotel and unpacked, and I took the longest, hottest shower of my life. I shaved every inch of my body, lathered myself up from head to toe, and shellacked my body with oil. I laughed as I watched the brown, dirty water going down the drain. It was time for a well-deserved nap.

The group was meeting up for a farewell dinner. I wasn't interested in seeing the group, but I did want to see Sameer. He was interested in what I was writing whenever he saw me journaling. It was cute, and he would try to read over my shoulder. I decided to buy him a journal as a thank-you gift and included a tip. I walked to the restaurant where they were meeting. I planned on arriving for the tail end of the party, but then I got lost on my way through the narrow winding streets of Kathmandu. I started to panic, realizing I was going to miss the party and miss the opportunity to see Sameer. At that moment, I realized how much I really liked him. I quickly paid a young Nepali boy to guide me to the restaurant. I got there just as they were finishing dessert. I sat next to Amelia, and Sameer came right over and sat next to me. He said he was glad I'd come; he was afraid he wouldn't see me again. I gave him the gift with the tip in it. Everyone paid his or her bill, and we left within ten minutes to walk back to the guesthouse. It was kind of surreal to have our dysfunctional group lined up and walking together again, but this time through the dirty streets, when just the day before we were walking in nature's glory.

I walked with Sameer and we flirted and giggled on the way back. I finally mustered up the courage and said, "Hey, Sameer, do you want to go out with me for a drink?" He said he was going to meet his friend at a local bar right then. Then came a long awkward pause, and he said, "You want to come with me?" He went on to tell me it's a cheap local dive bar, and I told him I have a secret love of dive bars. We agreed to not let the rest of the group know, so we finished our walk back to the guesthouse, we all said goodbye, and our expedition was officially over. I pulled Amelia aside and told her I was going out with Sameer and not to tell the group.

We walked together for ten minutes to find a small spiral staircase that led to my first Nepali dive bar. He was right, it was a total dive. His friend Kumar was already there. We played pool for about an hour and I bought them each a few beers. Sameer then pulled me close and said they were going to stay at his farmhouse, and he wanted me to come with them. He told me it was about an hour away and we would all three be traveling on one scooter. It took me about a second to say yes. If he could get me to Everest Base Camp and back safely, I could certainly trust him to go on this adventure. The scooter ride was uncomfortable. Kumar was driving, and Sameer was behind me—it was a Preya sandwich! The best part of the ride was that Sameer had his arms wrapped around me.

Chapter 26
NEPAL: THE FARMHOUSE

Everything was perfect, but yet so final, for in the depth of my heart I knew it was the last day in this lifetime I would spend with Sameer...

***

When got to the farmhouse, Sameer showed me where I would be sleeping and within minutes we were embraced in a passionate kiss. I could tell we had both been waiting for two weeks for that moment. I had decided by about the second day of trekking that if I was go going to have another passionate love affair before I went back to the US, it was going to be with Sameer. And so it was! His skin was the smoothest I had ever felt, like a baby's. After all of the physical exertion on the mountain, both of our bodies were strong and our sexual energy was high. He gracefully undressed me and I undressed him. We kissed, we giggled, and we made sweet beautiful love. I slept on and off the entire night and was eager for morning to come to have sex with him again.

We made love twice in the morning. I fell back asleep and Sameer woke me up with boiled potatoes he had made for breakfast. During breakfast we laid in bed cuddling and talking about our time on the trail. He told me that he thought I was beautiful the day we met, and I told him the same. We shared tender moments together over plain boiled potatoes. No butter, no salt, but the best breakfast I had in months!

We walked outside and in the daylight I saw his beautiful little farmhouse for the first time. The Nepali countryside was magnificent, so different than being in Kathmandu. The

Chapter 26: NEPAL: THE FARMHOUSE

mountains were carved with rows of green terrace farms. We meandered the garden, holding hands; it was a beautiful moment decorated by all the flowers in bloom. The sun was shining bright, and my heart felt so full of gratitude for my blessed trip, and for Sameer. I was pleasantly surprised when he asked me if I wanted to meet his family. Wow...I kept thinking that this was how it was supposed to be—you make love with a man and the next day he wants you to meet his family, not like Andrew, who never contacted me again.

We walked up the mountain to his home. It was a simple Nepali house: the kitchen had a fire pit for cooking, the floors were mud, and there was no running water. It was similar to the houses in my dad's village in India. Outside the house were two goats, several chickens, and a cow for milk. Sameer's father had died five years ago, and his mother was a hard-working woman. She spent her days climbing the mountains to gather grass for the animals, foraging wild plants for food, and carrying buckets of water for the house, along with the usual chores of cooking, laundry, and cleaning the animal pens. She didn't speak any English, but she was beautiful. Her smile lit up my heart, and she kept offering me food and desserts. She needed supplies from the neighboring town, and Sameer and I went on his scooter to get them. We bought rice, lentils, flour, and some sort of grain, along with potatoes, tomatoes, and onions. I paid for his family supplies and we also bought two bottles of Nepali wine and crackers. I was starving; my metabolism was on overdrive from the hiking and now from our love affair. I wanted to support his local village and I felt awkward dressed in my hiking gear. Sameer picked out a traditional Nepali skirt for me. It was a narrow cut wraparound skirt that had an ornate red and off-white design on it. I wore it with a loose fitting white cotton shirt. As we were driving home, Sameer pulled the scooter off to the side of the road and looked deep into my eyes. He said, "When you get back to America, are you going to forget about me?" I kissed him and said, "Are you going to forget about me?" He said, "No." I said, "Never in my life will I forget about you, my dear Sameer." It was a touching and emotional moment of feeling vulnerable with each other.

By the time we had gotten back to the house, his mother had prepared an early dinner for us. The main dish was a potato curry with a vegetable she had harvested that morning. She made fresh chapattis. I was really hungry, but it didn't seem like there was enough food for all three of us, so I ate a very small portion to make sure there was enough food left for her. We sat on the dirt floor in the kitchen and ate with our hands.

I kept thinking about what a cultural gap Sameer lived in. He spends weeks at a time with 'rich' Western tourists who waste so much food and money, and then comes home and lives an impoverished village life. I could tell he was insecure about me being there, and he kept apologizing for his simple life. I tried to reassure him, but I could tell it was hard for him to live a split life. After our early dinner, we walked around the village, and he took me to meet many of his cousins. One had a large mulberry tree in her yard, and I told him I loved mulberries. He went into the house, got out a big sheet, and placed it on the ground. Then Sameer climbed the tree and shook it as hard as he could so that the mulberries rained down upon me. We then feasted on the fresh Nepali fruit. It was such a beautiful spring day, the roses were in bloom, the berries were ripe, the birds were chirping…and I was in lust!

That evening Kumar came back over to the farmhouse. I opened the first bottle of wine, and we had a party. We put a couple blankets on the floor, I pulled out my 'emergency' deck of cards, and we started to play rummy. Kumar was hilarious; he told me some ridiculous joke about a flying angry bird laying an egg in his broken English. I had no idea what he was talking about, but I was joyful and we both laughed and laughed. He loved America, and talked about our old TV shows. He really wanted to learn Texas Hold'em. I tried teaching him, but after about one glass of red wine, Kumar was drunk, so I suggested we just go back to playing rummy. Kumar left shortly afterward, and Sameer was eager to get me back up to bed. I was a little buzzed and finally had the courage to tell him I wanted him to work at giving me an orgasm. I think he was a little shocked by my request. I suspect many Asian men are not accustomed to pleasing their women like American men are. He gave me a

Chapter 26: NEPAL: THE FARMHOUSE

long and sensual back rub and a well needed foot rub before going to be bed.

We woke up early the next morning and I asked Sameer if I could use his phone to call Amelia at the hotel. I left a message and told her I was returning later that day. He requested I ask her not to tell the others that we were together, which I did. Even though he was no longer my guide, he had a very good job and we both wanted to ensure he kept it.

Kumar came back over and we all went to the garden where I taught my first yoga class as a certified teacher. I couldn't imagine a more beautiful place or people to teach. They loved it. I was concerned since we had experienced a few physically intense days, but my body was stronger after climbing Mount Everest than after the month at the ashram. I was even able to hold the scorpion, my most difficult pose. Sameer had a hard time sitting still during yoga; I remembered those days also, when I first started yoga. After class we sat in the garden and Sameer shared his hopes and dreams with me; I felt like yoga had really opened us both up to authentic intimacy.

Later that morning, we took the local bus back to Kathmandu. It was awful; it was beyond crowded, and I felt like a sardine. I was being knocked, bumped, and stared at by everyone on the bus. Just like my first public bus ride in India, a creepy man sitting next to me kept rubbing up against me. I told Sameer we had to get out of the bus immediately and get a cab. He told me there were no cabs in the villages and this was the only way to get back to Kathmandu. I took my shawl out, covered my head, and tried to meditate. Finally, after an hour he said, "Okay, let's get out, we can get a cab from here." I literally had to push and climb over people to get off of the bus. The bus cost 12 rupees, and the cab ride from one side of Kathmandu to the other cost 250 rupees. I knew the average person had no other choice than to travel in that awful bus.

When I got back to the guesthouse, I saw someone from my group, and I felt like I just had been caught hiding out with Sameer. I tried to avoid seeing anyone who would recognize me, and luckily most of them had already flown home. It reinforced the fact that I wanted to check out of the guesthouse. It was my last night in Nepal, I wanted to spend it with Sameer, and we couldn't do it there. I saw Amelia, and she was full of questions, but I didn't feel like 'gossiping.' I did give her a quick summary, and told her I was going to be checking out of the hotel and spending my last night in Nepal with Sameer. I went to the Internet café and booked the only five-star hotel in Kathmandu, the Westin. I looked up the best restaurant in Nepal, and after a few possible choices, I decided on Dwarika's Hotel. I called Sameer, and he was eager to leave work early to see me. I told him to meet me in front of the guesthouse in an hour. I packed up and checked out in record time. I said my final goodbye to Amelia—she was leaving Nepal in two days and flying back to Detroit.

Sameer and I met in front of the gate and took a cab to the Westin on the other side of town. I felt transported back into Western living. A bellhop unloaded our taxi in front of the grand entrance. As we walked to the reception desk, the cool air conditioning refreshed us. I asked for the best room they had available and told them tonight was a special night. Sameer was a like a fish out of water, and after so many months in Asia, so was I. I felt like an American 'sugar mama' who was seducing a 'poor' Nepali man. I got over it as soon as we got to our top-floor room with amazing views of Kathmandu. It didn't take us long to break in the room. Somehow making love always feels better in an upscale hotel, and I had my first orgasm with Sameer. We raided the mini bar next, sat on the balcony in our plush white hotel bathrobes, and had a cocktail while we enjoyed the view of the city. We both were eager to go swimming, so we headed down to the pool. There were four other couples around the pool; they were all white, and I could tell Sameer felt awkward. It was a huge Olympic-sized pool, and I felt strong as I glided through the water with ease. My body finally forgave me for the weeks of hard work I had demanded of it. We sat poolside most of the day. We ordered beer, had lunch delivered to us on our pool loungers, and swam together closely. Everything was perfect, but yet so final, for in the depth of my heart I knew it was the last day in this lifetime I would spend with Sameer. One of our servers was his cousin. It felt uncomfortable having him serve us, and I could see Sameer's worlds colliding.

Chapter 26: NEPAL: THE FARMHOUSE

Sameer told me he had never played tennis before, and asked me if I would teach him. I told him he could have picked a better teacher, but I would be happy to try. We went back to our room and changed into our 'tennis clothes'; it was pretty much a joke because the only shoes Sameer had were lace up dress shoes or flip fops. There was perfectly manicured grass for acres around us. We were right in downtown Kathmandu, one of the busiest cities in all of Asia, yet all I saw around me were green rolling hills, rhododendrons in full bloom, and my sweet Sameer. We had so much fun together. I felt like a little girl again when I was with him. He was a decent athlete and picked up the sport quickly. I had years of tennis lessons as a girl, but I think my parents would have done better investing their money in finding gold in Alaska. The hour went by quickly, and we went back up to the room, showered, and got ready for a grand dinner.

We had a cab pick us up, and we arrived at Dwarika's a little past our reservation time. It was an old brick hotel with ivy growing on the walls; I could feel the history of this establishment that catered to the aristocratic class of Nepal. I was dressed in the fancy half sari I had bought in Vrindavan. When we walked in, the hostess said, "Welcome Mr. and Mrs. Shah," and gave me a flower and told us to follow her. We walked past many carved pillars and through wood archways to the main dining area. It was past dinnertime. The room was brightly decorated red, with lavish woodcarvings and ornate gold trim. I could visualize the lavish parties the royals must have had here.

Our table was amazing. There were bright red and black tufted cushions on the floor for us to sit on, our table was carved dark cherry wood, and we had round pillows on either side of us to rest our arms on or lean up against. Our silverware was heavy and made of brass. Sitting on our main plate was a personalized menu. On mine it said "Mrs. Shah" and on Sameer's it said "Mr. Shah." We both laughed about it especially since Nepal is similar to India culturally and is a paternalistic society, so to have my last name on the menus floored Sameer. We feasted on a seven-course vegetarian meal of traditional Nepali food. We spent most of dinner reminiscing about our trip to Everest Base Camp. We shared our feelings for each other freely. I tried to be present and enjoyed every minute of the amazing dinner in our almost private dining room. With each course Nepali dancers came out to our table. Each dancer was from a different region of Nepal and performed their traditional dance. After dinner I gave Sameer a card and a silver bracelet that I had bought for him.

We got back to the hotel late. We were both tired, but neither one of us wanted this perfect day to end. We stayed up late, we made love, we held each other, and we didn't talk about our goodbye the next morning. I slept for a few hours nestled closely against his silky smooth body. I woke up at 5:00 a.m. and meditated as the sun came up. I prayed to God that Sameer and I both found love and happiness in our lives. I lay back in bed after I meditated and Sameer held me tight; I felt very close to him after the weeks we had shared together. I took my final picture, one of the most memorable pictures of my trip—me wrapped up in a five-star hotel sheet, naked, nestled in Sameer's arms. I had no idea what would happen upon my return to America, or what my life would look like when I got home. In these eight months of traveling, I had found God, I had found love, and I had found peace. What more could a party girl from Detroit ask for from traveling the world alone.

***

ONE LAST THING...

Thank you for joining me on my journey. I hope reading about my evolution will inspire you to take on your own personal journey of self-discovery. If you enjoyed reading my story I request that you take a minute of your time to review my book on amazon.com

CONNECT WITH ME

Want to learn more about my journey? Please visit my website Preyashah.com for pictures, links to my podcasts, social media links, and videos.

ABOUT THE AUTHOR

Preya C. Shah has received her Bachelors and Masters Degrees from University of Michigan. Preya has been a practicing physical therapist for almost 20 years. In her personal journey of holistic healing she has become a Certified Yoga Master, Theta Healing Instructor, certified in Nutraceuticals, and a CranioSacral Therapist. She has received The Circle of Excellence Award and Outstanding Alumni Award from University of Michigan. She enjoys speaking at corporate trainings, and professional conferences. Preya's passions are traveling, yoga, backpacking, and helping guide her clients to a deep level of authentic healing.